Cuban Youth and Revolutionary Values

Cuban Youth and Revolutionary Values

Educating the New Socialist Citizen

DENISE F. BLUM

University of Texas Press ⏁ *Austin*

First edition, 2011

Requests for permission to reproduce material from this work should be sent to:
  Permissions
  University of Texas Press
  P.O. Box 7819
  Austin, TX 78713-7819
  www.utexas.edu/utpress/about/bpermission.html

♾ The paper used in this book meets the minimum requirements of
ANSI/NISO Z39.48-1992 (R1997) (Permanence of Paper).

Library of Congress Cataloging-in-Publication Data to come
Blum, Denise F., 1960–
Cuban youth and revolutionary values : educating the new socialist citizen /
Denise F. Blum. — 1st ed.
  p.   cm.
Includes bibliographical references and index.
ISBN 978-0-292-72260-6 (cloth : alk. paper)
1. Education—Cuba—History.   2. Education—Cuba—Evaluation.   3. Education—
Cuba—Curricula.   I. Title.
LA486.B58   2010
370.97291—dc22   2010015367

To the families of the La Flor neighborhood;
To my mother, Delphine Blum; and in
memory of my father, Herman Blum

Contents

Acknowledgments

This book is a product of love: the love the Cubans shared (and share) with me, and the love that keeps their stories from leaving my heart and mind. My heartfelt thanks go to the families I lived with, my neighbors, and the families whose children attended Granma Junior High School in La Flor. They were my inspiration for this book and for my continued interest in Cuba.

None of this research would have been possible without the research authorization given to me by the Cuban Ministry of Education and the mentoring provided by the Pedagogical Institute of La Varona. Thanks also go to the Cuban academics who provided feedback and direction along the way: Nancy Chacón, Carolina de la Torre, and Jesús Guanche.

In the early stages of my research, my U.S. comrades were a constant source of support and understanding on Cuban issues. I warmly thank Matt Childs, Joanna Swanger, John-Marshall Klein, Michele Reid, Marc McLeod, Jessica Montalvo, Nadine Fernández, Marvin Leiner, and Damián Fernández.

Final preparation of the manuscript would not have been possible without the help of the following individuals: Laurie Frederick, Kelly McCoy, Hector Amaya and Rebecca Rhyne. Special thanks go to Doug Foley for his mentorship throughout my research.

Funding for my fieldwork was provided by the John D. and Catherine T. MacArthur Foundation and by a Continuing University Fellowship from the University of Texas at Austin.

Cuban Youth and Revolutionary Values

Introduction

The radical has a passionate faith in the infinite perfectibility of human nature.
He believes that by changing man's environment and by perfecting a technique
of soul forming, a society can be wrought that is wholly new and unprecedented.
ERIC HOFFER, *THE TRUE BELIEVER*

Preparing students to be socially responsible citizens is of concern to educators and policy makers alike. During my years teaching school in different
Latin American countries and in the United States, this topic inevitably became the center of many conversations. Recognizing that the systemic structure of capitalism nurtured consumerism, egocentrism, individualism, and
competition, I wondered whether children in a noncapitalist society might
be more altruistic and socially responsible than those in a capitalist society. If
so, what mechanisms were in place in the school system to ensure a different
citizen outcome? Knowing Spanish, I set out to discover what was going on
in Cuban education.

On my first visit to Cuba, in 1995, to conduct research for my master's
thesis, I pursued stories and documents pertaining to the 1961 National Literacy Campaign, the Cuban government's massive attempt at expanding education to all and transforming the political culture through education (Fagen
1969). This project ultimately led to the topic of this book: How is socialist
ideology, or *conciencia*, taught, and in what ways are young people making
meaning of it?

In this introduction I briefly present my methodology (more detail can
be found in the appendices), then introduce the Cuban government's focus
on using education to create a new personality, "the new socialist man." The
New Man, *el Hombre Nuevo*, was to emerge from Fidel Castro's rendering of

society as "one huge school," with education transformed into a totalizing, society-wide, mass media process (Medin 1990) for value inculcation. A description of the work-study principle follows. This principle in praxis is meant to provide Cuban children with a socialist orientation toward work and communist conciencia. Motivation and incentives played important roles in gaining the support of the Cuban young people. My work in the schools and in the countryside gave me valuable opportunities to assess the degree to which different generations had absorbed revolutionary values and make a preliminary assessment of the success of the educational program's transformative agenda.

Methodology

My focus on secondary education is deliberate. Before going to Cuba, I had spent ten years teaching ninth graders Spanish in the United States and English as a second language in Latin America. From this experience I acquired a general understanding of ninth-grade behavior that someone outside the teaching profession might label disaffected. In addition, because Cuban schooling is required only through ninth grade, that is the year when students decide whether they will pursue further education or follow a vocational path. Thus, ninth grade seemed an appropriate time for exploring students' aspirations and the extent to which they coincided with the needs of a socialist society.

Although most researchers on education in Cuba focus on the stellar achievements in elementary education and try to pinpoint the formula for success in attaining literacy, little work has been done on secondary education in Cuba. Enrollment in Cuban elementary schools (99 percent) surpasses elementary school enrollment in the United States (96 percent) (UNESCO 2008). In contrast to the high secondary school enrollment in the United States, however, which remains at a steady 96 percent, Cuba's secondary school enrollment is much lower. In 1998–1999, while I was living in Cuba, secondary school enrollment reached 65 percent, up from an all-time low of 50 percent in 1993 (UNESCO 2008). This difference caught my attention. What were the teenagers doing if they were not in school?

The adolescent schooling years are of serious concern to the Cuban government, which considers them a time to hone revolutionary teaching, to form new cadres to lead and perpetuate socialist values and norms, and to "ferment" conciencia—but fewer Cuban students are electing to stay in school. What, then, are Cuban schools' role and responsibility in increasing secondary enrollment? How does low secondary enrollment affect society, and what options are Cuban students choosing instead of further schooling? My work with Cuban students and teachers, while it did not necessarily answer enrollment statistics, did uncover some students' feelings about the educational curriculum, aspirations for their own future, and attitudes toward school in the late 1990s, during a period of economic change.

It was at a celebration of the 1961 Literacy Campaign at Cuba's National Literacy Museum while I was in Cuba collecting data for my master's thesis that I met Lizabet, a former literacy worker, or *brigadista*. She not only shared the story of her experience as a brigadista, she also told me how much she loved teaching civic education to ninth graders and invited me to visit her school, Granma Junior High School (a pseudonym) in Havana.

The Cuban Ministry of Education (MINED) granted me permission to conduct my research at Granma Junior High School. During the initial stages of my research, I always referred to my school site by its revolutionary name (all Cuban schools are named after heroes or martyrs of the revolution). I also referred to it by the municipality in which it was located, never by the name of the neighborhood, and perhaps this missing link was what lay behind the reaction of MINED at the end of my study. As I was concluding my research visit, MINED officials met with me to review my data and my preliminary findings. In the course of the conversation I mentioned the name of the neighborhood, at which I received looks of shock as they suddenly realized they had granted me permission to conduct research in a school located in what they termed a "marginalized neighborhood." Surprised and concerned, during my last week in Havana the officials scrambled to grant me additional permission to observe in Ciudad Libertad,[1] an educational compound and showcase of experimental ideas in Cuban education.

I spent approximately five of my fifteen months of fieldwork observing and participating in activities at Granma Junior High School and with the families in La Flor (another pseudonym) neighborhood. I lived with a family and divided my time among consulting archival documents, conducting forty-five formal audiotaped interviews, making daily school observations, and participating in school, community, and family activities, through which I acquired hundreds of hours of taped field notes and interviews. Family members, teachers, education officials, and education researchers are equally involved in the educational process, and so I included the stories of their experiences as well. Because older people frequently commented on the differences between their generation's and their children's or grandchildren's generation's education and value inculcation, I have also used generational interviews to show the significance of historical context, socializing mechanisms, and general reception of educational policy by the Cuban population.

Receiving formal permission from the Cuban government to conduct long-term research in a Cuban school was unprecedented, according to MINED officials. Likewise, my methods of data collection, analysis, and interpretation were unique by the very activity of conducting research in this "forbidden research terrain" (Fuller 1988). It took me several years to gain access to a Cuban school, and when I did, I was assigned a Cuban mentor and debriefed by MINED before leaving Cuba. I began seeking permission for a long-term engagement during the initial years of fieldwork for my master's thesis. Even with the intense monitoring of my work by government officials, teachers and students wanted their stories told and navigated the political obstacles for me so that I would "see more" and tell the "real story." Moreover, primary informants became collaborators in data analysis and interpretation as they assisted in the transcription of my taped interviews throughout the study and met for discussion after each transcription session to give me feedback about the data and to guide me in my research strategies and interview techniques.

Although I expected heavy monitoring, what I did not expect was the intense suspicion my research methods ignited. Not a single Cuban educator and only a few Cuban anthropologists[2] had ever heard of ethnography. I was repeatedly asked why I wanted to go back every day to the school: what was I looking for that I had not already seen? Why was I constantly taking notes? Why did I not have a survey? Why did I spend so much time collecting data? What was qualitative research? What would my final dissertation contain, and how could this research possibly be scientific?

Because of the U.S. government's longstanding antagonistic and colonizing position toward Cuba, I was often accused of being a CIA agent, and even those who accepted me considered my research practices odd. Neither perception was easy to shake or to live with. Nevertheless, applying a survey instrument seemed to ease the tension as well as to open more opportunities for dialogue. So I did a survey.

With all of the political sensitivity surrounding my presence as a U.S. researcher investigating the prodigal child of the Cuban revolution, the educational system, what I found most surprising was the remark of a MINED official during my final debriefing. He asserted, "Criticism of the Cuban education system is okay, but with all of our difficulties, please do not leave us beaten up and on the floor. As you know, we have a history of being bullied by the United States. Recognize that we have implemented methods to save our educational system. We care about our people. Try to leave it on a positive note." In that moment I realized that researchers have the power to do what they want with data; we have full rein. I had the choice of describing the glass as half empty or half full. Candidly, I responded, "For me, it was not one extreme or another. I really did see marvelous things taking place at the school, as well as critical struggles for teachers and students. All countries struggle with many of the same issues. The U.S. school system, with even more material resources, has many problems. Instilling proper values is a major struggle for the United States, too." So it is with the goal of showing both the strengths and the weaknesses of the Cuban government's efforts to create and maintain revolutionary citizens and the Cuban populace's responses to their efforts that I have written this book.

Since schools have always reflected the government-endorsed normative framework for a society, Cuban schools are an interesting site in which to study the process of human transformation. Cuban schools are both the generators and the meters of the values implicit in this evolving socialist society, offering insight into Cuba's future political system and its particular flavor, and using explicit methods to inculcate revolutionary values.[3] Furthermore, the country's about-turn in politics and economics to accommodate a socialist ideology at the advent of the 1959 Cuban Revolution and again at a time of economic crisis in the 1990s makes its accompanying effects in schooling noteworthy.

The response of the Cuban people to their government and its institutions is crucial to cultivating and maintaining conciencia to reproduce and perpetuate socialism. Ernesto "Che" Guevara used the term *conciencia* when he formulated his ideas about moral incentives. For Guevara, the word meant more than is implied by the English translation of "consciousness" or "awareness." Conciencia was created through education with explicit political goals and participation in revolutionary activities; it involved a commitment to action (Guevara 1965). Fidel Castro has defined conciencia as "an attitude of struggle, dignity, principles and revolutionary morale" (Castro 1980, 59).[4] Conciencia, during the Cuban Revolution, was at the very heart of socialist ideology. Therefore, my goal became to document the methods of its inculcation and internalization in Cubans.

Education has always reflected the political and economic structure of society. As a result, schooling will be explicitly aligned with the means of production. Insofar as Cuba before 1959 was a capitalist country, the radical change to socialism necessitated the schooling or socialization of a new personality, the new socialist man or woman. The means to inculcate this ideological orientation was the implementation of Fidel Castro's totalizing concept of the country as "one huge school," and the most salient mechanism for inculcating this new orientation was the Marxist-Leninist work-study principle, the dominating principle in schooling from kindergarten through college and even in professional life.

Creating a "New Personality"

Educating society has been the key to creating both the material abundance and the social consciousness required by the sought-after ideal communist society. Educational policy in post-1959 Cuba established transformational tasks for the schools and defined new standards of conduct that required active cooperation among schools, families, and the organized community. When questioned about the obvious reflection of Cuban revolutionary ideology in the schools, Cuban educators never deny it. Abel Prieto Morales, an official of MINED, was asked at an educational conference in Italy, "Is the school in Cuba an instrument of the state?" To which he replied, "Yes, of course. Just as it was before the triumph of the Revolution and as it is in present-day Italy" (cited in Leiner 1975, 6). What does it mean for education to be an instrument of the state? Is this beneficial or detrimental, and to whom?

In the process of cultivating revolutionary values, the Cuban leadership repeatedly pointed to the need for a "new personality training" as part of the effort of building a socialist society (Figueroa, Prieto, and Gutiérrez 1974, 3). Che Guevara was the chief promoter of pursuing these ideals in educational policy, especially in the initial phases of the revolution. He embodied the revolutionary ideals bundled in the new socialist man concept. "We are building a new society—a just and human society in which exploitation of man by man will have no part. As a part of that, our schools need to form the New Man—one who is motivated not by greed or self-interest but by the good of all," he said. In this process of total societal transformation, schools were given the responsibility of creating new socialist men and women. As Castro proclaimed, "All revolution is an extraordinary process of education. . . . Revolution and education are the same thing" (1961b, 271). In other words, the revolution could not occur without proper education, and schooling had to explicitly serve the revolution.

Like other countries, Cuba has used education along with economic and political measures to resolve basic developmental problems. In contrast to many countries, however, the Cuban government has rejected traditional development ideologies and strategies. Instead of partial, incremental reforms it has opted for a major structural transformation. More important, instead of treating the economy as a means to improve the human condition, the Cuban revolutionary government has targeted transforming human mentality and behavior as key to economic development, and revolutionary education as the primary means to this end (Barkin and Manitzas 1973; Jolly 1964; Leiner 1975). Revolutionary education, therefore, was marked by an overt ideological constancy and expansion to all ages and levels of education (Carnoy 1990). To what degree would an explicit ideological emphasis improve Cuban citizenship and the island's future?

Cuba Is "One Huge School"

With the goal of educating Cubans not only through the institution of schooling but also through every medium of society, education authorities point to the Cuban Revolution as both the prime motivating force for educational innovation and change and the source of the educational or ideological message. Transformation of the bourgeois capitalist mentality to one that served the country and the people was necessary for a socialist society to thrive. Transformation was based on reeducation to understand the former imperialist domination, the relations of production, and class structure. Not surprisingly, Samuel Bowles (1971) has claimed that every major economic and social objective of the Cuban Revolution has been manifested in some aspect of educational change. Similarly, every major dilemma in constructing a socialist economy has had a counterpart in the Cuban school system.

In transmitting the values of the new society, the Cuban government has consistently emphasized educational ideological activities such as massive campaigns and mobilizations to actively engage as many people of all ages as possible. As Richard Jolly (1964, 181) reported, based on a 1962 visit to the island, the Cuban government "has acted simultaneously on a large number of educational fronts, mobilizing economic and human resources with a massiveness seldom if ever seen." One of the most significant examples is the 1961 National Literacy Campaign, which reduced illiteracy nationwide from 23.6 percent to 3.9 percent in eight months, making Cuba the nation with the highest literacy rate at the time in Latin America (Lorenzetto and Neys 1965). In the twenty-first century, mobilizing for national participation in education-based endeavors continues.

Fagen (1969) argues that the results of the Literacy Campaign, when measured against the costs and tangible results, might have been less than what the revolutionaries claimed. However, he also notes that if the goal was mobilizing and changing Cuban political culture, the campaign was an unquestionable success. Political culture includes "patterns of action as well as states of mind," Fagen writes (16). In this way, the Literacy Campaign was

> seminally important in the evolution of the institutional and political culture of the revolution. . . . [E]ven those who were most cynical about the peda-

gogical achievements of the campaign would probably admit that the widespread cultural and psychological barriers inhibiting adult education in Cuba were broken in 1961, even if functional literacy were not achieved for very many of the so-called new literates. (55)

The Literacy Campaign had an additional side to it, one critical to the development of the new socialist man: it connected what had previously been separated by capitalist development, bringing the urban educated sector into contact with the poor and illiterate all over the island. From 1961 on, sending young people, generally in their early to mid-teens, to the countryside for agricultural labor became a dominant theme. Its goal was to break down barriers and dissolve differences between urban and rural areas (such as differences in production, distribution, measures, and values) as an integral part of the Cuban development process (Carnoy 1989).

The campaigns and the work brigades, the mass organizations and the newly trained young people as the vanguards of the revolution, were just some of the signs of a new political culture in the 1960s. To make the transition to a new political culture, Marxist-Leninist concepts were projected in political messages in all realms of life, including educational, cultural, artistic, and social arenas. By proclaiming that he would make the island "one huge school," Castro emphasized that education occurs beyond the walls of school buildings. Furthermore, education includes all socializing mechanisms, and therefore the government must use all channels of dissemination, including schools, workplaces, media, and recreation, to inculcate new revolutionary norms. These sites and channels, as well as mass organizations and nationwide activities, reflected Castro's need to strengthen his base of popular power and to perpetuate that base by developing a revolutionary consciousness in the masses to take the place of merely transitory enthusiasm (Fagen 1969). Through the many modes of education, the state intended to transform the culture of a nation to serve immediate and long-term national goals, focusing on productivity (work) and the development of a revolutionary consciousness to respond to economic and ideological needs.

The Work-Study Principle

The work-study principle is fundamental to the process of forming the new socialist citizen. Innovations in educational programs that sought to create the new socialist man included combining work, production, and study; emphasizing the study of socially useful subjects; incorporating voluntary labor;

stressing moral rewards; reinforcing emulation and cooperative study; and, in 1968, introducing military training in all but elementary schools (Castañeda 1973). In this new political culture work had new meaning, especially in relation to pedagogy. Part of my work has been to probe this relationship between political culture and pedagogy in contemporary Cuban society. I describe its evolution in the later chapters of this book.

The work-study principle combines both mental (academic study) and manual (physical labor) activities on a regular basis. The manual activities take different forms at different grade levels, from school maintenance, participation in recycling programs, attending to *educación laboral* (woodshop, sewing, and the like), and working in the community garden to intensive weeks of living and working in the countryside performing agricultural labor. Students undertake "socially useful work" several times a week for a few hours, and the time devoted to this work increases with each age group, but never consumes more than three hours a day. The only exception is when secondary students go for their weeks-long stint of agricultural work in the countryside. Through these work activities, which everyone from kindergarten through twelfth grade participates in, the Cuban government hopes to communicate the equal importance of all professions, eliminate class stereotypes, encourage empathy for and solidarity with the proletariat, and foster "a love for work" and a devotion to *la patria*.

According to Cuban officials, the hallmark citizen virtues and behaviors of the New Man include not only patriotism but also what Fagen (1969, 147) calls "the moralization of work." This type of work is a "Cuban revolutionary variant of the Protestant ethic, stripped of its overtones of salvation by means of privatization" (ibid.). Like other prescriptions for behavior, the Cuban revolutionary work ethic fuses work and societal service into an idealized vision of a clean, hard, useful life, reinforcing revolutionary values such as conciencia, egalitarianism, self-sacrifice, patriotism, internationalism, anti-imperialism, laboriousness, and loyalty to the revolution.

In the end, the most salient feature of the Cuban educational revolution is the linking of productivity and consciousness by including a strong ideological component based on collective work and moral incentives. The intention is that the value-laden curriculum and work activities will yield productive, loyal citizens by creating both the material abundance and the social consciousness required by the sought-after ideal communist society. For its ideological and economic importance, Cuban officials have regarded the work-study principle as "the cornerstone of Cuban education"; without it, Cuban communist education would cease to exist (Guerrero and Socarrás 1979). With the work-study principle so central to the operation of Cuban education, it became my primary focus. I therefore sought to evaluate the future of the system and its sustainability with the fall of the Soviet bloc in 1989.

The Philosophical Underpinnings of the Work-Study Principle

The work-study principle in Cuba is rooted in the ideas of the philosophers Karl Marx, Vladimir Lenin, Friedrich Engels, and the poet-philosopher and national hero José Martí. Lenin held that the relations of production determine the development of each generation. In a capitalist society, for example, the education of the working class is limited, and therefore the lower classes are involved in work that alienates the individual from his or her creative capacities. In the ideal Marxist-Leninist society, in contrast, socioeconomic and pedagogical conditions are created to convert work into a decisive factor in the holistic development of an individual. This highlights one of the most important conditions for communist development—the linking of study and productive, socially useful work for students. In this way the students participate directly in practical tasks of constructing socialism and, in the process, form their convictions and consciousness through collective activity.

Marx's belief in the transformative nature of labor is evident in his critique of the Gotha Program (an educational program for the German principality of Gotha). He stated, "an early combination of productive labour with education is one of the most potent means for the transformation of present-day society . . . every child from age nine should become a productive worker" (cited in Tucker 1971, 300). However, Marx realized the tenacity of the old economic order and the need to address its legacies:

> What we have to deal with here is a communist society not as it has developed its own foundations, but on the contrary, just as it emerges from capitalist society; which is thus in every respect, economically, morally, and intellectually, still stamped with the birth marks of the old society from whose womb it emerges. (6)

Woven into the revolutionary work concept in Cuba as developed by Marx, Lenin, and Engels are the ideas of Cuba's nineteenth-century philosopher, political theorist, and literary figure José Martí. Based on an understanding of Cuba as an underdeveloped nation, with a society that depended mainly on the country's agricultural resources, Martí postulated the need to bridge the gap that existed in education between theory and practice, work and study, and manual and intellectual labor. Quotations from Martí (1975, my translations) are often used to support the practice of physical labor as the educative task of the school: "To educate is to prepare for life" (308). "Behind every school a field" (287). "In the morning the hoe, in the afternoon the pen" (53). "Physical, mental, and moral advantages come from manual work" (285). "Man grows with the work of his hands" (285). The blending of Marxism-Leninism and Martíism allowed the Cuban leadership to virtually graft Marxism-Leninism—a relatively foreign system of ideas to the Cubans—onto Cuban nationalism (Medin 1990).

Rooted in the perceived needs of Cuba's new communist society, a combination of work and study became the backbone of a new kind of pedagogy from the time of the Literacy Campaign. Referring to building the base of the Cuban educational revolution, Fidel has said, "It is impossible to think of education in communism without this idea of the combination of work and study" (cited in García Galló 1973, 10), and "The participation of our students in productive work is a great tool of revolutionary pedagogical work and contributes to their ideological formation" (ibid. 17). Through meaningful work—work that would truly become a part of national development—students would learn what it meant to work in a Marxist tradition. Specifically, they would learn the meaning of labor and production; most important, their own potential for transforming the nature of work would in turn transform not only the natural world but also human beings themselves. Thus, the incorporation of physical labor into the Cuban curriculum is part of a transformative process, one aimed at bridging the gap between theory and praxis.

Broad participation, symbolizing acceptance and comprehension of national efforts, was viewed as the path to transformation. Economic prosperity under socialism required changes in attitudes as well as individual sacrifices of material items on behalf of the collective well-being. Rather than acceding to the ever-rising demands for consumption characteristic of capitalist countries, the Cuban government has strived to create a consumption pattern and structure of rewards based on group participation and identification with national achievements. Individual consumption of material goods has been restricted, while collective participation in social services has expanded. Making this transition from an emphasis on the individual to an emphasis on the collective requires a change of incentives and ways of motivating people.

Motivation and Incentives

Motivational changes start with the Cuban children, who must learn to be motivated more by moral incentives than by material ones to fulfill the moral and material ideals the socialist government has for its citizenry. To achieve the state's socialist vision, Castro's goal since the mid-1960s has been a "synthesis, a search for the ever-elusive balance between moral and material incentives to unglue an inefficient economy" (Black 1988, 376). Reflecting this vision, Che Guevara introduced the mechanism of moral incentives into the various volunteer work projects in the 1960s.

Cuba's society-wide economic distributive system is based on *conciencia comunista*. It is a form of learned behavior channeled from above by various mass and state organizations for social honors. The preference for Cuba's nonmarket methods, according to Robert Bernardo (1970, 120), "is bound up with the goal of instilling a new work ethic in which workers, including managers, are internally motivated to work for the net social good." Insofar as this goal is achieved, it forms the decentralized or voluntary aspect of the system of moral incentives.

The Cuban model of development is unique in its primary reliance on moral incentives over material ones, both for intensifying the work effort and for raising total work hours in socially needed tasks, particularly in the unpopular area of agricultural labor. Converting the workforce to address the emphasis on agriculture required a heavy investment in education to provide training that would be more directly relevant to the new productive needs of the country (Barkin and Manitzas 1973). One of the hallmarks of socialist educational methods is emulation. Emulation involves competition by group instead of by individual, as in capitalism. Those who succeed have the duty to help others gain access to the same level of success. In the process, the outstanding groups, or brigades, are rewarded with public recognition, and frequently with certificates or an honorary pin or medal. Two of the most important elements in the educational process of forming the New Man have been the emphasis on agricultural labor and the reliance on moral incentives. Therefore, it is important to ask: What is the current state of students' involvement in agricultural labor? What is the place of moral incentives today, and how effective are they?

The Importance of Youth

In the Youth Congress of 1962, the nation's youth were praised as the embodiment of the future of the revolution, as only the young could come to the revolutionary experience uncorrupted and pure enough to be formed into true communists (Fagen 1969). They were valued for their future contribution to the development effort and for their potential to bear the seeds of the new political culture.

According to psychologists, young people are more available psychologically for recruitment into new experiences. Erik Erikson (1968) describes how young people are searching for a sense of self that is relatively unambiguous, action-oriented, and ideological,

> because in adolescence an ideological realignment is by necessity in process and a number of ideological possibilities are waiting to be hierarchically ordered by opportunity, leadership, and friendship. . . . At no other time as much as in adolescence does the individual need . . . oversystematized thoughts and overvalued words to give a semblance of order to his inner world.

Erikson's formulation is relevant to understanding the fusing of the system requirements of the Cuban government with the personal identity needs of Cuban youth. The mobilization programs launched by the Cuban educational system meet the implied conditions of Erikson's analysis, with adolescents submitting to rough physical conditions, a scarcity of material items, and the challenges that accompany mobilization to the countryside. Their sense of self-importance is strongly reinforced by participating in activities that not only make a visible transformation in the physical environment but are also of national importance and pride. Students' energies are channeled into prescribed patterns of behavior, such as societal service, where students are given serious responsibilities and collectivism is encouraged to stave off egoism. As Fagen (1969) suggests, the formative environment of Cuban children ameliorates many of the most profound uncertainties and difficulties that are usually characteristic of the search for identity.

Yet contemporary Cuban youth are at a juncture of judging the Cuban political system not only for its promise but also for its performance. The state realizes that it must meet two different but related demands, affective and technocratic. The young people of the 1960s became the solid base of support for building socialism—the vanguard. However, the factors that imprinted a strong socialist value system on those young people have had a somewhat different effect on their children and grandchildren.

Most recently, attempts to mold a new consciousness have consistently met economic obstacles. Events such as the fall of the Soviet bloc, the Helms-Burton Act, and the decades-long U.S. embargo have forced Castro to create a mixed economy with capitalist incentives, such as new jobs in low-skill sectors like agriculture and tourism. Dissatisfied with the career options and Cuban peso salaries that have not corresponded with a dollar-driven[5] or euro-driven economy, many have questioned the revolutionary ideals of patriotic sacrifice, equality, and hard work (Díaz-Briquets 1993; Martín 1991).

The Cuban educational system has been one of the main institutions held responsible for "rescuing" revolutionary values (Addine Fernández 1996; Báxter Pérez 1990, 1999; Charcón Arteaga 1998; Menéndez Quintero 1994; Romero Fernández 1994; Trujillo de la Paz 1999). As Romero Fernández (1994, 149; trans. mine) has written, "What is certain is that with the appearance of new necessities, of new challenges to society, and to humanity, values that have structured the destiny of humanity and many societies are being reordered." More specifically, Cuban sociologist Juan Luis Martín (1999, 144) states that "the truly strategic objective of the coming years will be the development of a social consciousness with an important ethical component, one of its main features being love of work." A common saying in Cuba is, "They pretend to pay us and we pretend to work." How do economic changes shape labor issues in Cuba, and how do labor issues in turn shape the role of schooling for Cuban citizenship? What values are schoolchildren holding on to in their changing context?

Political Religion, Affect, and the Performative Dimensions of *Conciencia*

To understand how Cuban young people are making meaning of their world, I draw on the theoretical work of Damián J. Fernández (2000), who argues that the Cuban government crafts an affective attachment to and among the citizenry to cultivate human motivation and conciencia. Fernández defines the government's "affective discourse" as its "political religion, giving meaning to the official discourse of Marxism-Leninism in a culturally authentic language" (67). It is clearly the emotional connection that crafts the story between the Cuban government and its people. As James Loewen (2007, 342) writes in *Lies My Teacher Told Me*, "emotion is the glue that causes history to stick."

Cuba's political religion taps into and appeals to *cubanidad*, or Cuban identity. The affective discourse touches the Cuban people directly, for it couches issues of national immediacy in moral language—emphasizing, for example, the importance of working in the fields to support the national economy and *la patria*, or crusading against economic dependence, imperialism, injustice, laziness, illiteracy, exploitation, and selfishness. It is important to note that the revolutionary values are tied to moral goals and therefore are driven by an explicit emotion—for example, instilling a love for work, devotion to *la patria,* self-sacrifice, solidarity, loyalty to the revolution, hope, faith, and so on. The promotion of conciencia is facilitated by a political religion that is infused with "notions of unity and harmony for high moral ends" (Fernández 2000, 69) and dependent on a charismatic leader—who has been growing weaker. Building on the emotional codes of Cuban political culture, the state generates politics with affect and passion, hoping to link the masses with the leader. Political religion complements Marxism-Leninism by viewing human nature in a spiritually optimistic way with possible emancipation. The political religion presumes a faith in the perfectibility of human nature in general and in Cuban exceptionalism in particular.

This emphasis on affect in the theoretical framework is not meant to reduce the importance of other material and nonmaterial factors in the formation of the New Man, nor is it to say that emotions play the primary role in political developments in Cuba. Instead, I suggest that while historical, international, economic, geographic, cultural, social, and political factors can help us understand the politics and peoples of a country, the analytical category of emotions and its influence on Cuban politics and policy can provide useful insights often overlooked by traditional research.

With respect to the role of affect in politics, epistemologically, emotions are interpretations of reality, if we hold to the understanding that all reality is interpreted subjectively. Emotions are products of both of heart and mind, exist both privately and publicly, and yield both irrational and rational responses. Likewise, passions are judgments about the world and are usually moral and normative. Feminists like Ruth Behar (1993, 1996), Donne Kondo (1990), Chandra Talpade Mohanty (2003), and Michelle Rosaldo (1984) argue that politics are personal, but Fernández understands emotions as an analytical category to be considered in the struggle for power and legitimacy. He underscores the affective: "Emotions in their social cultural setting reflect the community's outlook, its normative map. They are indicative of political culture, that is, values, norms, and affective codes that influence how people in particular groups relate to politics" (2000, 2). Notably, Fernández calls revolutions and transitions "affairs of the heart," because they are emotionally charged situations. He says that the specific role played by emotion is shaped by particular historical, social, and economic factors, making the affective attachment to the system crucial for governability and legitimacy.

Other social scientists have identified emotion as a factor in the promotion of systemic change. Human frustration, argue Ward Goodenough (1963) and Harry Mtonga (1993), causes people to discard old beliefs, replace them with new ones, and carry out rapid reconstruction. This desire for society's members to create a more satisfying culture has been termed a "revitalization movement" by anthropologist Anthony Wallace (1966). Furthermore, Rolland Paulston (1971) has observed that the new cultural system (resulting from revitalization) specifies not only new relationships but also new behaviors. The new behaviors result from a new reality, or at least a reinterpretation of existing power relations and institutions. This new worldview, or what Paulston terms a "mazeway," may necessitate changes in the social system to bring the mazeway and social reality into congruence. In attempts to replace the old mazeway of capitalist culture with one based on communism, political bonding becomes an ethical phenomenon, a crusade against imperialism, corruption, illiteracy, exploitation, and economic dependence.

Gerald Read recognizes the Cuban government's movement for societal transformation and regeneration of the masses as a form of "ideological evangelism" (1970, 142). Frei Betto similarly states, "The Cuban revolution is an evangelic creation" (1999, 5). Maintaining this same religious tone, Read says that through participation in the revolution, Cubans are free and can "prepare themselves through education for their ultimate fulfillment, or state of 'grace'" (1990, 134).

A major component of Cuba's political religion is the Manichean myth, which reinforces the totalistic character of confrontation, where enemies are stigmatized to maintain or increase their perceived polarization. The language and symbols of the Manichean myth are teleological and instrumental, charting the "right" track toward utopia for the Cuban people and promising hope for the faithful and hard-working. The language of Manicheanism is comforting, as it clearly divides the world into good and evil, with no middle ground, thus dispelling confusion in a time of transition. Its polarizing character reinforces the totalistic character of confrontation. The government's political religion draws on Manicheanism to create an axiological and emotional atmosphere conducive to the mobilization and discipline needed to confront the enemy, real or imaginary (Fernández 2000; Medin 1990). Through the polarization of values, the goal is to stigmatize the enemy (especially the United States and capitalism) and idolize the heroes and martyrs who represent the revolution. The binary choice, either revolution or treason, represents a for-us-or-against-us mentality. Any potential diversity or heterogeneity is neutralized, and the concept of self-image becomes exclusive in order to impose a monolithic identity.

The Performance Dimensions of *Conciencia*

These Manichean images, binary discourses, and polarization of values, with affective attachments, are part of Cuban culture. The New Man, *el Hombre Nuevo*, is evolving into a "Newer Man," or what Frederik (2005) terms *"el Hombre Novísimo,"* [6] a combination of past and future images. While discourses may remain formalized, standardized, immutable, and replicated from one context to the next, as Yurchak (2005) observes, a duality exists. The performative dimensions of speech acts (Austin 1971) must be considered to recognize and interpret this lived duality and the conciencia that is taking shape within the "velvet prison" (Haraszti 1988) of everyday life, where Cubans negotiate chambers of constraint with the creativity, ingenuity, and inventiveness that mark cubanidad.

The even newer socialist man of Cuba's twenty-first century is one who has learned the values inherent in *el campo:* hard-working, humble, and altruistic, with an identity connected to the land and a strong patriotism. Frederick (2005) describes this even newer man as a *"pura cepa"* (pure stalk), grounded in the values of the countryside, yet at the same time *culto* (cultured) in the arts and letters, taking an interest in both national and international issues. The *pura cepa* reflects a person schooled in the Marxist-Leninist work-study principle, a principle that produces a person who knows how things work, has experience with agricultural labor and *el campo*, and values *lo espiritual* over *lo material*, even as he adapts to the ever-changing circumstances—social, political, economic, and historical—of the twenty-first century. It is precisely the work-study principle, which ties physical labor to mental or intellectual labor, that has been responsible for cultivating and inculcating an emotional attachment to *la patria*, its people, and ultimately the state.

Damián Fernández's work is helpful in highlighting the affective dimension of the state's attempts to achieve conciencia by appealing to Cubans through a hyperattachment to affective language, symbols, and the Manichean epic myth to evoke a pro-revolutionary emotional bond with the pueblo cubano. Yet Fernández maintains a binary framework of private and public behaviors in tension that fails to capture the paradoxical mix of alienation and association with the ideals and realities of socialist life that coexist in everyday Cuba. It is important to consider, as Yurchak (2005, 135) notes, that Cuba's socialism is "both everlasting and steadily declining, at the same time full of vigor and bleakness, as well as dedicated to high ideals and devoid of them." None of these values is a façade, as they render seemingly contradictory behaviors and attitudes that are many times simultaneous and overlapping. In fact, both Yurchak's keen understanding of this duality and Fernández's rendering of affectivity inform what I call a *doble conciencia* (double consciousness), a play on words of the official schooled conciencia, that has been and is being subtly and explicitly socialized into Cuban young people.

The affective bonds between the state and its people, and between teachers and their students, are pivotal to creating and sustaining a politically stable society. This book presents a portrayal and analysis of the ongoing operation of the *doble cara* (double face), *doble moral* (dual morality), and resulting *doble conciencia* in Cuba's schooling that coexist and contribute to the country's political stability while changing it.

To understand this pivotal time for the Cuban state and its youth, in the first three chapters I provide a brief overview of the political and economic dynamics and their influence on educational policy since the late 1950s, in an effort to show the linkages between the goals of the Cuban government and Cuban schools' role in socialization. In this way I offer insight into changes in the role of Cuban youth with regard to society as a whole — changes shaped both by the transformations in the country's economic and social situation historically and by the age group's internal dynamics.

In Chapter 1 I introduce the construction of conciencia from 1953 to 1969. In Chapter 2 I briefly examine policy and planning from 1970 to 1985, attending to the more overt forms of Soviet influence and market changes in the political, economic, social, and educational arenas — the struggles in fomenting revolutionary consciousness as youth became more removed from the revolutionary tasks of the 1960s. Chapter 3 provides an overview of what came to be known as the "rectification of errors," which entailed a reemphasis on and revamping of the moral aspect of the economy, politics, and the educational system. Rectification started in 1986 and is still in effect today in policy.

The historical overview of Cuba's policy and planning is meant to promote greater understanding of present-day measures in its educational system and to contextualize the stories I collected on my visits in 1998, 1999, and 2000. My personal experiences in 1998 and 1999 are recounted in Chapters 5, 6, and 7 through ethnographic portrayals of the schooling process, both formal and informal. Chapter 5 introduces the reader to the research site, the La Flor neighborhood and its junior high school, Granma. This chapter provides some snapshots of the connections and disconnections between official discourse and the Cuban people regarding educational institutions such as MINED, the Pedagogical Institute, and Granma Junior High School. Chapter 6 presents an overview of the Pioneer organization, a student mass organization that actively structures school life politically, academically, and socially. I also provide vignettes of a few of the Pioneers' different programs, including interest circles, clubs, FAPI (Fuerzas de Acción Pioneril), and the Explorers. Chapter 7 is devoted to a unique program, Escuela al Campo, or "school to the countryside," which involves the temporary mobilization of urban students as a class to do farmwork in a rural area for a few weeks. The final chapter addresses the implications of my findings for Cubans today. The details of my methodology and documents showing the evolution of my survey instrument are included in the appendixes. The translations from Spanish to English are mine unless otherwise indicated, and I assume full responsibility for any errors in translation or documentation.

Using a lens of political religion combined with a recognition that structure and agency are mutually constitutive, I hope to broaden current understanding of the Cuban educational system's methods and the results of value inculcation in relation to the work-study principle. Focusing on the affective and the performative, dramaturgical aspects of the state and state-run educational system (Austin 1971; Edelman 1971, 1985; Fernández 2000; Geertz 1983, 2000; Turner 1974, 1982, 1992) complements earlier political economy approaches to the study of Cuban education (Bowles 1971; Carnoy 1989; La Belle and Ward 1990; Paulston 1971; Read 1970) and adds a new dimension to the study of Cuban educational policy making (Lutjens 1996). I have set out to shed light on the ways in which resistance to and the accommodation of educational goals regarding work are emotionally and axiologically constructed. Moreover, by focusing on the evolution of the Cuban work concept in schooling and its reception by Cubans over time, I propose implications for educators and policy makers around the world who seek more and different ways to involve schoolchildren in service learning and community development.

I hope that, by being exposed to the chronological juxtaposition of historical, economical, and political contexts with educational policy, the reader will gain a greater appreciation and understanding of the current ideological, axiological, and material struggle that the Cuban people at all levels are engaged in and seeking answers to. A second goal in writing this book is to demonstrate the commitment of the Castro government to form the proper conciencia through schooling, and the tension and complexity that often result, owing to economical, political, or affective factors. In education, order flourishes and finds its reputation.

CHAPTER 1

1953–1970: Constructing *Conciencia*

*A communist society, Fidel has expressed, implies that man
has reached the highest degree of social conciencia ever.*
FIDEL CASTRO, "EDITA 'EL MILITANTE,' (TRANS. MINE)"

Affection and passion played central roles in the advent and consolidation of
the Cuban Revolution, as well as in its leadership and the strategies pursued.
A foundation of sentiment was laid to promote a new conceptual world and a
socialist-humanist mind-set. An important role was played by affect, which,
along with historical, political, and economic factors, strengthened and
loosened the bonds of politics and social mores in the early years of Cuban
revolutionary planning and development. The Cuban revolutionary government needed all these factors and applied them with intent in constructing a
communist *conciencia*.

Several affective themes, the subject of this chapter, influenced the construction of conciencia. Among these were the moral imperative and affective dimension of the revolution, which were realized in a variety of ways; the
idealizing of youth; the affective underpinning of the guerrilla-focus theory;
Fidel Castro's leadership; and the affective dimension of political unity or one-
ness of self with the nation. Through the projection of these themes (Medin
1990), the goal was for Cuban people to acquire conciencia. The sociologist
Joseph Kahl notes that in the 1960s, "*conciencia*" was "perhaps the most repeated word in the Cuban language of revolution" (1969, 32).

The Affective Dimension and the Moral Imperative of the Revolution

Fernández (2000) observes that revolutionary movements are rarely motivated by material factors alone. Rather, he contends that the personal and the affective have been just as important as the structural in determining support for and the initial course of the Cuban revolutionary process, from the early 1950s through the 1960s. Struggling against the encumbrances of capitalist ideology and U.S. imperialism, the revolutionary leaders attempted to create a new rational, emotional, and ideological world (Medin 1990).

Fernández (2000) cites feelings of resentment, frustration, indignation, and aggression over economic, political, and social conditions as providing the emotional basis for revolutionary change. Values such as a collective spirit, egalitarianism, self-sacrifice, patriotism, internationalism, and conciencia would displace the old society's emotional base of resentment and frustration. The new values and sentiments would be the clay from which to form what Che Guevara called the "new socialist man." The New Man ideal type would be consumed with passion for the nation and the revolution, denying any emotions that were not useful to the regime.

This normative agenda of creating the New Man as part of creating a new society was driven by a moral imperative that infused politics with idealism and intensity—what Fernández (2000) calls "the politics of passion." The politics of passion are characterized by a hyperattachment to emotionally charged myths and symbols. The moral-emotional political fervor had a staggering impact on the Cuban people. A line was drawn in the sand; one was either for the revolution or against it. Moral conviction allowed no deviation; one had to be willing to live, work, and die for *la patria*, the fatherland, and for political ideals. These themes were promulgated in the media to create the New Man for the new society. The revolutionary government employed emotionally evocative themes that corresponded with the sociopolitical context (Fernández 2000; Medin 1990).

The New Man ideal would not appear when communism was achieved but rather was necessary for constructing communism. Thus, there was an urgency to the task of forming a new consciousness in which the moral would predominate. This consciousness would express itself in the production process in the form of a readiness to work on a voluntary basis. With the understanding that material incentives would work against the development of the socialist ethic, Che Guevara believed that the development of consciousness could, in a short time, do more for the development of production than could material incentives (Guevara 1964).

The emphasis on moral incentives was expected to complement a revolutionary regime that sought to replace a sociocultural system based on hierarchical elitism, individualism, and private ownership with values that supported a socialist system, such as collectivism, egalitarianism, and mass mobilization (Moreno 1971). Thus, the mark of being fully integrated into the revolutionary process was to acquire conciencia (to internalize these values) and to live according to revolutionary praxis. Conciencia was at once the way of achieving the goal and the way by which the individual could know that he or she was achieving it (MacDonald 1985). This type of consciousness became the government's cultural and behavioral objective for the newly transformed Cuban society (Azicri 1988; Fagen 1969; MacDonald 1985).

Emphasis on Youth

From the beginning of the revolution, the Cuban state envisioned the young as embodying the New Man image more fully than any other age group:

> The Revolution is born in the soul of the Cuban people, with the vanguard of youth which desire a new Cuba, free of past errors and petty ambitions. It is a revolution emanating from new men and new procedures, prepared with patience, bravery and decision of those who dedicate their life to an ideal. (Castro, cited in Dubois 1959, 33)

Castro was clearly imbued with a sense of generational renovation, which further manifested itself:

> We need men of character and it is logical that this generation cannot be as good as future generations, because this generation was not educated in revolutionary doctrine; it was not educated in good examples. The formidable generation, the marvelous generation, will be the coming one; and that one will truly be more perfect than us. (*Revolución*, March 13, 1959, 11)

Revolutionary struggle separated the young from the older generation in the 1950s because of the latter's more generalized abstention from the aims and activities of the anti-Batista movement (Fulgencia Batista was president at the time). The older generation had more family responsibilities and, in many cases, was more disillusioned with Cuban politics (González 1974). Under the younger generation, the political rebellion assumed an encompassing, redemptive character. The Cuban government held the fundamental belief and hope that the young were malleable enough to come to the revolutionary experience uncorrupted and pure enough to be formed into perfect communists (Fagen 1969).

To this end, the state established a series of institutions and drafted a code of conduct to socialize youth. The objectives were twofold: to answer some of the labor needs of the developmental effort, which had been made even more acute by the mass exodus of Cubans at the beginning of the revolution, and to foster the revolutionary personality (Hart 1962). The young were expected to model their behavior on the guidelines set forth by state institutions, especially the national educational system.

In the 1960s, Cuban young people became the vanguard in the great tasks of the day: the literacy campaigns, national defense work, coffee and sugar harvests, the construction of public works, and so forth. From their ranks came the officers and cadres of the armed forces and the new intellectuals to replace those who had emigrated. The youth of the 1960s were to form the solid base for building socialism, and the Cuban educational system played a major role in giving young people an appropriate political and ideological orientation (Martín 1991).

The Sierra Maestra and the Guerrilla-Focus Theory

The experimentation with suitable political and ideological programs in the Cuban educational system is largely rooted in the early revolutionaries' experience of consciousness raising and guerrilla activity in the Sierra Maestra. During the 1950s, Fidel Castro and his Rebel Army lived the rugged life in the mountains, taught campesinos to read and write, and gained their participation in the revolutionary struggle. Without the peasants, in turn, the guerrillas probably would not have survived in this environment. In 1957, after living for several months in the mountains, Castro proclaimed the role of education in the Sierra Maestra Manifesto. As part of a ten-point program for the provisional government, the manifesto decreed "the immediate start of an intensive campaign against illiteracy and for civic education, a campaign stressing the citizen's duties and rights with respect to society and the Fatherland" (cited in Dubois 1959, 166). Thus, the role of education was to create revolutionary citizens.

Theorizing about revolutionary consciousness a posteriori and projecting it as a general revolutionary thesis, Fidel Castro and Ernesto "Che" Guevara developed what has become known as the guerrilla-focus theory to explain how a new consciousness was to come into being (Medin 1990). Che Guevara, as Castro's first lieutenant, was one of the model guerrillas in the Sierra Maestra. He interacted with the peasants not only as a guerrilla but also as a medical doctor. In guerrilla-focus theory, the camaraderie of the Sierra Maestra guerrilla fighters became the template for reshaping Cuban society. As Guevara (1964, 627) wrote,

> The guerrilla struggle in Cuba had developed in two different spheres: [the still-]slumbering masses, who had to be mobilized, and, in their vanguard, the guerrilla band, the driving force behind mobilization, generator of revolutionary consciousness and enthusiasm for combat. This vanguard was the catalyzing agent that created the subjective conditions necessary for victory.

From Guevara's words, it is important to note that one of the basic goals of implementing guerrilla-focus theory to effect social change was the creation of conciencia. Of course, the Marxists had their party, but the specifically Cuban element came from the mountains and the rebels' experience of integrating their lives with the campesinos' (Fagen 1969; Kahl 1969). Thus, even before Castro's pronouncements of 1961 and 1962, explicit efforts were already under way to create a conciencia, which set a pattern for future programs designed to inculcate values.

Much in line with Paulo Freire's (1970) dialogical theory, Guevara did not conquer people for the revolutionary cause. Instead, he gained their following through dialogue, cooperation, and communion, treating the peasants as "subjects who meet to name the world in order to transform it" (Freire 1970, 148). Freire's dialogical theory, characterized by collaboration, union, organization, and cultural synthesis, involves communication and interaction with others in order to liberate oneself and discover the world; such a situation requires humility and constant dialogue on the part of all participants. In Freirian dialogical theory, at no stage can revolutionary action forgo communion with the people, which brings leaders and people to the fusion described by Guevara when he was in the Sierra Maestra:

> As a result of daily contact with these people and their problems we became firmly convinced of the need for a complete change in the life of our people. The idea of agrarian reform became crystal-clear. Communion with the people ceased to be a mere theory, to become an integral part of ourselves.
>
> Guerrillas and peasants began to merge into a solid mass. No one can say exactly when, in this long process, the ideas became reality and we became a part of the peasantry. As far as I am concerned, the contact with my patients

in the Sierra turned a spontaneous and somewhat lyrical decision into a more serene force, one of entirely different value. (Guevara 1968, 56–57)

Freire implies that this fusion can exist only if revolutionary action is really human, empathic, loving, communicative, and humble. Che Guevara was successful in creating a fusion between the peasants and the goals of the revolution. His type of emotional interaction and investment as a medical doctor and a literacy worker exemplified revolutionary values, and thus became a model for future educational projects of the Cuban government. Guevara became the embodiment of the New Man, the symbolic figure at the core of revolutionary morality.

The experience of the guerrillas interacting with the peasants in the Sierra Maestra became the model for the forging of conciencia. In the midst of and by dint of struggle, it became clear that revolution was not just a spontaneous overthrow. Even at this early stage, the guerrillas understood that conciencia was not formed by mere propaganda and interaction but arose from revolutionary praxis: armed struggle, agrarian reform, participation in militant action, and a change in living conditions (Fagen 1969). As Guevara wrote,

> Those poor, suffering, loyal inhabitants of the Sierra Maestra have never suspected the role they played as forgers of our revolutionary ideology. . . . We convinced them that once they were armed, organized, and had lost their fear of the enemy, victory was certain, and the peasantry . . . imposed agrarian reform on the revolution. (Guevara 1968, 57)

Again, in Guevara's famous "Man and Socialism in Cuba" (1965), and as Castro has reiterated several times, the Cuban leadership measures the success of the revolution first by its progress in creating and sustaining a conciencia, and second by pragmatic economic productivity. However, this consciousness could not survive without the economic assistance and solidarity of other socialist allies, and this need for allies clashed with Guevara's insistence that Cuba operate its government independently from the Soviet Union.

Castro and *Conciencia*

Castro and his cabinet members modeled the ideals of the revolution in a socialist patriarchy in which even the socialist citizen was called *el Hombre Nuevo*, the New Man. Albert Padula (1993) suggests that the ideal Cuban citizen's revolutionary profile was generated not only by policy but also by the structure of the patriarchal Cuban regime. Although a noticeable glass ceiling for women existed in the governmental ranks, the Federation of Cuban Women (Federación de Mujeres Cubanas, FMC) tacitly supported this subordinate relationship, urging women "to think of Fidel as their father" (ibid. 25). This persistence of patriarchy is paradoxical in a revolution that imagined itself to be quintessentially modern. However, in many ways the Castro regime follows a traditional family model. Since its foundation, the FMC has been headed by Vilma Espín, one of the revolutionary leaders and coordinators in the underground struggle against the Batista regime. Espín is also the wife of Fidel's brother, Raúl, who has held the position of minister of defense and first vice president and, since 2008, when Fidel decided not to run again, president. In addition, in the 1980s, one of Fidel's sons, Fidelino, became the head of the nuclear power commission of Cuba. Around this central family there grew up another political family, those who had been guerrillas in the 1950s.

Initially, the armed struggle had been confined to an isolated attack on the Moncada army barracks in July 1953. The attack failed, many were killed, and Castro was imprisoned on the Isle of Pines. In the island penitentiary he started his own school for prisoners to raise their awareness about Cuban reality, with classes in philosophy and history. After his release from prison in 1958, during the fight against U.S.-backed President Batista, this informal educational experience was continued in orientation classes given to the Rebel Army, both in the Sierra Maestra and in the mountains in Las Villas (Fagen 1969).

To carry out the revolutionary tasks at hand and in the near future, adult cadres were needed who had the necessary social consciousness. Castro spearheaded the birth of the Escuelas de Instrucción Revolucionaria (EIR) on December 2, 1960, in an attempt to bring together the mixed revolutionary factions at the time and build a cohesive ideological mission. Much secrecy surrounded their planning, maneuvering, and founding. The first EIR course was attended by more than 700 students, cadres, and revolutionary activists from the M26 and the Popular Socialist Party (the renamed Cuban Communist Party) and a few from the March 13 Revolutionary Directorate (an anti-communist group that opposed Batista in 1957). The Revolutionary Directorate attached special, even transcendental, significance to the founding of the EIR, because the schools were set up before the different revolutionary political forces came together in a single organization. Therefore, the EIR schools were symbolic and responsible for the origin of political integration of various revolutionary organs (Soto 1963).

The mission of the EIR schools was to teach classes in Marxism-Leninism, and the student selection process followed a policy that consciously favored those of lower social origin and "*absolute fidelity to the revolution, class spirit, and practical action in support of the revolution*" (Soto 1967, 42; emphasis in original, trans. mine). It was also understood that philosophical thought was not enough, that in accordance with the philosophy, people must be engaged in revolutionary praxis. The praxis included participation in work brigades for literacy, agriculture, and construction. By 1963, 87,036 students had passed through the EIR courses, which lasted two to three months. Lionel Soto, the national director and founder of the EIR, noted that in those years, "the study of Marxism became a mass phenomenon" (1965, 69; trans. mine). The EIR schools had concentrated "all of their efforts in the mass dissemination of the brilliant ideas of scientific socialism, of Marxism-Leninism, and the decision to win over the consciousness of the masses to socialist ideas" (Soto 1963, 35; trans. mine). By 1961 the EIR schools were able to provide the rebel leaders with revolutionary adults newly trained in Marxism.

This added internal ideological security, coupled with the external increasing aggression of the United States, paved the way for Castro to make his formal declaration of the revolution as socialist endeavor on April 16, 1961, during the Bay of Pigs Invasion. Later that year, in December 1961, Castro proclaimed himself a Marxist-Leninist. In January 1962, in a radio interview with Moscow Domestic Service, he added, "When we began this struggle, we already had some knowledge of and sympathy for Marxism. But we could not for this reason call ourselves Marxists. . . . We were revolutionary apprentices" (Castro 1962).

The context and timing of these pronouncements, December 1961 and January 1962, are important for showing Castro's attempts to educate others in revolutionary ideals and the practical factors that may have influenced him. With the U.S. government still putting strong pressure on Cuba, Soviet protection and aid became essential for the survival of the revolution (Domínguez 1989). The more Castro could portray himself as a Marxist-Leninist, the more secure Soviet help would be. In light of these developments, Castro's repeated denial of being a full-fledged Marxist prior to 1959 makes sense.

Many factors shaped Castro's ideology, including his personality and upbringing, both of which were key to defining the political direction of the country, conciencia, and the schooling of a revolutionary society. The transcendental voluntarism promoted by the Cuban leadership had both a historical and an emotional basis. When recalling their schooling by Jesuits, Castro and the majority of the Cuban leaders have admitted they were shaped and influenced by the religious education they received. Indeed, Castro has noted that "all qualities that make a priest are qualities needed to make a good revolutionary" (cited in Kirk 1989, 122). In an editorial note in *Juventud Rebelde,* Cuban sympathizer Frei Betto said, "Here a society of cooperation, collaboration, and international spirit has been constructed. All of those socialist values are essentially Christian" (1999). According to Nelson Valdés (1992), even if the Cuban revolutionary politicians did not accept the political content of the Catholic ideology, the politicians internalized the Catholic-Hispanic values of willpower, discipline, self-sacrifice, total dedication, ethical norms, and a strong character.

Castro also had an electric and messianic link with the masses, ranking as one of the twentieth century's greatest charismatic leaders. In many respects a textbook case of a Weberian stereotypical-ideal charismatic leader, "Castro in power came to be seen as an ascetic, devoted to the revolutionary cause" (Eckstein 1994, 20). He made ordinary people feel a sense of worth and dignity. Indicative of how he appealed to them, Castro (1972b, 169–170) noted that "You all know very well that we are not capable of imagining that this phenomenon [charisma] is the mere consequence of personal magnetism. . . . A revolution is not the work of a man . . . or a group of men. Revolutions are the work of an entire people." Castro was, as Max Weber (1978) has noted of charismatic leaders, obeyed by virtue of personal trust in him and treated as if he were endowed with superhuman qualities, defying great odds to deliver a people from doom, and perhaps leading some of his followers to see him as providential.

Castro's leadership was established at a time of profound crisis and during a power vacuum. His charisma may have had the capacity to transform society, but charisma is inherently an unstable source of power. Charisma is a feeling and, like beauty, is always in the eye of the beholder. Also like beauty, charismatic rule is prone to become strictly personal and transitory. It depends not only on the leader's extraordinary qualities but also on the even more important aspects of performance and the subject's belief in his mission. To remain a charismatic leader one must prove one's worth. Thus, the affective dimension and the political culture cannot be ignored when assessing the bond between Castro and the Cuban people, and its relation to the governing strategies employed by the revolutionary leadership.

The revolutionary leadership, which included Castro's cabinet members, might be best understood as the charismatic leader's organization of disciples. Weber recognized that only a small group is likely to be sufficiently idealistic after the initial stages of a revolution to devote their lives purely to its call. However, this aspect of what Weber terms "routinization" tends to produce its own challenges, with followers seeking to make their living materially from their calling. In the process, they are prone to appropriate power, control, and economic advantage for themselves, whereas the leader strives for the fulfillment of his mission (Suarez 1971; Weber 1947). The leader determines the limitations of the disciples' power, usually guided by the exigencies of the moment (Weber 1978). Faced with this issue, Castro periodically purged party members who, in his estimation, were failing in their duties.

Castro's core philosophy is based on the belief that the direction of history can be perceived, and that conscious revolutionaries can and ought to accelerate the rate of change. He tapped the deep roots of the mid-nineteenth-century insurrections against Spanish colonialism and its themes of nationalism, radicalism, and social justice populism. He became the "supreme symbol not only of the revolution, but also of Cuban nationalism" (Medin 1990, 54). Whatever the timing of Castro's private allegiance to Marxism, he waited more than two years after the takeover to identify himself publicly with socialism and Marxism. The wait may have been tactical, but it also represented a recognition of the feelings of Cubans toward their history and the revolution.

Moreover, the political culture of Cuba since the colonial era was steeped in a sort of romanticism in pursuit of a moral and material utopia. Later, José Martí, the hero of the nineteenth-century Cuban independence wars, reignited this millennial vision. It is no coincidence that both Karl Marx and José Martí have become political icons in socialist Cuba. However, from the outset, José Martí seems to have been Castro's personal role model. This idea is explicitly expressed in a poem by the Cuban poet Nicolas Guillén (1964, 129–130): "Te lo prometió Martí / y Fidel te lo cumplió" (Martí promised it to you / and Fidel kept the promise). Furthermore, it is Martí's, not Marx's, bust that stands guard at every Cuban school, even at the small schools the revolutionaries built in the remote mountainous areas. Nevertheless, it must be recognized that Martí's image constitutes the expression of a specifically Cuban origin of the revolution, and therefore, according to Medin (1990, 56), "any trend of tolerance reflected in the image of the revolution always derives from the underlying Martí motif."

With an ideology well grafted onto compatible aspects of Cuban culture, the revolution evoked feelings and relied on those feelings to muster popular support. Strong affective reactions stemmed from a moral sense of justice expressed as a radical nationalism, based on Cuba's past and proposed future. The adoption of Marxism-Leninism as the official ideology was successful because it resonated with the passion and affection sparked by their charismatic leader. Castro sustained the traditional Cuban foundation that had been built on liberal, informal, corporatist norms. He provided continuity in political culture despite a change in ideology and regime.

Revolution and Political Unity

During structural transition and revolution, emotional appeal is paramount in garnering much-needed popular support and fostering political unity. The one-party system and strong political unity of Marxism-Leninism were crucial to the survival of the Cuban Revolution, especially in the early years. In light of the state of international affairs in the 1960s, becoming a Leninist benefited Castro and the Cuban people. Yet Cuba's ongoing economic stress and survival required political centralization and alliance with the Soviet Union, assuming that socialism and democracy would be achieved under a one-party system (Domínguez 1978).

An external enemy, the United States, served to heighten the need for unity in the name of national security. The small island nation had to withstand military attack with CIA-directed sabotage and assassination attempts on Fidel Castro in the Bay of Pigs Invasion and during the 1961 Literacy Campaign. These acts of U.S. aggression increased the need for political loyalty and collective support. Moreover, the U.S. embargo encouraged and affirmed the need for a concentration of political power in Cuba. The embargo also enabled the Cuban government to call for a degree of conformity among its people to combat the "market mentality" of the enemy, the United States (Leiner 1994).

The political religion constructed from these politics of passion provided what other ideological institutions, such as the Catholic Church, had not been able to up to this point: the sense of a nation united in the quest for a moral absolute. Passion, in this case, polarized politics.

Passion was also structured by a Manichean technique of dividing the world into good and evil. Especially in times of confrontation, use of this technique has proved to be highly effective and to have a strong affective value. The enemy became stigmatized by the constant repetition of *gusano*, or worm (a term used for traitors), and the enemy was identified with other enemies already unanimously repudiated by the Cuban people. The term *gusano* is an emotionally charged and evaluative expression of total contempt for anyone who was not on the side of the revolution. The United States, representing imperialism and capitalism, was demonized as "the great enemy of humankind" (Guevara 1964, 650) and "the executioner of nations": "It does not limit itself to sucking the blood and devouring the flesh of the peoples that fall victim to its insatiable appetite for wealth" (*Verde Olivo* 1961, 7; trans. mine). The greater the polarization, the more the enemy was stigmatized through the use of stereotypes—the scaffolding of the Manichean scheme.

The Manichean conceptual world is used to reflect a political strategy; it reinforces the totalistic nature of confrontation by stigmatizing the enemy. The stigmatization is fueled by stereotypes that, Medin (1990) contends, are purposeful in creating an emotional charge that will, in turn, mobilize and discipline Cubans to confront the enemy, real or imagined. Medin proposes that while the projection of the image varies with the changes in political strategy, many times the Manichean image precedes or prepares the way for the explicit or official presentation of the strategy to the masses. This was especially true during the 1960s, when Castro waited more than two years after he came to power to identify the revolution as a socialist effort and himself as a Marxist. He chose for the context of his announcement a moment at the apex of imperialist domination and confrontation, the Bay of Pigs Invasion. The official socialist character of the revolution was grafted onto a robust body of Cuban nationalism and anti-imperialism. At the same time, even as the Cuban *pueblo* (village) was being primed, one of the largest mobilizations of the populace was successfully launched—the 1961 National Literacy Campaign. The Cuban leadership used the Manichean scheme to its advantage. The regime was by no means enslaved to it in the 1960s; however, over a period of time, the Manichean scheme may have become normalized as the exclusive conceptual and emotional frame of reference for the leaders themselves.

The revolution was not merely a hostile reaction to the policies of the United States and its allies, it was an attempt to create a better world with a more humane worldview. According to Domínguez (1989, 117), "The Cuban government's evolving ideology has provided a means for the leadership to interpret reality; it serves as a lens through which to see the world or as a framework within which to evaluate the evidence." Moreover, Domínguez states that the ideology of the Cuban leaders has both "descriptive and prescriptive content," especially in its belief in revolution. The conceptual framework of this ideology, according to sociologist Bob Hall (1975), consists not only in the humanistic ideal of Cuba's New Man but also in the support for revolution with the language of *lucha*, or struggle, and a millennial vision. The discourse—a language of passion—gave way to a political religion, not an ideology narrowly defined (Fernández 2000). The political religion advocated duty to the revolution, which was compatible with Marxism-Leninism, although it did not necessarily arise from it.

A Moral Economy

What was emphasized in socialism—morality—was rarely mentioned during the U.S. capitalist domination of the island. During pre-revolutionary times, Cuba's economic growth and dependence on the United States by means of the sugar crop and tourism resulted in a stronger economic structure and better qualified human resources than in most other countries in the region. However, Cuba did not profit from import substitution or from an industrial diversification policy. Instead, money was invested disproportionately in expensive urban housing, gambling casinos, and major hotels catering to U.S. tourists. Meanwhile, the country suffered from corruption characterized by crime and rampant prostitution, especially in Havana. Commenting on this complex phenomenon, Edward Boorstein noted in his firsthand account of the developing revolutionary economic policy, "Until the Revolution, the central fact about the Cuban economy was its domination by American monopolies. . . . It was from imperialist domination that the specific characteristics flowed. Unless this is recognized, the Cuban revolution cannot be understood" (1968, 1).

In the initial days of the revolutionary regime, Cuba was in political crisis, and a command economy was established to combat the extreme inequalities of wealth and underdevelopment. The country had become too dependent on the sugar industry, and the decision was made to diversify agriculture and become more self-sufficient. Development was sought through rapid industrialization. As Minister of Industry Che Guevara, architect of this strategy, phrased it, "there can be no vanguard country that has not developed its industry. Industry is the future" (1964, 14).

At the beginning of 1961, the ideology of the revolution was still undefined, but the policies of the previous two years had set in motion a dynamic that was becoming increasingly difficult to reverse. The alliance of Castroites and communists had subdued or won over most of its rivals. The problem of control, therefore, was being resolved with the emergence of a new elite sprung from previous dominant groups, but identified with the aspirations of the peasants and proletariat (Malloy 1971).

Along with state socialism, proletarianism became the decisive vision in 1962. Cuba was a socialist society in self-definition and practice, and a member of the socialist bloc of nations. However, the tactical reality of making the socialist model function and achieve success over time proved challenging. Putting socialism into practice revolved around the delicate issue of balancing political agendas and economic reality.

In confronting this new dilemma at the beginning of 1962, the Cuban leadership had the advantage of working with a Cuban population that, for the most part, was primed by the consumptionist policies of the previous three years and thus recognized an affective commitment on the part of the new regime. Hence, the fledgling socialist society was in a position to utilize force and the somewhat eroded but still significant revolutionary fervor as basic mechanisms for generating support.

Cuba was utterly unprepared, though, for a centrally planned economy. It lacked both technical personnel (who were in exile in the United States or imprisoned in Cuba) and statistics. With spectacular growth targets, a sharp decrease in sugar production, and little success in agricultural diversification, industry suffered greatly, leading to the collapse of the Cuban economy in 1962 (Domínguez 1993).

The shift to economic logic began in March 1962 with the imposition of a rationing system to help address product scarcity and demand satisfaction. With overall consumption cut, at least all available goods, as well as services, were equally distributed. Outside of collective consumption, a limited number of material incentives were used to reward the work of individuals. A minority of workers could win bonuses, refrigerators, motorcycles, automobiles, and trips in the socialist competition for productive output. The government continued to use a limited number of material incentives and to meet the general level of demand for services as a means to gain political and economic support (Malloy 1971).

Although the economic goal was to become more self-sufficient, by 1963 Cuba had discovered that it could not escape from the role of exporter of agricultural products, especially sugar. Sugar became the economic engine of the revolution. The important point is that in the last part of the industrialization phase, and particularly during the return-to-sugar phase, the dominant logic was that of accumulation and investment primarily paid for by increasing restrictions on mass consumption (Malloy 1971; Mesa-Lago 1971).

The Soviet Union and Cuba made their first long-term agreement in 1964, one that guaranteed better, more stable bilateral sugar prices. Soon after signing this agreement Castro started to publicize the unprecedented goal of producing 10 million tons of sugar in 1970 (production was 3.8 million tons in 1963) (Domínguez 1993). His proposal did not go without dispute. Opposition from administrators and technicians in the sugar industry was overruled, and this utopic goal, like others, became a point of pride for committed revolutionaries.

During this stage, Cuba followed the classic state-socialist model. The guerrilla spirit waned as the more mechanistic Soviet and East European model was adopted. A command system was established that entailed central planning, the central allocation of resources, and central wage fixing. Socialism was also broadened as the state progressively eliminated, particularly in agriculture, more private economic activity (Malloy 1971; Mesa-Lago 1971).

This centralization and organization of the economy was accompanied by more control mechanisms, namely, the army and a yet undefined national party. In 1963, compulsory military service was initiated. With that measure the Cuban army swelled to become the largest single standing army in the hemisphere outside the United States (Malloy 1971). However, the roles of the Cuban militia were very broad. The army represented more than an instrument for organizing and deploying military force. Many sections were militarized, including unarmed brigades that worked in agriculture and on construction projects. Even sections that were trained in warfare performed tasks such as cutting sugarcane (a form of cost allocation). Thus, the regime introduced to the army a form of compulsory mobilization and production functions, a move that was to have a profound influence on the course of the revolution, particularly after 1966 (Malloy 1971).

However, the broadening reach of the army did little to diminish the heated debate over the nature of socialist economic organization. Che Guevara represented one side, which argued that all enterprises should be branches of central ministries owned by the state. Material incentives were to be phased out, and the law of supply and demand was to be eliminated. The other side saw the state not as a single economic unit but as a variety of enterprises independently owned and state operated. Material incentives were essential to maintaining productivity and quality and reducing costs. Guevarism prevailed.

Guevara's policies were not generally adopted until after he left Cuba in 1965 to participate in revolutionary campaigns in other parts of Latin America. In his absence, the implementation of his policies was carried to extremes. Ironically, as the economy became thoroughly centralized, the means for central planning and control were neglected. Castro would later acknowledge his chaotic administrative practice in a dramatic speech he made on July 26, 1970, when the Cuban economy lay in ruins.

Regardless of administrative foibles, Guevara's precepts continued to shape economic and ideological practice. Castro (1972b, 413) recognized that the customs of the past would be the greatest obstacle during the initial stage of building a socialist society: "[the] ideas instilled and maintained and propagated by the economically dominant classes, by the imperialists and by the capitalists in our country; these prejudices, beyond a doubt, constituted one of the most powerful forces with which the revolution had to contend." The pre-revolutionary capitalist order sanctioned social inequalities, which motivated people to work solely for the pursuit of money. Work in a capitalist society was motivated by fear, and competition was seen only in destructive terms. To combat these values, the revolutionary regime shifted from material to moral incentives as part of official policy in 1965.

According to Guevara, moral incentives guided economic production as well as other social relations. With the transition from material to moral incentives, the new socialist leadership hoped that the Cuban people would comprehend the need to work for the common good, with no need to strive for profitability, and abundance would follow. Ultimately the whole economy would produce for the population's needs (Azicri 1988; Kahl 1969; Pérez-Stable 1993; Silverman 1971).

Prior to 1966, Fidel Castro skillfully avoided committing himself on the substantive controversy over material versus moral incentives. However, after the political structure consolidated with the final formalization of the Cuban Communist Party, in 1965, and his own position was secure, he launched the revolution on a new course, one that veered sharply from the orthodox socialist forms of the Soviet Union and Eastern Europe: the path of moral incentives.

From a political point of view, moral incentives are a means for "achieving political support, by creating a mental state of generalized affectivity and commitment" (Malloy 1971, 39). It reverses the classical liberal theory of political obligation, which sees affective commitment as a product of material reward. Instead of the capitalist social contracts involving advantage-seeking individuals, moral incentives are based on a preexistent "moral community" that transcends individual members (Malloy 1971).

The notion of a moral community is critical to understanding the new political culture at this time, because a moral community can be a double-edged sword. On the one hand, it can be a positive, noncoercive generator of support, rewarding conformity with abstract moral signs of approval. On the other hand, moral incentives have a highly coercive potential in that behavior considered deviant can be curtailed through public shame, forced labor, or, in extreme cases, excommunication from the community. Thus, in Cuba, especially during the 1960s, many mass revolutionary organizations maintained a moral vigilance over the population. Those who rejected the revolution were excommunicated from the community, stripped of their material possessions, sent to work in agriculture, and subjected to humiliation before they left the country as gusanos—worms (Malloy 1971).

According to Malloy (1971), moral communities cannot be simply declared, they must be constructed. In revolutionary Cuba this end is sought with mobilization and value formation. This formation process is applied in a unique way according to generational lines, which I outline below. The different ways in which children and adults are addressed illustrate the different ideological expectations for each on the part of the revolutionary government.

Much emphasis has been given to youth, because young people are malleable and so are considered to be the clay out of which the ideal New Man can be formed. The educational system is given major responsibility, starting as early as day care, to form students according to revolutionary values, even when such formation is at odds with the parents' wishes. For example, when students reach eighth grade, they are mobilized to rural areas for long stints to perform agricultural work and are involved in work projects on weekends in the community. Additional on-campus hours are supplemented with Pioneer interest circles, Pioneer Explorer activities (Pioneer Explorers are like the Boy Scouts and Girl Scouts of America organizations), and other Pioneer activities. All of these activities involve separating children from their parents, the older generation.

This separation of generations ensures that children spend more time with secure, proper formative mechanisms (revolutionary-primed teachers and curricula) and that the value formation channeled through the school will override any family opposition. Moreover, if need be, the children are likely to cultivate a stronger affective bond with their peers in their collective experience than with their own family.

In a sense, the school is creating a new awareness of belonging and family, a possibly competing moral community to that of the nuclear family. The school community pledges allegiance to the revolution and inundates those who follow with reinforcing affection, attention, friendship, and pride. Through the collective revolutionary schooling experience, the student from a young age ideally gains social consciousness to be motivated by moral commitment alone, becoming a self-mobilizing adult and rendering material reward unnecessary.

With adults the process is reversed, in that the mobilization precedes the formation. Since adults are considered to be the product of a previous "degenerate" society, their formation is more complex and is expected to be imperfect. Thus, positive and negative moral incentives are employed. Through various mobilizations, such as collective work projects, it is hoped that the proper formation will occur. In a few cases, material incentives are employed when the need is urgent; some examples are the housing built for farmers in the Green Belt around La Habana (*Granma* 1968b, 3) and the hiring of professional cane cutters needed to lead the cane cutting in 1970. In addition, bonuses in the form of kitchen and home appliances and the like were frequently given to exemplary workers.

Constructing a moral community required different elements for different generations. The revolutionary leadership recognized the history and experience from pre-revolutionary times as an obstacle to forming conciencia, what Fidel Castro called "the burden of the past." Whereas the Cuban elite has bet first of all on the moral commitment of the young people, in dealing with adults the more classic carrot-and-stick approach for social control has been employed, with increasingly more emphasis on the stick in the latter half of the 1960s.

Guevara's economic proposal, which included this moral dimension in cultivating social consciousness, has always been a goal of the Cuban government, but it has not gone without question and experimentation of sorts since the early 1960s. The balancing act has involved teetering between material and moral incentives, centralization and decentralization of the economy, and different strategies of market exchanges. During the early sixties, budgetary planning operated in industry and self-financing operated in agriculture following an economic strategy based on overdiversification and self-sufficiency. By the late sixties, a version of budgetary financing prevailed, as the Cuban government launched a radical plan for centralization that included mass mobilizations and increased attention to moral incentives (Pérez-Stable 1993).

The first decade of the revolution was a time of experimentation in all realms of government. Revolutionary fervor had been mounting prior to the 1959 takeover, and the decade of the sixties saw an outflowing of this built-up passion: will was all, and everything seemed possible. From the outset of the revolution there was a strong participatory impulse that, according to Fernández (2000), was due to the leadership, the pre-revolutionary history, and consciousness-raising events. From 1962 to 1965 the state-socialist model was consolidated both politically and economically. In the political realm, Castro brought the major factions of the revolution to heel and brought into being two powerful state instruments, the army and the national party. Moreover, Castro became the person who defined the future of the revolution.

Economically, the emphasis shifted from consumption to development. Support was generated by an amalgam of affective and economic interplays, including (1) an appeal to affective commitment, based on Castro's charisma and the demand satisfaction from 1959 to 1961, (2) a reduced but equalized level of demand satisfaction and social service with limited material incentives, and (3) the increasing use of militarization, force, and mobilizations to control political dissidents.

The army is an important institution of social control, especially in effecting the mobilization of human and material resources and in providing technological skill. Unlike in orthodox socialist states, where military institutions come under strict party control, in Cuba the army is the real locus of power. The Communist Party is the chief organ of political coordination, but its command structure is infiltrated at all levels by the military. Indeed, Cuba's top military men also hold key positions in the party, thereby guaranteeing not only the interests of the military institution but also a preponderance of military values and style (Malloy 1971).

This militarization of society, as well as other internal transitions and transformations, took place with unprecedented speed during the 1960s and the first half of the 1970s. By 1968, the "revolutionary offensive" had rapidly eliminated what remained of private property and material incentives. Nearly 56,000 small businesses were confiscated by the government, completing the total collectivization of the nonagricultural sector. The revolutionary offensive also promoted large labor mobilizations in order to increase agricultural production, exhorting the masses to work harder, save more, and accept the scarcity of goods in a revolutionary spirit. Through these measures the state hoped to increase capital accumulation, even at the cost of further reducing consumption (Mesa-Lago 1971).

Another move to increase capital accumulation was the expropriation first of foreign enterprises and later those of the national bourgeoisie. These measures, together with support from the socialist camp, allowed for accelerated growth of investment, which generated a significant increase in and diversification of employment. For instance, fifty-nine types of technical occupations existed in 1953 and 118 existed in 1981 (CETSS 1981, 204–205, Table 54 and Resolution 654). The transformation of property relations caused an emigration of upper-class owners, people imbued with the values of this class who saw their expectations of consumption or accumulation blocked by the new socialist model of society. The conjunction of these factors opened up a social and economic space for previously marginalized groups, such as women, people of color, and young people (Martín 1991).

With this objective in mind, the role of education in the development of society and individual personality was fundamental in transforming culture in ways that were supportive of the immediate and long-term goals of social change. In the Cuban view, without the education and reeducation of the Cuban masses there could be no successful and lasting Leninist politics, agrarian reform, economic transformation, or international realignments (Fagen 1969). The revolutionaries saw a direct link between economic development and education. Therefore, the fastest way to move away from underdevelopment was through education.

In 1966, at a closing session of the National Meeting of School Monitors, Fidel Castro spoke of the tasks of the revolution: "The most sacred of all of our obligations has been that of how we are going to form our children and youth . . . [O]ur triumph in this great historic mission will depend upon the measure in which we are capable of solving correctly the problem of the formation of our new generations." Education was entrusted "with the delicate function of forming new generations, of forming the new man for the new society" (1966b). Furthermore, the Cuban educational system was charged with a mission that went beyond expansion and mass education, which are ambitious goals in themselves. Revolutionary pedagogy involved promoting the adoption of the conceptual, cognitive, emotional, axiological, and terminological world projected by the revolutionary leaders (Medin 1990).

CHAPTER 2

The Revolution in Education

The revolutionary government's strategies to construct communist *conciencia* through political and economic restructuring had their counterpart in education. From the beginning of the revolution, Fidel Castro focused considerable attention on the matter of widespread illiteracy and on education in general. For the revolutionary government, the Literacy Campaign was understood as a fundamental act of social justice. At the same time, the campaign and subsequent education programs became vehicles for integration into and participation in the revolution, reinforcing Castro's immediate power base, the Rebel Army, and his broader power base, the peasantry. The revolutionary Cuban educational system was designed to reinforce and reflect the new political and economic goals in an effort to construct political unity, to respond to production needs, and to transform the hearts and minds of people to become new socialist men and women.

The educational efforts that followed the Literacy Campaign took on a political importance that transcended the pedagogical. The radical changes in the political and economic structure were reflected in the educational system and in a revolutionary pedagogy. The more urgent goal was to prepare the different generations for revolutionary confrontation. This goal meant that the pupil had to acquire a new conciencia, one that would adopt a conceptual and axiological worldview based on revolutionary struggle against imperialism and the forces of the past. How did revolutionary pedagogy function in the 1960s to transform the Cuban population into New Men and New Women with a communist conciencia?

Pre-revolutionary Education in Cuba

The revolutionary educational system initiated in Cuba in 1959 bore little resemblance to the educational system that had earlier been introduced in Cuba by the United States. Cuban public education during the U.S. military occupation and under American tutelage from the early 1900s until the 1959 revolution was a paternalistic system that imposed its own set of values on a subordinate culture (Epstein 1987). Thus, the extent to which foreign intervention succeeded in expanding access to education is questionable. In 1955, the proportion of primary school–aged children enrolled in school was 51 percent, only 6 percent higher than in 1902. Moreover, the percentage of primary school–aged children enrolled in Cuban schools was lower than in all but three Latin American countries, and well below the 64 percent average for Latin America as a whole (UNESCO 1962, 146).

During the pre-revolutionary years, structural obstacles and corruption plagued the Cuban educational system. Although nearly one-fifth of state expenditures went toward education in 1958, the massive outlay had little effect on primary school enrollment, inadequate school facilities, or the poor literacy rate. Prior to the revolution, 23.6 percent of the population was illiterate, including more than one million adults. However, national averages fail to disclose the uneven cultural development throughout the country. There was great disparity between literacy rates in rural and urban areas: in 1953, while the illiteracy rate in Havana province was 9.2 percent, in the less developed provinces of Oriente, Pinar del Rio, and Camagüey it was 35.3 percent, 30.8 percent, and 27.3 percent, respectively. Moreover, there was an acute deficiency of classrooms: in 1958 there were only 17,000 classrooms, whereas, according to independent estimates, approximately 35,000 were needed (Valdés 1971).

The *Report on Cuba*, underwritten by the World Bank, describes public schooling at the beginning of the 1950s as being in a state of "disquieting deterioration" (Paulston 1971, 379). The report notes that whereas some progress had been made toward developing secondary school education and specialized schools during the 1940s, the general trend since the late 1920s had been retrograde. Instruction had dropped from four hours a day to only two. Apathy and absenteeism prevailed among teachers. In addition, teachers were granted life tenure as government officials and received a full salary whether they taught or not. Teacher appointments were reported to be a major target of patronage, being bought and sold at high prices. Furthermore, from the mid- to the late 1940s, the minister of education stole millions of dollars from the education budget and rapidly became one of Cuba's richest men (Paulston 1971).

The Castro government's accomplishments stand in stark contrast to the miserable state of pre-revolutionary education. In little more than a decade, the revolutionary government managed to enroll close to 100 percent of eight-year-old children and more than 90 percent of all children of primary school age (Epstein 1987).

Revolutionary Education: Educational Expansion and the 1961 Literacy Campaign

Whereas before 1959, the educational program was stagnant, serving to maintain a well-defined class structure and providing only a relatively small percentage of Cubans with access to the foreign-dominated sector, the revolution's educational reform was geared toward developing all Cubans into a skilled labor force and toward creating a generalized socialist consciousness (Carnoy 1990). To achieve these ends, a new political and ideological orientation was necessary. The expansion of education to all was regarded as essential to achieving the economic, social, and political objectives of the new society.

To transmit the values of the new society, mobilizations emphasizing the participation of Cuban youth were launched. The most notable of the early mobilization campaigns was the 1961 National Literacy Campaign. Close to 100,000 teenage literacy workers accepted Fidel Castro's challenge to go to remote areas of the island to live and work with *campesino* families. Once there, the *brigadista* literacy workers integrated themselves in rural culture, working in the fields for eight months while teaching the campesinos to read and write at night, an effort that reduced the illiteracy rate from 23.6 percent to 3.9 percent in less than a year (Lorenzetto and Neys 1965).

The involvement of the young brigadistas on the front line of the campaign was one of the unique features of this endeavor, but adults were not excluded. Adult contingents were asked to participate in the workplace, in urban slum areas, and in the countryside, as lead teachers for the brigadistas. "Each literacy brigade headquarters thus formed a focus of intellectual and political life, from which the ideas of the Revolution radiated far and wide" (Karol 1970, 37).

Literacy instruction occurred on a wide scale. Altogether, more than 1.1 million Cubans, roughly 894,000 students and more than 270,000 working as teachers, directly participated in this "passionate, turbulent, sometimes desperate" campaign (Kozol 1978, 84). The campaign represented a "large-scale government effort to advance the level of education and break down the psychological barriers to participation by adults in an effort to educate them" (Domínguez 1978, 165).

The Literacy Campaign became a template of the means by which to achieve the ends of the Cuban Revolution, as well as an outstanding model of revolutionary pedagogy. When I spoke to participants—now education officials, teachers, or parents—during my time in Cuba, all of them mentioned the Literacy Campaign as setting the stage for educational innovation, achievement, and value inculcation. In addition, in conversation, all of them cited a personal experience that broadened their perspective on life.

Before reviewing the older generation's perspective on the 1961 Literacy Campaign, it is important to note that the campaign became a hallmark event in Cuban history and an educational fulcrum for Cuba's future. We might ask, then, in what ways the role of affect, through the Literacy Campaign, was used to forward the goals of the Cuban government, and to what degree the affective component was incorporated into later future educational programs and policy.

The bond between the Cuban leadership and the masses and its influence on the governing strategies must be seen in the light of a political culture that tried to shape not only how one thought and felt about politics but also one's behavior as result of these thoughts and feelings. The new regime sought to change the political culture to adhere to a new ideology.

I follow Richard Fagen's definition of ideology as "a symbol system linking particular actions and mundane practices with a wider set of meanings" (1969, 163). The function of an ideology, according to Daniel Bell (1965, 591), "is to concretize the values, the normative judgments of the society." The ideology of the revolution did not rely necessarily on literal truth but rather on its evocative or motivating power for its success. In this way, the "battle" against illiteracy, the formation of the "New Man," and other symbolic language of the revolution, according to Clifford Geertz (1964), should not be discounted on the grounds that these terms and slogans are not scientific. Rather, metaphors and symbols should be taken seriously and considered successful insofar as they multiply meanings and enlarge understanding for their intended audiences.

Recognizing the symbolic value of terminology and cultural motifs, I use the model of the Literacy Campaign to illustrate the ways in which "codes of passion," to use Fernández's (2000, 38) term, have been incorporated into Cuba's revolutionary pedagogy. For Fernández, codes of passion are "cultural motifs running throughout Cuban political history . . . essentially romantic norms of conduct . . . that carry an intense emotional and moral charge." The motifs I have identified include the perfectibility and redemptive power of youth (Fagen 1969; Valdés 1989), the existence of a moral absolute or a moral imperative as part of a millennial vision (Fernández 2000; Kahl 1969; Valdés 1988), and behaviors derived from the guerrilla-focus theory (Medin 1990), initiated in the Sierra Maestra experience and characterized by mobilization, combat, and the Freirian notions of humbleness and empathy to cultivate a "communion" with the people. These motifs have been noted in other aspects of Cuban revolutionary society but to date they have not been used in aggregate to analyze the affective dimension of Cuban revolutionary pedagogy, of which the Literacy Campaign serves as a model.

The Perfectibility and Redemptive Power of Youth

Since the early days of the revolution, the focus has been on youth. In 1959, Fidel Castro called on those who had graduated from the sixth grade to become *maestros voluntarios* (volunteer teachers) to pilot the would-be literacy program. The younger generation was perceived to be the embodiment of courage, idealism, and purity of heart, and therefore prime material for creating the new socialist man and woman (Fagen 1969; Valdés 1992). Once trained, the young would become the vanguard of the revolution and, according to Castro, redeemers of the masses.

Brigades of student volunteers were sent to the Sierra Maestra for training, and then to the remotest areas to carry out literacy efforts. After their "veritable revolutionary bath in the Sierra Maestra," it was thought that the student workers could live under any conditions, no matter how trying (Hart 1962, 14). (Unlike their predecessors, the literacy workers who followed did not undergo a revolutionary bath before beginning their literacy work.) Working to the government's advantage, however, were the younger generation's energy, enthusiasm, and willingness to engage in an adventurous and exciting project.

The sacrifice and in some cases the martyrdom of a few young people served to fuel the Manichean image of a battle being waged against evil imperialism and the serpent's nest of capitalism, the United States. One death that was eulogized occurred in the pre-campaign efforts of 1960. A young pilot literacy worker, Conrado Benitez, was reportedly tortured and murdered by counterrevolutionaries. When the official Literacy Campaign started in April 1961, the student brigades took on his name and were called the "Conrado Benitez brigadistas." Moreover, they were issued military-style, olive green uniforms with a badge bearing the martyr's initials. Poems were written in his memory, and the hymn of the Conrado Benitez brigades was broad-casted six times daily (Fagen 1969).

Even though the literacy workers consisted of more adults (*alfabetizadores*, numbering 126,069), professional teachers (33,960), and workers on paid leave (13,882) than child brigadistas (100,000), more publicity and recognition were accorded the sacrifice and heroism of the children (Valdés 1972). Forty percent of the brigadistas were in the 10- to 14-year-old age group and 47.5 percent were in the 15- to 19-year-old age group; the average age was 14–16 years. Almost three-quarters of the students came from urban homes and were assigned to rural provinces (Lorenzetto and Neys 1965).

The Literacy Campaign tapped the resources of the young by deemphasizing credentials and allowing thousands to become teachers. This strategy enabled the revolutionary government to move with existing resources on a broad mass base, and then, at a later stage, to focus on raising the quality of the teaching personnel.

When the student literacy workers returned eight months later from the countryside, they were heralded as heroes in scale and spirit, very reminiscent of the way the guerrillas were hailed when they entered Havana at the time of the revolutionary triumph in 1959. The child brigadistas returned with stories of hardships, of crossing raging rivers, sleeping in hammocks, and working in the fields without seeing their families for months, much like old soldiers recalling past battles. Most students had a sense of having fulfilled a national duty, with the added benefits of personal experience gained and the satisfaction of seeing the results of their literacy attempts. The élan, the image, and the exploits of the youth captured national attention and met the revolutionary goal of forming young people to be the vanguard of the revolution. As a result of this tremendous literacy effort, the year 1961 came to be called, in Cuba, "The Year of Education."

The Existence of a Moral Absolute or Imperative as Part of a Millennial Vision

Following Castro's issuance of the Sierra Maestra Manifesto, eliminating illiteracy became a right and a duty for all citizens. It was held out as a just measure that would end inequality by elevating the educational level of workers and farmers and carrying forward the socialist goals and ideals of the revolution. So strong was the moral imperative to participate in the Literacy Campaign that all schools closed during the campaign to free children and teachers to respond to Fidel's call to "raise the cultural level of the country."

A common slogan of the campaign was "Every student a teacher, every teacher a student." This slogan was seen on posters and emblems and was accompanied by an image of a double handshake (one between a white arm and a black arm, the other between a black arm and a white arm) illustrating the unity and integration of the Cuban people in the campaign (Leiner 1987).

In addition, for the urban students, the countryside became a setting in which to experience another reality. Participation was one imperative, integration to foster political unity was another. Marvin Leiner (1987, 182–183), in an interview with a literacy worker, provides a clear example of the achievement of a mutual learning experience, a moral imperative for all Cuban citizens:

The peasant is a very respectful person. They themselves had offered their homes. I never felt that they manifested any negative attitudes because of my youth. In fact, they always called me "*usted*." When we were studying they were always attentive and respectful.

We tried to help the peasants in their work whenever possible. When we didn't have classes we'd go with them in to the fields. In this we learned a great deal. For instances, peanuts—what you get peanut oil from—I'd never seen a peanut plant before. . . . I'd go out with him and help him gather peanuts. . . . I missed my family very much. I'd never been away from them. But I was determined to carry out the Campaign as I had decided to.

I recall it was difficult because in addition to teaching them to read and write, we also had to explain the Revolution: the issues, how life was in the past, the things that the Revolution planned to carry out, those which it had already done. And in that aspect I must say I did have difficulty. For as much as they had explained it to us, at that age, there were still things I didn't understand. Sometimes the students, the peasants themselves, though they couldn't read, had lived more, so it was they who would explain things to us. The OEA [OAS] for example. I had some idea of what it was but the peasants, they knew. They had the knowledge—I'd call it historical knowledge—related to the history of Cuba—what they had lived through and what they'd spoken of.

The themes presented in the literacy primer paralleled the revolutionary undertakings of the government. The Literacy Campaign offered the possibility of reaching every Cuban and encouraging him or her to identify with the reforms and ideals that were being promulgated, such as agrarian reform. The instructor's manual included twenty-four political lessons with titles such as "Fidel Is Our Leader" and "Imperialism." One lesson, titled "The Revolution," includes the following passage:

People need revolution in order to develop and advance. When a nation is dominated by another more powerful nation, only through revolution can it drive out foreign domination and establish its own government not subject to such domination.

This type of moral idealism is infused into each lesson to create feelings, such as a sense of honor, duty, conviction, and dignity. Stressing moral learning, argues Wallace (1961), will always be a part of revolutionary societies. Revolutionary morality is more than conformity; it involves heroic self-sacrifice for the betterment of society. In this way the moral behavior of a revolutionary society seeks not only the interests of the community but also a higher ideal that advances the welfare of all. According to Paulston (1971), in revolutionary societies like Cuba, the primary concern of education must be the moral transformation of the population to facilitate the destruction of the old society and to guide in the creation of the new. The Literacy Campaign attempted, and reportedly succeeded, in doing just that: destroying the pre-revolutionary understandings that did not correspond to the goals of the revolutionary government and replacing the old ideology with the new.

The Guerrilla-Focus Theory

The Literacy Campaign was modeled after the Rebel Army's Sierra Maestra experience. Drawing on the image of the heroic guerrillas of the revolution, the Literacy Campaign became another battle to be won, and its implementation revived a watered-down version of the guerrillas' strategies of communion with the people, mobilization to the rural, rugged countryside, and militarization.

The Literacy Campaign training closely resembled the Sierra Maestra experience. Starting in 1959, these *maestros voluntarios* went through an intensive training program in Minas del Frió that entailed climbing Turquino Peak (in the Sierra Maestra) three times.

Later this program was extended to include all future elementary-grade teachers. Students who had graduated from sixth grade were eligible to become teachers. They spent seventh grade in Minas del Frió, then spent eighth and ninth grades in Topes de Collantes (in the Sierra de Escambray), and finally ended their training with two more years of study and practicum at the Makarenko Pedagogical Institute at Tarará Beach (Huberman and Sweezy 1969; Martuza 1981). This teacher-training program, known by the shorthand "Minas, Topas, y Tarará," was a life-changing experience for many of those who went through it. Miguel A. Ortega Fernández (cited in Arias Medina and Ares Valdés 1997, 53–54; trans. mine) tells of his experience:

> Today, thirty-six years later, I consider that my training as a *maestro voluntario* has determined my attitude before life and the revolution. . . . It was a school for life, for confronting questions of life, for tempering our character, and . . . it made us strong for analyzing the character of others who did not have this background. Thus, it made us uncompromising in our principles.

Another *maestro voluntario*, Esteban, recalls, "I came to know a Cuba that I had never seen, the experience of strength and personal sacrifice. Friendship that is born out of sharing a difficult life. The pureness of ideals and the disposition of sacrifice of those there remain with us" (ibid. 54; trans. mine).

Both the pre-campaign efforts of the young volunteer teachers and the Literacy Campaign proper were noteworthy in their attempts to break down psychological barriers between the urban literacy workers and the illiterate rural workers and create an environment of social cohesion. The UNESCO report on the campaign (Lorenzetto and Neys 1965, 18) indicates that the text used for the campaign was not only political and motivating "from the historical and psychological standpoint but also expressed this motivation in an accessible and comprehensible form, adjusted as much as possible to the language and expression of the peasantry." This report also notes that during teacher training, the literacy workers studied recorded conversation guides to ascertain the language of the illiterate worker as well as the person's social, political, and economic outlook. In addition, the literacy workers were also given an orientation for using the new curriculum.

At the beginning of each lesson was a photograph intended to stimulate conversation between the student and the teacher (the global aspect). In this way the teacher learned about the illiterate student's experiences and knowledge and had the opportunity to clarify concepts while helping to overcome timidity and promote expression in the student. Next, using the orientation provided in the manual, the teacher covered the essential points of the lesson, inviting the student to discuss the lesson or, in Freirian terms, "to read the world." By cultivating a critical consciousness (*conscientização*), or understanding of the broader social and political issues, the literacy lessons helped break down the "culture of silence," giving the once alienated a voice in determining their role in society and its future. Participants in the Literacy Campaign became, in Freirian terms, subjects — those who know and act — instead of objects (which are known and acted upon) of their own historical process of transformation (Freire 1970). By the end of the Literacy Campaign all of its participants would acquire a "new language"—the language of the revolution, a language that brought them into the conceptual and axiological fold of the socialist revolution.

A CONSTANT MOBILIZATION OF THE PEOPLE

The experience of mass mobilization creates a common denominator that transcends the individual experiences of, and cultural differences among, participants. In the Literacy Campaign, mobilization helped unify Cubans socially and emotionally, reinforcing nationalistic and revolutionary values. Cognitive advances must be recognized, too: city dwellers came to understand the lived reality of rural workers. As a result, mobilization continued to be an integral part of the educational system even after the Literacy Campaign had ended. In 1961, Fidel Castro acknowledged the merit of mobilizing urban youth to the countryside in the Literacy Campaign:

> You are going to teach, but at the same time you are going to learn. . . . You are
>
> Going to teach them [the peasants] what you learned in school, and they are going to teach you what they have learned in the hard life they have up until now. . . . They are going to teach you how many hundreds of thousands of peasants have had to live without highways, without parks, without electric light, without theaters, without cinemas. . . . [T]hey are going to teach you that there is a harder life than the life we have led. (Pogolotti 1967, 17; trans. mine)

As the younger generations were put in direct contact with reality, they discovered their country. In effect, this was a recycling of the model of the heroic guerillas in the Sierra Maestra, with revolutionary consciousness arising from revolutionary praxis, reviving the romantic myth epic.

The Cuban government utilized mass organizations, such as the Committee for the Defense of the Revolution (CDR) and the Federation of Cuban Women (Federación de Mujeres Cubanas, FMC), both in existence since 1960, to organize the mobilization necessary for the Literacy Campaign. After the end of the Literacy Campaign the Cuban government relied on these organizations to effect mobilization activities for a new developing economy, in a transformation associated with the new socialist man, and in defense.

Mobilization as a conventionalization of collective behavior is central to the purposes of the revolutionary government. Collective behavior keeps alive the political ideology and maintains linkages among the Cuban people and between the people and the leadership. By encouraging people to participate in revolutionary projects, such as the Literacy Campaign, the revolutionary government put in place a mechanism for identifying the lukewarm, the potentially deviant, and the true believer (Aguirre 1984). Mobilization in Cuba thus not only facilitated the organization and execution of an action intended to achieve a certain goal, it also helped equip and unify social consciousness emotionally and axiologically. It produced a common experiential reference to meld individual experiences and different political axiological outlooks, with the hope of transcending cultural differences and fostering political unity.

COMBAT AND MILITARIZATION COUCHED IN THE IMAGE OF CONFRONTATION AND HEROISM

Confrontation and heroism were constant features of the Literacy Campaign. Fidel officially put the Literacy Campaign into action the day after the Bay of Pigs Invasion. His charge to youth to fulfill a national duty drew not only on the present reality, the imperialist invasion, but also on evocative accounts of the torture and murder of Conrado Benitez. The story of Conrado Benitez became part of the teacher training, providing reason to confront the enemy, be it counterrevolutionaries or illiteracy itself. Like soldiers, the student literacy workers were given olive green military uniforms, a knapsack, and a Chinese lantern.

As literacy was achieved in each province, special victory literacy flags were raised in each locale. The progress of literacy in the countryside became a focus for the media, with advances tracked on a map and accompanied by personal testimonies and images, as if the campaign were a war to defeat a vicious, deadly force. In the testimonies, many literacy workers spoke of the threat of counterrevolutionaries as well as of environmental struggles. The theme of confrontation and heroism was the "quintessence of the conceptual and emotional content of the messages designed to shape revolutionary consciousness" (Medin 1990).

The literacy workers returned to Havana from their battle against illiteracy by train, bus, and boat, to be welcomed by cheering masses of parents and family members. A parade was organized, and literacy workers carrying giant pencils marched into Plaza de la Revolución (Revolutionary Plaza). Medals were awarded. The military themes of heroic self-sacrifice and combat that were woven into the campaign reinforced the affective undertones of a national duty performed, a service executed, dignity upheld, and pride earned.

A hedonistic or materially gainful conception of existence would render these affective themes or concepts meaningless.

The 1961 Literacy Campaign, the earliest of many similar efforts, lit the path by demonstrating how to integrate all of the revolutionary mechanisms—large organizations, mass mobilizations, work-study programs, and revolutionary value inculcation and informal instruction—important to the revolutionary agenda. It also lent momentum to the program of continuous mass education for all, a program that has had notable accomplishments especially in elementary and adult education. However, the appeal to the affective in the Literacy Campaign was instrumental in capturing the sentiment and support needed to advance the regime's revolutionary goals and ideals.

Educational Planning and Experimentation

In the 1960s, the task of the Cuban educational system was to develop the skills needed for economic growth and industrialization. To advance the economy, the focus switched from the pre-revolutionary emphasis on the humanities to an emphasis on the sciences and technology. In addition, to coincide with the radical economic changes, a "new personality," the new socialist man, was needed to build a communist society. To this end, teachers were to use a "revolutionary pedagogy" that emphasized "the creation of a new scale of values in which man and his complete development are the fundamental considerations" (Llanusa 1969, 69). The new socialist man created through this pedagogy would be one "for whom work is enjoyment and not obligation, and for whom study is a permanent process. A man of culture, science and technology" (ibid. 70). This type of pedagogy was aimed at creating a humanist culture and a mentality that identified personal and community interests as one and the same. Individuals were to be fully committed to equality, brotherhood, solidarity, and sacrifice; they were to be filled with heroism, abnegation, and enthusiasm, with no need for material incentives and devoid of selfishness (Castro 1969, 4). In short, the Cuban Revolution "made education a synonym for incorporation into the revolutionary process" (Carnoy 1990, 153).

It is important to recognize that the ideas underpinning the 1961 Literacy Campaign did not suddenly surface in 1960. Rather, the Literacy Campaign represented the culmination of much prior thought, experimentation, and planning. In fact, according to the memoirs of Mario Llerena (Castro's public relations foreign correspondent), which included a documented conversation between the two men in 1956, Castro seemed to feel that the formation of proper values in children was of paramount importance:

> When Castro mentioned educational reform, I hastened to stress the utmost importance that in my opinion should be given to education in the revolutionary program, and told him how, at the request of our friends in Havana, I was just working on one such project.
>
> "*¡Magnífico!*" he said, adding immediately, "Why don't you include in it my plan for school-cities?" Then he proceeded to describe with visible enthusiasm what seemed to be one of his pet ideas.
>
> As he explained it, Castro's "school-cities" were simply educational centers located in certain rural areas where the students would live permanently (away from their homes and families) since the beginning of primary school until the end of their secondary education. (Llerena 1966)

The Work-Study Principle: The Cornerstone of Cuban Revolutionary Education

The idea of the school city was the beginning of Castro's efforts to put the Marxist-Leninist work-study principle into practice. During the 1960s manual labor or work in the countryside was included in the school year. The work-study principle was instrumental in linking urban and rural areas, as urban children either boarded in secondary schools in the countryside or participated in a mobilization for short-term agricultural labor there. Prior to the revolution, the countryside offered few educational opportunities. Forty-three percent of the rural adult population could neither read nor write (Leiner 1975). By linking education with economic development, especially in rural areas, the revolutionary government sought to create a classless, egalitarian society that would become sovereign within the framework of cooperation with other socialist countries. Socialist education put work at the cultural and multidimensional focal point of personality development to create the New Man; the student was to develop the values required of the working class, the new society.

The emphasis on connecting study and work became apparent in the school cities, the Literacy Campaign, and all educational innovations that followed. The Literacy Campaign and the mobilizations to the rural areas were in part an attempt to duplicate the results of the guerrilla experience in the Sierra Maestra: to mobilize and incorporate citizen participation on a large scale in the revolution, to hone leadership skills in young people, and to repeat what Che Guevara claimed to have achieved—a communion with the people that went beyond mere theory.

All these aspects of the Sierra Maestra experience were put into play as the revolutionary government experimented with different implementations of the work-study principle. One of the most important goals was to generate a strong affective attachment within the school community through participation in revolutionary tasks, so that young people would become loyal, productive laborers and revolutionaries who rejected the idea of material incentives. In this section on Cuban education, I explore the history of the manifestations of the work-study principle, focusing on the school cities, the boarding schools, and the Escuela al Campo, or school to the countryside, program. As the Cuban educational system addressed the moral imperatives, the task involved not only curriculum reform but also a deep engagement of teachers and students in society as a whole (MacDonald 1985). The creation of Escuelas de Instrucción Revolucionaria or EIR schools for forming the adult cadres, as well as the school cities, the Literacy Campaign, and other early developments, are evidence of how urgent it was to the Cuban government to involve the channels of education as soon as possible, realizing the critical significance of conquering social consciousness in the early years of education.

School Cities

Castro's idea of the school city became a reality when two major school cities were established in 1959. One was established in Santiago at the Moncada barracks, where the Rebel Army had made its first attempt to overthrow Batista's government in 1953. The other was located at Batista's most important military base, Camp Columbia, in Havana. The military buildings at both sites were converted into several new elementary and secondary schools and a pedagogical institute; the one in Havana initially housed the national headquarters of the Ministry of Education (MINED). The circumstances and timing were not just coincidence but rather were highly symbolic of the change in government and its priorities. The symbolism of transforming barracks into schools has been much bruited by Castro and his followers to emphasize the draconian contrast between the benevolent, humanitarian "revolutionary style" and the immoral, unjust "Batistiano style."

Most school cities were intended for the education of the mountain-dwelling campesinos, who before the revolution had had neither the time nor the facilities for schooling (Castro 1961). The first school city included nine such schools in the Sierra Maestra environs. An article in *Turquino* published at the time describes them as follows: "They have the capacity to house 20,000 students, who will be educated in the most modern pedagogies. . . . [O]f the 350 acres this institution will occupy, 24 will be dedicated to the cultivation of fruits" (1959, 42; trans. mine). The most intelligent students would be selected starting at the fourth-grade level, with the school city boarding students through ninth grade. The selected students were scholarship students, or *becados*, and the state provided food, clothing, and study materials for them free of cost. The emphasis was on study and production (Castro 1961). The school city also included a normal school for teacher training and a technological school.

Granjas del pueblo

Another similar schooling compound, *granjas del pueblo*, consisted of *granjas infantiles* and *círculos infantiles*. The *granja infantil* accommodated elementary students, who would work in the mornings, study in the afternoons, and go home with their parents after work. School subjects taught at the *granja del pueblo* focused on agriculture. In addition, the *círculos infantiles* operated as day-care centers, receiving children as young as one month old. While children were monitored in their work and study, parents, especially women, were "liberated" from home child care so they could join the workforce in the countryside during the day. As long as the children were productive, the food, clothing, and school supply costs were covered. However, if production were low, parents would have to subsidize the fees (Castro 1961).

Boarding Schools

By 1966, boarding schools had been created in rural areas for all students entering the sixth grade, in an effort to create revolutionary citizens who would have the conciencia of the new socialist man, thus making them productive workers in creating the socialist society. The following year all fifth graders would also be grouped in boarding establishments in the countryside. On June 28, 1967, a model of the forthcoming boarding units was opened in Pinar del Rio province. The *Report of the Cuban Government to the Thirtieth Session of the International Conference on Education* (MINED 1968, 53) described it this way:

> This school has been organized on a new concept of the life and education of children in a boarding school. In it, use is made of new teaching methods, of connection between the school, the family, and the work of parents.

The teacher is an educator, an instructor, and a guide who shares fully the life of the students, their daily routine, their sports and their cultural and recreational activities.

The boarding schools have a communal system of living and the instructors organize the lives of the students. Under this type of guidance it is expected that no one will go astray and that the students will acquire the spirit of cooperation, egalitarianism, hard work, sacrifice, and solidarity that goes into making the new socialist man (Leiner 1975). By 1971, many more permanent schools in the countryside had been built for boarding secondary students, in a plan that incorporated agricultural work with academic studies.

A Special Emphasis on Women

Boarding schools also had a special purpose for *campesinas* (farm women): to integrate them into the industrial and agricultural revolution. It was necessary to school the women in ways that would liberate them from social and economic subjugation and promote them professionally. The *círculos infantiles* made it possible for many women to work or study. In 1961, Ana Betancourt schools (Las Escuelas de Ana Betancourt) were created, and more than 150,000 young women came from the mountainous area and rural zones of the Oriente to attend the boarding schools in the city. The students attended classes in home economics and sewing, but major emphasis was placed on academic studies. The most outstanding students went on to specialize in agricultural technology in other schools (Fernández 1981; MacDonald 1985).

On May 25, 1964, MINED issued Resolution 392, which stated, in part: "students [are to] go to cooperatives, state farms, or other areas and remain in these fields harvesting coffee or other crops, or participating in other types of agricultural work. The period of time will fluctuate from two to seven weeks." Beginning in 1966, after the founding of the Communist Party of Cuba, a shift in ideology resulted in a far-reaching change to both educational culture and educational structure (Domínguez 1993; Paulston 1971): the school to the countryside program became part of the national school system, no longer an experiment or a tool for use with only some populations. The pilot school to the countryside program took place in April and May 1966 and involved some 20,000 junior high school students. The students worked together with teachers and campesinos at a rural campsite in Camagüey province. In addition to performing agricultural labor, the participants engaged in cultural, sport, and recreational activities. According to José Aguilera Maceiras, vice minister of general and special education, the Camagüey experience provided a concrete way to put into practice the Marxist principle of educating new generations through work and for work, of forming the new society a new man for whom work would be an eternal and natural condition of human life, as Karl Marx foresaw, and of utilizing work as the main element of training, since, as Fidel said, "work must be the best teacher for the youth." (cited in Leiner 1975)

The Camagüey experience was unique because, for the first time, working in the countryside had been incorporated into a school program that recruited large numbers of students. In the 1966–1967 school year, the school to the countryside program was systematically incorporated into the school program for junior high and pre-university (high school) students for forty-five days. Cuban educators were convinced that the school to the countryside program was an important step in the educational and revolutionary transformation of Cuba. G. Jorge García Galló (1967) wrote:

Its development and consequences have as much vital importance for Cuban education . . . as that of the great literacy campaign carried out in 1961, since its adequate application will become the main link that will allow us to pull the whole educational chain, transforming in this way the structure, the contents, the technique, and the spirit of learning.

Ideologically, plans that integrated work periods and study were complementary to the goal of cultivating the values of responsibility, patriotism, sacrifice, hard work, and solidarity. The mobilization and involvement of large numbers of students, especially those from urban, more privileged families, may be viewed as a relatively successful attempt to bind youth to ideological constructs calling for struggle and sacrifice to eradicate a deeply embedded capitalistic and imperialistic inheritance. Campaigns and mobilizations were regarded by the revolutionary government as powerful socializing and motivating experiences that served as a means to eliminate vestiges of the imperialist-capitalist mentality and strengthen personal identification with and understanding of the larger revolutionary effort (Paulston 1971).

By the late 1960s, the heroism and sacrifice of the revolution—the days of the Sierra Maestra, the National Literacy Campaign, and the Bay of Pigs Invasion—were known only second-hand to most Cuban children. Therefore, in terms of mass psychology, the revolutionaries' children's lack of personal experience had an alienating effect, for they had not personally contributed to the revolution. It was considerations such as these that motivated the creation of the school to the countryside programs and other mobilizations, so that each new generation could be made directly aware, in the most practical sense, of its contribution to the revolution.

The conscious provision for revolutionary involvement embraced more than school-age youth. For instance, in 1968, Centennial Youth Columns were founded for 17- to 30-year-olds to provide "shock troops" for productive work and to meet production targets. The army organized the troops along military lines, but participation was strictly voluntary. The program called for a three-year commitment, with volunteers exempted from compulsory military service. However, only about half of the original 50,000 volunteers completed the demanding three-year duty (MacDonald 1985). The only penalty for noncompletion was loss of honor. The Young Communists (UJC) oversaw the columns and were active in encouraging and recruiting volunteers. One veteran of the columns commented:

> This was our way of making our mark. When you're working overtime every day, when you spend sixty such days without a pass to leave camp, you realize you're in a battle of heroic proportions against the sugar cane (or whatever the task is) and also against yourself. For those of us who finished the three years, that was survival—just like the heroes of Moncada. (Márquez 1972, 22)

Student organizations emerged early, though membership in the Pioneers was initially selective and extracurricular. By 1966 the Pioneers had opened to all elementary Cuban schoolchildren, and in 1968 the Pioneers became totally intertwined with the schools, from the classroom to the school council (Wald 1978). Both the Pioneers and the Federation of Secondary Students planned academic and extracurricular activities. Another mass organization, the Federation of University Students, was created for university students. Many more mass organizations, such as the CDR and the FMC, were created for adults and were closely networked with the schools.

The FMC has encouraged women to learn technical skills, including agriculture, tractor driving, specialized farming techniques, cattle raising, and political instruction. Women have found jobs in the rapidly growing social sector, particularly in health care and education, but the glass ceiling has persistently barred them from high-ranking policy-making positions, and political power has remained in the hands of men (Padula 1993).

Of the student organizations, the UJC is considered the vanguard youth organization. Members are selected starting at age 13. The UJC responds to the Cuban Communist Party to organize different activities for all ages of children. As leaders, their model behavior and attitude are scrutinized. In a 1962 pamphlet to the FSLN entitled *What Should a Young Communist Be?*, Che Geuvara mentioned that the UJC "could be defined in one word: vanguard. . . . The first in sacrifice. . . . The first in work. The first in study. The first in defense of the country" (4). Going by the motto *"Estudio, Trabajo, Fusil"* (Study, Work, Rifle), the UJC's first priority is ideological work, which entails systematically teaching and publicizing the history of liberation struggles and the revolutionary process and preaching the political line as indicated by the Communist Party and Fidel Castro (*Verde Olivo* 1972). The UJC is part of an organizational network that not only covers different sectors of social life but also provides a generational continuity with other organizations, such as the Pioneers, the Young Communists, and the Communist Party.

Participation in these student organizations is one of the ways Cuban youth are honed for leadership. Such were the sky-high expectations of the Cuban government that during the First Youth Congress in 1962, sponsored by the Association of Rebel Youth (the predecessor of the UJC), the congress bestowed on them the responsibility of constructing the socialist society, the new utopia. The congress's organizers promised that the young Cubans would eventually "live in the bounty of socialism" because they lacked "the vices, the limitations, and the unenlightenedness of the past" (*Bohemia* 1962).

Participation in mobilizations and "massifications" was part of the emotional infrastructure that shored up the policies of the revolutionary government and was intended to win the affection of the Cuban people (Fernández 2000). The guerrilla-style interaction with the peasants in the mountains of the Sierra Maestra—intense, daily, one-on-one—became a model for the collective spirit, action, and consciousness of the revolution. It was not enough that the new socialist man merely recite the revolutionary catechism perfectly. The test would be how he behaved—whether or not he worked, fought, studied, cooperated, sacrificed, and contributed in the prescribed manner. Because participation was organically related to socialization, the regime sought to forge the new political culture in the crucible of action, reflecting the experiences of the guerrillas in the mountains. The revolutionary institutions became both the training grounds and the testing grounds for the participatory Cuban citizen (Fagen 1969).

The training of maestros voluntarios, the Literacy Campaign, the coffee harvest, and the various mobilizations were conscious efforts to recycle and revitalize the Sierra Maestra guerrilla experience "to construct a more satisfying culture": living in rugged conditions, coming into contact with a peasant reality, valuing agricultural work, and achieving victory through collective effort (Wallace 1966, 264). Like Che Guevara's rebels, the young people in Castro's mobilizations left their urban environment to gain direct experience with the real needs of the rural workers (Márquez 1972).

The application of guerrilla-focus theory to organize these maneuvers was born out of an educational, economic, and moral formula understood as disalienating the pedagogy of the oppressed (Freire 1970). The achievements credited a collective effort, thereby reaffirming the revolutionary ideology of collective struggle, a millennial vision, and the creation of the New Man and New Woman (Hall 1975). What mattered most was the personal and collective involvement of the Cuban population in building a new society with new ideals.

Polytechnical Education

Polytechnical education was understood as a Marxist pedagogical contribution to educational reform (Price 1977), and in May 1964, the Cuban government adopted Resolution 392, stressing the incorporation of polytechnical education in Cuban schooling. It was a method by which children "from the outset in the primary schools learn the scientific principles underlying all subjects and acquaint themselves with the handling of tools and machines so as to acquire abilities, habits and dexterity, and communist attitude toward work which are important to society today" (Lorenzetto and Neys 1965). Various countries, such as Cuba, Mozambique, and Tanzania, "in transition" from one type of government to another have looked to Marx's idea of polytechnical education to bridge the gap between mental and manual work. The purpose was largely ideological: "Since the traditional separation between the working class and the bourgeoisie in conditioned capitalist societies is between manual and mental work, the incorporation of the collectivized individual into the new people-nation requires breaking down these previous classifications" (Carnoy 1990, 72–73). The attempt to give equal status to different types of schooling was to reflect the economic changes of salaries and wages in a communist society. According to Carnoy, while in capitalist societies academic education is distinct from vocational education "as if it served a different purpose rather than simply supplying different kinds of knowledge and access to social/material status" to different youths from different social class backgrounds, transition societies define all education as vocational, "and the state attempts to minimize material and status differences among vocations" (90).

In Cuba, the need for more technically qualified workers to support agricultural and industrial development led to vastly expanded technical and professional educational programs. For example, in the 1960s the Cuban government founded thirteen industrial-technological institutes to train scarce medium-level specialists in thirty-three fields related to engineering. Forty-five technical institutes were established to prepare skilled workers and agricultural technicians, along with a number of fishing schools to prepare skilled workers for the new and rapidly growing fishing fleet (Gillette 1972; Huberman and Sweezy 1969; Paulston 1971).

The shift to technological and scientific education reflected an effort to make education more practical. Cuba's schools and universities have become partners with farms, factories, and other enterprises in the ongoing work-study effort. Often, however, the practical education takes place outside the formal schooling effort because of lack of time in the formal curriculum or a lack of facilities. An example is the highly popular *círculos de interés* (interest circles), which were begun in 1963 to encourage technical vocations among elementary and secondary students. Activities range from zoology and biochemistry to animal husbandry and other aspects of agriculture. Ideally, the *círculos de interés* help bridge between the school curriculum and the student's later life of productive activity. Adults in these professions volunteer their time, bring the necessary equipment, and usually make the session a hands-on class that requires no grades or examinations. Other cultural *círculos de interés* exist, such as circles for ballet, cinema, painting, and sewing. The interest and motivation reflect both the wholeness of the educational experience and the real contribution being made to the productive capacity of the nation. By 1968, more than 300,000 students were taking part in interest circles (Bowles 1971; Lamore 1970; Leiner 1975).

By tying the educational experience more closely to the economy, the interest circles perform an important function. Since Cuba is a society that has forgone the use of wage incentives, the interest circles provide an alternative way to inform young people about specific occupations while at the same time stimulating interest in careers likely to be needed for national development (Bowles 1971).

As a further stimulus to parental and community involvement in the school system, the *padrino* system was established. The padrino system, which is based on a system similar to that of the East European socialist countries, encourages cooperative arrangements between neighborhood institutions and the schools. Padrino sponsors usually include factories, which agree to adopt a school and to offer special services and assistance on a voluntary basis. For example, the padrino organization may assist with mechanical repairs, transportation, supplies, or arrangements for a collective birthday party. Not only do the padrinos provide important skilled labor and materials that might be in short supply, they also give guided tours and offer students opportunities to work together in agricultural work brigades. In this way the padrinos serve a function in revolutionary education, tying the school to the factory and providing the children with practical confirmation of the revolutionary values of respect for all types of work and of working collectively to improve the nation as a whole (Leiner 1975).

The goal of national development has driven changes to higher education as well. Upper-level education was turned toward meeting manpower needs instead of maintaining the pre-revolutionary focus on humanistic, legal, and social science careers. Enrollment is controlled by the state, and the enrollment shifts between 1959 and 1967 are telling evidence of the change in focus. The proportion of enrollment in humanities and law, for example, declined from 15.5 percent to 2.9 percent over the period, whereas enrollment in engineering and the natural and agricultural sciences increased from 24 percent to 43.2 percent. Notable increases were achieved both in the medical sciences and in education. During the period of rapid industrialization (1959–1963), the most remarkable increase was registered in engineering. When the emphasis later switched to agriculture, the decline in engineering enrollment was matched by an increase in agricultural sciences. The decline in enrollment in the social sciences, such as in schools of commerce (later to become economics), was due to the state's deemphasis of the self-finance system of management (JUCEPLAN 1968).

Castro envisioned universities being replaced by technological institutes and Cubans becoming "an engineer, an agronomist, a soil technician, a livestock specialist" (Castro 1966a). Castro stressed not only the ideological and pedagogical purposes of education but also its pragmatic aim and necessity. Therefore, the educational system is guided by an overriding concern to produce students who know how to learn, and who understand the scientific approach to problem solving and how things work. Castro has stated the issue on a number of occasions: "What place can the scientifically illiterate man, the technologically illiterate man, possibly have in the community of the future?" (1968, 2). And in his famous speech, "La historia me absolverá" (History Will Absolve Me), Castro stated, "We are going to educate, teach to think, teach to analyze, give you elements of judgment so you will understand" (1972a).

Promoting the Scientific Character of the Revolution

From this sort of scientific perspective, however, critical autonomy seems to be conceived of only as the ability to reach the scientific conclusions of Marxism and to explain them rationally. As a qualitative alternative, this mode of critical thinking would strike many as antiscientific and counterrevolutionary. The scientific character of the revolutionary ideology and praxis justified maintaining the revolutionary mystique, with an emphasis on ideological unity (Medin 1990). To anyone familiar with the general partiality of Latin Americans to more traditional, even mystical ways of knowing, however, this stress on science and empiricism as a way of knowing is truly revolutionary (Paulston 1971).

The scientific character of Marxism-Leninism as defined by the socialist regime became a source of fortitude and faith, offering assurance of a final victory and the unconquerable strength of the revolutionary movement. Indeed, science, monolithic unity, and the revolutionary mystique appear closely united, forming what Fernández (2000) calls a "new political religion." Fernández describes political religion as an affective discourse "produced as a conscious decision of the top leaders and through interaction with and by the people" (67). In the 1960s, political religion resurrected intense feelings because it responded to a moral concern for the national project in crisis, as well as making sense out of the uncertain times of the revolution. As part of a political religion, the Cuban leadership relied on traditional symbols and myths that would resonate with long-held beliefs and desires, to contextualize and advance national goals. These symbols or guideposts rendered what Geertz (1964, 64) described as the ideological remaking of cultural symbols, making "otherwise incomprehensible social functions meaningful, to so construe them as to make it possible to act purposefully within them."

Addressing the Older Generation

Most Cubans credit the initial formation of a revolutionary consciousness to the mass participation in the 1961 Literacy Campaign. Barely two months after the Literacy Campaign ended the Seguimiento, or follow-up courses, started for the recently literate graduates of the Literacy Campaign. The material taught corresponded to grades one through three of primary school, and the program consisted of arithmetic, reading and writing, natural history, social studies, and hygiene. In addition, Worker Improvement courses, or Superación Obrera, corresponding to grades four through six of primary school, were initiated for literate but underschooled adults. These courses were designed to capitalize on and consolidate the educational gains from the literacy program.

Once implemented, the programs grew steadily. Flexible formulas permitted continuous, organized study by workers in various settings, such as factories, shops, on farms, and on boats. The Seguimiento program was so successful that its goal was pushed up from third-grade equivalency to sixth-grade equivalency, and the "Battle for the Sixth Grade" became a well-publicized event. By the end of 1973, more than 500,000 adults in the Seguimiento program had graduated from sixth grade through this program (Cánfux 1981; Leiner 1985; MacDonald 1985).

In 1968, of 30,000 teachers active in Seguimiento programs, only 8,000 either already had had some type of pedagogical training or were currently acquiring the training. As a substitute for professional training they were encouraged to seek advice from a veteran teacher or their own students. Humility was held out as a virtue, and being self-critical about one's performance was seen as one of the most effective ways to self-improvement (MacDonald 1985).

High on the list of priorities in the Seguimiento program was to make the curriculum relevant to the students' new identity, the New Man. Reading and writing, for example, included some of Che's more cryptic aphorisms, the poetry of José Martí, and Spanish translations of Gorky and Charles Dickens. Throughout, the student was expected to identify with the oppressed and to recognize the conditions rendering such oppression, particularly capitalism (MacDonald 1985).

Although creating the New Man identity was stressed, methodology issues arose in learning basic skills in mathematics and other subjects because of the deficiencies in teacher training. Much of the material was learned mechanically, without understanding of the psychology of cognition. For example, in mathematics the syllabus reflected a greater concern for procedures than for understanding. The challenge for both teachers and the Seguimiento plan instituted by the ministry was to cultivate an intrinsic motivation for learning in the newly literate that would combat the lack of concrete teaching aids and the teachers' insufficient time with students.

The likelihood that newly literate people will relapse into illiteracy is quite high. Maintaining literacy can effectively weaken a newly literate person's social bonds with an illiterate subculture, resulting in social and psychological pressure to regress to the comfort of illiteracy (MacDonald 1985). The goal of the literacy campaign was to move the learner completely out of the illiterate subculture and into the "causative 'teller' group" as delineated by Freire (Mac-

Donald 1985, 91). Therefore, the newly literate struggled with considerable pressures, both internal (psychological) and external (social), to relapse into what was familiar: the illiterate community of which he or she was a part.

During the early years of the Seguimiento program, vigorous efforts were made to avoid regression to illiteracy. A magazine called *El Placer de Leer* (The Pleasure of Reading) was published and widely distributed to those who had just completed the basic literacy program. Designed to develop the reading habit, the magazine was a great success. It included easy vocabulary with summaries of current events, so that literate learners could discuss the new reality of the revolution and be fully confident that they had a role to play in it (MacDonald 1985).

The Facultad Preparatoria Obrero-Campesina (Preparatory School for Peasants and Workers) sought to prepare industrial workers and peasants ages 18 through 40 years for university study. A significant innovation at the university level, this preparatory program attempted to link farming, industry, and higher education more closely. After several years of preparatory courses held at the universities, the candidates began a regular program of studies. Enrollment increased from eighty-five students in 1959–1960 to 8,156 in 1967–1968 (Lataste 1968; Leiner 1985).

The Mínimo Técnico program, begun in 1962, sought to give workers in industry, agriculture, and business a minimum technical understanding of their work and machines. Classes were held at the job site and sought to increase productivity and responsibility by explaining to workers how their contribution related to the total production process (Gillette 1972; Paulston 1971). The adult education programs revealed a different side of the work-study principle. Whereas students were to acquire a new conciencia related to work and to value work equally with studying, now adult workers were to become students and understand education as lifelong learning. For the adults, it also ensured the ideological education that the regime sought as a way to unify generations, and therefore society.

Particular to women was the night school for former menial workers and prostitutes that opened its doors in Havana at the end of 1961. A year later some 20,000 former domestic servants were attending night school classes organized in more than sixty schools in the capital and surrounding districts. The courses were varied but typically included typing, shorthand, commercial secretary, administration, and driver training (Azicri 1988; MacDonald 1985).

As for giving adults in the city an agricultural experience, the Cordón, a green belt of 10,000 ha, was created around Havana. The goal was to make the urban complex self-sufficient in foodstuffs by bringing adjacent lands under cultivation. Ideologically, agricultural labor was considered essential for all citizens, especially city dwellers, who needed to be liberated from their city ways and bourgeois values (Fagen 1969).

The magnificent effort to supply educational opportunities to the adult population of socialist Cuba was matched by achievements in education for children. From 1958 to 1962 the enrollment of all children ages 7–14 increased from 50 percent to 80 percent (Jolly 1964). In addition, there was an increase in the construction of schools, in teaching materials, and in teacher training, and all students were provided with uniforms, new textbooks, and in some cases meals on the premises. From 1965 through 1969, twenty-one substantial changes were made to the secondary syllabus and twenty-five variations of subject offerings were tried at the high school level before the curriculum became fairly standardized in 1970. These changes created some confusion for recently trained teachers, who might find themselves teaching subjects for which they had no preparation.

By 1969 Cuban high schools were turning out eleven times the number of university entrants as in 1963 (MacDonald 1985). The university entrants were reported as having a "higher aggregate standing" in 1969 than in 1963 (*Educación contemporanea* 1976, 191). Because new mathematics came to Cuba in 1964 and new entrance examinations were implemented in 1963, it is unclear what "higher aggregate standing" might mean in light of syllabi, curricular, and examination content changes made after 1963. Regardless, all of the changes were made in the name of a new socialist society.

Fulfilling the Revolutionary School Mission

The early sixties were years of experimentation in unifying the vision of the Cuban people using the heroic guerrillas as models of the revolution to achieve the revolutionary mythic epic. Therefore, the formation of new citizens was to be an integral and crucial element of all programs developed under the new educational philosophy. As stated succinctly in the Cuban report to UNESCO (1962, 25),

> The teaching programs must help to develop a love of country and a love for the workers and peasants—for the people as the creators of labor and the source of all social wealth. They have to indicate what is represented by the struggle against exploitation and misery. . . . They must encourage a moral sense founded on the struggle against social inequality. They must stress the underlying causes of inequality and its terrible consequences.

Clearly, the teaching goals illustrate the importance of the constant features of confrontation and heroism (Medin 1990). Furthermore, the role of the teaching profession is important in the social, economic, and political development process. As shown by a study of fifty-seven Cuban exiled teachers by Provenzo and García (1983), teachers' potential for succeeding in the new educational system depended on their ability to adapt to the new revolutionary and socialist ideology. In the preface to Jonathan Kozol's 1978 book on the literacy program in Cuba, Paulo Freire mentions that Kozol was writing "about the Cuban revolution, about the people reborn in the process." However, Kozol's study, like many others, dealt only with the participants in the revolution.

Projection and Reception in the 1960s: The Manichean Scheme

The Manichean message was imbued with a call for emotional attachment and was often resorted to in exhorting young people to gain firsthand acquaintance with the rugged life of self-sacrifice experienced by the guerrillas in the Sierra Maestra. Mobilizing young, urban schoolchildren and sending them into rural areas would, the regime hoped, forge the requisite revolutionary consciousness. These mobilizations were in part an attempt to incorporate citizen participation in the revolution, to hone leadership skills in the young, and to repeat what Guevara claimed to have achieved: a communion with the people that went beyond mere theory.

However, not everyone jumped on the bandwagon. Another group, the exiled teachers, failed to be "reborn" as a part of the new educational system. The revolution necessitated their adopting the values of the new Cuban society, engaging in a normative agenda, and integrating themselves into a new educational system, or giving up their profession as teachers. Noteworthy is that most of the exiled teachers did not resign or were not fired immediately. The majority made considerable attempts to integrate themselves in the Literacy Campaign and in the schools, leaving in the early 1960s (Provenzo and García 1983). The history to be taught was markedly different, and this new history was infused across the curriculum: from literacy primers that taught "A" is for agrarian reform and "F" is for *fusil* (gun of the militia) to mathematical problems that included the evil imperialistic character of the United States. The first step in building a foundation for teaching the new materials about Marxism obtained from the Soviet Union was to teach the political religion of a future communist utopia and disdain for the imperialist enemy.

The same passionate political religion of confrontation and heroism, a type of revitalizing of the guerrilla experience within a Manichean scheme, was embedded in the educational methods and curriculum. This was done in an effort to create "an axiological and emotional atmosphere conducive to mobilization and discipline needed to confront enemies and real or imaginary dangers" (Medin 1990, 40). In this polarization, the United States came to represent the negatives of imperialism, *gusanos* (traitors), counterrevolutionaries, and capitalism. At the positive pole of the Manichean axis were the Cuban Revolution, socialism, communism, the Soviet bloc countries, the Third World, and humanity. Anyone not on the revolutionary bandwagon was suspected of being either a traitor or a counterrevolutionary.

The absolute ends of these politics of passion (Fernández 2000) demanded social solidarity and relied on the convergence of the social with the political. Nonetheless, opponents, such as teachers and others who did not agree, became more than adversaries; they became evil and inhuman. In this situation, passion both polarizes politics and is an indication of the polarization.

The middle ground was untenable for all, but a teacher's loyalty to the revolution was more visibly on trial than in any other profession. In the early sixties, the militia was put in charge of monitoring all classrooms to make sure proper instruction was being provided. It is no surprise that teachers from all levels of the educational system formed the largest single professional group to go into exile: approximately 50 percent of the entire teaching population in Cuba left. Whereas one out of every nine Cubans emigrated to the United States during the early sixties, one in two teachers did (U.S. Department of Health, Education and Welfare 1976). From 1960 to 1962, net out-migration from Cuba amounted to about 200,000 people, or an unprecedented average of well over 60,000 per year (Domínguez 1993). The massive emigration to the United States was a consequence of the dramatic reorganization of Cuba's internal political and economic affairs.

To maintain political and economic unity, in the mid-sixties the Cuban government cracked down on all workers, seeking to eliminate absenteeism and loafing and to increase productivity. Work camps known as Units for Military and Agricultural Production (UMAP) were created around 1965 for those who deviated from the norm, who had divided loyalties, such as clergy and laypeople, or whose behavior ran counter to the ideals of the new socialist man (Azicri 1988; Leiner 1994; Pérez-López 1995). Located in chiefly agricultural areas, these camps were used to intern loafers, political prisoners, homosexuals, school dropouts, and others exhibiting "antisocial behavior" (Córdova 1992). The "Yellow Brigades" were created in the UMAP labor camps to toughen up "effeminate" boys as an educational form of aversion therapy, as was suggested by antigay commentators and psychotherapists in other countries (Leiner 1994). The camps held people from all levels of society, and the measures employed, which included not only physical labor but also, in some cases, electric shock treatments, constitute a darker side of revolutionary life that remains unofficially explained (Johnson 1993).

Until 1966, Cuban leaders also sent political opponents of the revolutionary government to detention and rehabilitation work camps on the Isle of Pines. As many as 15,000 men may have been detained there until they "demonstrated their willingness and readiness to be reincorporated into the new social order" (Fagen 1969, 176). The model prison on the island used a reeducation program called Three Steps to Freedom, consisting of lectures, studies, and work (McManus 2000). Beginning in 1966, these camps and the prison were converted into schools, and the detainees either were set free or were detained on the main island.

The year 1967 saw endless movement on the Isle of Pines. Trucks with people, animals, equipment, food, and supplies moved across the new roads and construction sites. A reservoir was built to irrigate some 96,000 acres of land. Many young people made up the workforce for this project. As the story goes, after the young people were congratulated on their tireless efforts to finish on time, they asked to have the island renamed the Isle of Youth. Castro supported the idea, but qualified this notion with meeting a list of goals first. "Here we propose not only to revolutionize nature, but also to revolutionize minds, to revolutionize society. . . . Why not also make this the first communist region in Cuba?" (1968, 5). The sparsely populated Isle of Youth became an incubator, away from the influences of the city, for the first generation of truly new socialist men. The Spartan atmosphere of the Isle of Youth was to serve up young people who exemplified the values of sacrifice, cooperation, selflessness, discipline, and hard work. The rich land was cultivated for citrus crops, combining agricultural work with schooling. Most of the young people who boarded at the schools on the island made a two-year commitment. In the sixties, this was the school to the countryside movement taken to its logical extreme.

What constituted a proper education became a moral crusade that split the country in two, each half fighting for a different set of ideals. On one side were parents and children who abided by the political religion, which offered extensive opportunities to work in the countryside collectively: as one of the 100,000 children who signed up as brigadistas to teach, learn, and live with a campesino family in a remote area of the island; as one of 43,000 students engaged in the coffee harvest; as one of the hundreds of thousands of students in the school to the countryside program; as a scholarship student at a boarding school; as a young child working in a *granja del pueblo;* or as one of the 2,000 scholarship students sent to the Soviet Union in 1961 and 1962. On the other side stood parents who feared for the safety of their children in the outback, the separation, and the education, which they understood as abusive indoctrination involving child labor, and who took every measure to remove their children from this milieu. The dispatch of Cuban children to the Soviet Union conjured up memories in some families of older relatives who had lived through the Spanish Civil War, during which more than 20,000 Basque children were sent to other countries, including the Soviet Union (Conde 1999). As shown by these examples and bears repeating, passion both polarizes politics and is an indication of the polarization of politics. The factional responses from the parents were based on their emotional attachments.

Those parents who were not in agreement with the new forms of education made clandestine arrangements for their children's departure to the United States, in the hope that Castro's attempts at socialism and communism would fail and the family would soon be reunited. In this program, dubbed Operation Peter Pan, more than 14,000 Cuban children were sent to the United States—the largest exodus of children in the Western Hemisphere and the only foster care of refugee children that the United States has ever federally funded; it cost the U.S. government more than $4,000,000 in assistance to relief agencies (Conde 1999). In each situation—participating in the Literacy Campaign, being schooled in the Soviet Union, or being schooled in the United States—parents were willing to send away children as young as eight years old, responding to either fear of punitive measures if they did not or the hope that their child might receive a better education.

Perhaps an image of a revolutionary family, fervent in beliefs, but its members also at odds with one another, helps explain the outcome of those prodigal children who challenged or rejected the system in the 1960s. Brutal attacks were waged on those believed to be counterrevolutionaries, including homosexuals, Jehovah's Witnesses, clergy, and other unfortunates with minimal recourse to legal action. Individuals caught fleeing the country on rafts were imprisoned. No one knows the exact number of political prisoners, but it was widely assumed in the 1960s to be in the tens of thousands.

To guide Castro's intelligence and security systems, in 1959 more than 100 KGB advisers were sent to Cuba. In an ironic twist of history, many of these agents had come from the group *"los niños,"* children of the Spanish communists who had been sent to Russia alone by their parents during the Spanish Civil War (1936–1939) (Conde 1999). Because they spoke both Spanish and Russian, they were a logical choice for a Cuba-Russia link (Andrew and Gordievsky 1990) in a process of Soviet-style institutionalization, which took place from 1970 to 1977.

By the late 1960s the response of the Cuban people, especially the young people, to the call for collective endeavor had made history, as evidenced by Fidel Castro's words in an interview with K. S. Karol (1970, 487): "Yes, *Hombre Nuevo* is no longer an empty phrase, no longer a pipe dream! We have many *Hombres Nuevos* in this country!"

It is difficult to assess to what degree people were transformed into Hombres Nuevos, and what kind of lasting effect such a transformation had. It was important to secure the future of communism by securing the formation of conciencia in those who would become the country's future leaders. The revolutionary government took radical measures during the sixties, including the Literacy Campaign and the use of mass organizations, rehabilitation camps, and new ways of schooling for all ages. The Cuban population reacted to the radical nature of these new measures differently. Some welcomed the changes and others feared them, taking whatever means to leave the country or at least to secure the safety of their children by sending them abroad. Meanwhile, those who stayed on the island participated in or were subjected to the educational molding plans for becoming new socialist men and women.

CHAPTER 3

1970–1985: Reconciling Revolutionary Fervor with the Requisites of the Modern State

The institutionalization of the 1970s was intended to unify revolutionary feelings and give them an organized form (Fernández 2000). However, the Cuban government apparently found it difficult to reconcile the tension between feelings and institutions, between utopianism and performance, between the moral and the material dimensions of the revolution. The outcome was periodic oscillation between the poles, with, as might be predicted, inconsistent results. This chapter briefly describes the swinging pendulum in the Cuban economy and politics during the 1970s and early 1980s, then takes up the repercussions of these economic and political measures as reflected in the educational system. Many modifications were in place to secure the means of revolutionary consciousness, to advance the concept of the new socialist man, and to attend to production needs.

The Institutionalization of the 1970s

By the end of the 1960s, the government had modified many of the policies it had promoted earlier. Whereas the revolutionary economic policy of the second half of the 1960s gave priority to the development of the new socialist man, it ignored many basic economic laws. Extreme idealism, labor mobilization, egalitarianism, moral incentives, and the Ten Million Tons Campaign to harvest sugarcane characterized economic policy until 1970. In the end, however, the sugarcane harvest goal was missed by approximately two million tons. The honor of the revolution had been staked on making the 1970 sugar harvest target. In the end, the intense mobilization and voluntary work demanded by the arduous campaign left the population exhausted and ready for a change. Missing the target prompted a reevaluation of the mode of economic organization of the 1966–1970 period, which from then on was characterized as "idealistic and voluntaristic" by Fidel Castro (1987). In 1972 Cuba joined the international communist Council for Mutual Economic Assistance, or Comecon, and the First Communist Party of Cuba Congress in 1975 consummated the break with Guevarism, with its emphasis on volunteerism and moral incentives. In fact, Che was the victim of several years of silence, to such an extent that his name was not even mentioned at the First Party Congress (Habel 1991). Failure to reach grandiose targets, the economic dislocation of 1970, and increasing Soviet pressure for economic rationalization were the main determinants of the policy shift (Mesa-Lago 1978).

Previously the leadership had emphasized moral incentives, such as emulation, to stimulate production. For example, the worker who each year cut the most sugarcane was honored throughout the country. Other workers were singled out for their exemplary contributions. Work sites were similarly honored for the excellence of the collective efforts of their workers. Exemplary workers were to encourage the others. While emulation still existed as an incentive, the setback with respect to the 1970 sugarcane harvest caused the revolutionary regime to reanalyze the equation between revolutionary consciousness and productivity (Maurer 1975).

The relationship between the leadership and the workers should be understood historically. Although the entire labor force joined the unions soon after 1959, the state ministries spoke as one voice on behalf of all the workers. With the 1970 setback, the unions were revitalized and the mass organizations were reemphasized. These political and historical changes with regard to work are an important link to the changes in educational policy that took place in the 1970s.

The relations of production, the foundation for the economic and political Marxist-Leninist state, were being restructured. One result of this restructuring was a fundamental change in how decisions were made with respect to production goals. A discussion chain linked every workplace with the national ministries, allowing workers' individual and collective concerns to be aired and reflected in the final plan, along with the needs and resources of the economy as a whole. Other results included the installation of a quota system, the introduction of material incentives, and less reliance on voluntary labor.

The change in the relations of production was reflected in political reforms. The First Party Congress solidified the sociopolitical and economic changes achieved in the 1960s. Ideologically as well as institutionally, as a result of the increased leverage of the USSR Cuba was, in its structural and political setting, a Marxist-Leninist state (Azicri 1988; Mesa-Lago 1978). Structurally, the new 1976 socialist constitution was organized along the lines of the constitutions of existing Marxist-Leninist states, such as the Soviet Union and other socialist countries. However, the new constitution also reflected Cuban traditions, in this way combining change and continuity in a single instrument. It safeguarded the changes of the 1960s while laying out the mechanisms for future change in a socialist polity.

The expanding economy provided more room for female workers. In the 1960s, many had worked as volunteers. In the 1970s, however, the picture changed: aided by various affirmative action programs, women's share of the labor force rose from 12 percent in 1959 to 38 percent in the 1980s, with women finding jobs in the growing health and education sectors (Federación de Mujeres Cubanas 1990). New social legislation also allowed generous maternity leave. Nevertheless, there were very few women in high-ranking policy-making positions; political power remained in the hands of men. This subordinate relationship was tacitly approved by the head of the Federation of Cuban Women (FMC), who urged women to think of Fidel as their father (Padula 1993).

Within this restructuring process, the Organs of People's Power (Poder Popular, or OPPs) were established as the nation's new political and legislative structure. To neutralize the threat of bureaucratic routinization, the revolutionary leaders wanted the masses to participate, and the OPPs provided a mechanism for greater communication and responsiveness at the local level. Whereas prior to this time, Cubans had had little input into the decision-making process, the OPPs provided an avenue for channeling a limited amount of criticism. Delegates to the Poder Popular were nominated at neighborhood meetings, with "the masses freely and spontaneously realiz-[ing] their proposals" (*Verde Olivo* 1976, 44), rather than by the revolutionary organizations, as in the Soviet Union. The vast network of municipal assemblies at the local level, moreover, offered easier access to state officials and a device for resolving local problems. The OPPs were still structured within the framework of the Leninist one-party system, but their mere creation was an indication of the importance given, even within the process of institutionalization, to the active, conscious involvement of the masses.

Options for both the worker and the consumer were expanded in the mid-1970s with the new System of Economic Management and Planning (Sistema de Dirección y Planificación de la Economía, SDPE). It introduced some market-oriented adjustments, similar to those seen in the Soviet Union in the pre-Gorbachev era, with the expectation that the new plan would be fully operational by the early 1980s. Parallel markets and a dual price system were established, which improved the choices available to consumers. The objective was to impose budgetary discipline while giving state enterprises more managerial independence. Although prices were set by the state, managers were able to make decisions regarding product lines and volume after complying with the centrally planned quota.

Not everyone favored the planning process. As managers began to make decisions involving the reallocation of resources to increase profits, some eyebrows were raised (Pérez-Stable 1993). Castro (cited in Jatar-Haussmann 1999, 32) expressed his sentiment toward the SDPE strategy:

> With the system called SDPE we are supposedly trying to increase economic efficiency and labor productivity. Now, there is no system in socialism by which you can substitute politics, ideology and people's conscience. The factors that have determined efficiency in a capitalist economy are others. They cannot exist in socialism where the political, ideological and moral aspects are still fundamental factors in the system.

While there was economic growth and development throughout the 1970s and early 1980s, production, material quality, diversification, and distribution problems persisted. At each turn, Cuba confronted an assortment of domestic and international factors that influenced the relationship between the state and the market (Domínguez 1989; Jatar-Haussman 1999). The result was a politically charged dichotomy between the drive for economic efficiency and adherence to socialist principles.

By the late 1970s the emphasis on moral incentives, coupled with the constraints of the U.S. embargo, had resulted in food shortages and growing inefficiencies throughout the economy, and Cuba turned to the protective arms of the Soviet Union for military and economic aid. After Cuba joined Comecon, the Soviet bloc alliance, a few decidedly capitalist threads began appearing in Cuba's socialist fabric (Suchlicki 1997) as the Cuban government began advocating a move toward material incentives, decentralization, and the introduction of some market exchanges.

Some problems stemmed from the tension between a central planning system and the use of material incentives to stimulate increases in production. Prices were centrally administered, not determined by market mechanisms. This resulted in shortages of products, whether consumers had the money to buy them or not. In this context of product scarcity, the material incentives may have appeared as a deceptive mechanism to increase production. Notwithstanding the shortcomings of the SDPE, Cuban authorities seemed cautiously satisfied with the results obtained through its implementation. Overall, the economy performed at a higher level of productivity and efficiency in the 1970s than in the 1960s. The higher price of sugar during the early part of the decade improved economic conditions, although economic growth declined toward the end of the 1970s (Azicri 1988).

Educational Reform in the 1970s

State building in the 1970s fostered a more pragmatic development strategy and new expectations for education. The closer relationship with the Soviet Union, the increased use of material incentives, and more centralization had their counterparts in educational reform. Whereas the 1960s were a period of quantitative gains in the Cuban educational system, the 1970s emphasized qualitative improvements.

According to Lidia Turner, director of Cuba's Central Institute of Pedagogical Sciences, Cuban education has witnessed two powerful spurts of educational change since 1959. The first occurred during the initial years of the revolution, when Cuban education was placed on a new footing, and the second occurred between 1975 and 1980, the years of radical reform, when the educational system underwent a major overhaul in structure and content according to the Plan de Perfeccionamiento (Improvement Plan). As Turner notes, the plan arose out of a process of critique and reflection marked by two significant events, the First National Congress of Education and Culture, held in Havana in April 1971, and Castro's speech at the end of the Second Congress of Young Communists (UJC), in April 1972 (Turner 1987).

Delegates to the First National Congress on Education and Culture put forward some 3,000 proposals and recommendations for change and improvement. The achievements of the Cuban Revolution in education were remarkable: a reduction in the illiteracy rate, a doubling of the number of elementary schools, and an increase in the proportion of school-aged children in school. However, the Cuban government reported serious problems and deficiencies in the educational system. In April 1971, out of the total number of school-aged children (ages 4–16), 300,000 neither studied nor worked. (The Anti-Loafing Law of 1971 apparently reduced this number to 215,513.) The dropout rate was very high: in elementary schools, 79 percent of those who entered in the class of 1965 had not finished by 1971. The dropout rate was worse in rural areas (88 percent) than in urban schools (66 percent). The dropout rate in junior high school was higher (86 percent) than in elementary school (Mesa-Lago 1978). Other concerns included an out-of date curriculum; poor use of school time; inefficient organization of the school system; poor co-ordination between different types and levels of schooling; inadequate teacher training; inappropriate textbooks and materials; internal inefficiencies caused by low promotion rates, repetition and dropout; failure to keep abreast of developments in science and technology; and operational weaknesses in the "school to the countryside" scheme for urban secondary school pupils. (Richmond 1990, 109)

Some of the reasons given for this dropout phenomenon were of a material nature: poor school facilities, difficult access to schools, and the deficient training of teachers—in elementary schools, only 39 percent of the teachers had finished their studies; in junior high schools, only 27 percent had finished (Mesa-Lago 1978). Additionally, it was reported that the students did not show enough motivation or enthusiasm, which Castro said was the result of being spoiled by the revolution, which was providing them with everything. "Students in general are willing to do anything, except to study hard," he said (Castro 1972d, 2).

The state turned to institutionalizing its policies through the First National Congress on Education and Culture in April 1971. Cuban officials made a series of statements to reinforce a social atmosphere that would combat any form of deviation among Cuban youth. Referring to governing fashions, customs, and behavior, the delegates stated that "the necessity of maintaining the monolithic ideological unity of our people and the struggle against all forms of deviation among our young make it imperative to implement a series of measures for their eradication" (Declaración 1971, 5). The state would take direct action to eliminate "extravagant aberration." Those homosexuals who, by virtue of "artistic merits," worked within institutions designed to attract youth would be transferred to institutions without youth programs. In addition, homosexuals would be barred from representing Cuba abroad as performers. The state believed these policies would strengthen the revolution, but later policy reversals suggest that the officially imposed isolation of homosexuals only weakened Cuba internally. The state eventually realized that these policies would only lead to greater alienation of the international intelligentsia, which had long favored Cuba for its commitment to the improvement of education and culture (Johnson 1993).

In the declarations of the First National Congress on Education and Culture, various areas received more detailed discussion. Teachers were asked to maintain art and literary interests within the objectives of socialist morality. At the same time, radio and television were recognized as the "most efficient instruments for the formation of the *conciencia* of the New Man" (Declaración 1971, 17). Cinema was recognized as the "art *par excellence*" among the mass media. Furthermore, the congress recorded its opposition to "all elitist tendencies," calling for the broad cultural development of the masses (16).

The Second UJC Congress in 1972 indicated that although the organization had achieved some of its objectives, problems had emerged within the UJC between the organization and the youth. Addresses at the congress pointed to a "serious weakness" in the previous political work of the organization, and the UJC launched a campaign to recruit hundreds of thousands of young people, or at least to exert political influence on them. Recognizing the crucial period of childhood in the future formation of communist ideology, the political work of the UJC was extended "to make every young person a self-sacrificing fighter" for increased production and productivity, reduced production costs, the careful use of material resources, and the donation of overtime work when necessary. The UJC agenda continued to imbue the young with Marxist-Leninist values and revolutionary attitudes toward work, education, and defense of the fatherland. Internationalism was added to these qualities at the 1972 congress (Mesa-Lago 1978).

In addition, the Second UJC Congress called attention to the problem areas that would probably persist in future decades. Among the issues of conflict was the mechanical and formalistic style of the UJC, which distanced the organization from problem youth. Other issues of concern included the attitudes and behaviors of youth toward work and the increasing dropout rate, especially among girls. To address these challenges, the UJC proposed a reinvigoration of ideological work among the organization's cadres and among youth at large. The aim was to increase the membership of the UJC and to attract young people to the tasks of production and defense (*Bohemia* 1972, 50).

One of the plans that emerged from the Second UJC Congress called for the UJC to work closely with the Ministry of Education (MINED) to reduce student dropout rates and direct students to the fields in which they were most needed. The UJC requested that "strict, revolutionary measures be taken in the shortest possible time" against young people who had antisocial behavior, especially those who neither worked nor studied and those who were careless, negligent, and irresponsible in handling socialist property (*Granma Weekly Review* 1972). These measures included reducing the student dropout rate through drafting by militarily organized labor squads, as in compulsory military service. In 1973 the Youth Centennial Column and the former Military Units to Aid Production (UMAP) were merged into the Youth Army of Work (EJT), a paramilitary body dependent on the Ministry of the Armed Forces that is devoted to agricultural work (Mesa-Lago 1978). In addition, a new Social Service program, with a commitment of three years' service in rural areas, was made mandatory for secondary school graduates who had not been drafted into the military or had not served in the Youth Centennial Column. Finally, those who had neither been drafted into the military nor had served in the Youth Centennial Column or the Social Service program were assigned three years with the EJT (Dolgoff 1996).

The reformist impetus, evidenced by the thousands of proposals to the First National Congress on Education and Culture and fueled by Castro's address to the Second UJC Congress, resulted in the Plan de Perfeccionamiento. This plan adopted a comprehensive perspective in restructuring both the curriculum and MINED. At a national plenary in 1972, the minister of education encouraged problem solving at a local level and the adoption of a "rational" approach to finding solutions (Lutjens 1996).

The Poder Popular was a part of the solution through the influence it could have on the structures of education administration. In July 1976 a separate Ministry of Higher Education was created that included shared authority over the pedagogical institutes. The Center for Education Development was transformed into the Central Institute of Pedagogical Sciences (Instituto Central de Ciencias Pedagógicas, ICCP). The ICCP became the educational research branch of MINED; its researchers were drawn primarily from MINED and from the ranks of professors in the pedagogical institutes (Miranda 1984).

MINED continued to be at the center, establishing short- and long-range plans in line with the party's decisions for social and economic development. Planning included every activity within education—material, pedagogical, and administrative. In addition, the municipal and provincial offices of education were to be subordinate to MINED in normative and methodological areas, but also to the local Poder Popular. Prior to the creation of the Poder Popular, MINED had been responsible for physical maintenance, providing material resources, and similar functions. Inspections were organized to identify problems and develop policies for improvement, with the results shared with the president of the Poder Popular. After 1976, investment was calculated at the municipal level and reconciled at the provincial level. Thus, the Poder Popular, with its decentralizing reforms, provided new avenues for popular participation in education after 1976 (Lutjens 1996).

Restructuring also extended to the school council, a legacy of the 1960s, which was revamped to fit the institutionalized process. The school council was a means to link the school to the community, affording parents and others participation in school activities. As part of the 1975 Family Code, parents were expected to be actively involved in supporting school activities. In addition, parent-teacher committees were created to expedite the process of creating a new conciencia, with school administrators and teachers taking new steps to reverse exploitive stereotypes. For example, MacDonald (1985) cites children's essays, and one in particular that boys were to write about washing dishes. After 1976 the school council was expected to be guided by ministerial resolutions and to be another example of the decentralization of educational administration (Lutjens 1996).

During the years of the Improvement Plan, participation in education was stressed in teacher education. In a manner reminiscent of John Dewey's learning by doing, the Plan de Titulación de Maestros in 1970 was to prepare "teachers who understand the essence of the educational process and who are able to dominate this process; teachers with a mastery of the subjects they teach; and teachers capable of teaching children not encyclopedic facts, but how to learn" (*Granma* 1970b, 3). The plan was to upgrade the preparation of in-service schoolteachers, with attention to the rationale and tactics for the certification of primary and secondary schoolteachers.

To accommodate the increase in secondary student enrollment in the 1970s, the Pedagogical Detachment of Manuel Ascunce Domenech was established in 1971. This detachment was created to encourage the selection of students for a teaching career. At the Second UJC Congress, Castro announced this new task to the youth: the creation of "a movement to call students currently in tenth grade to go and teach at the secondary schools in the countryside, under the direction of experienced teachers, and to enroll in the Pedagogical Institute for preparation courses" (Castro 1972c).

Revision also included programs and textbooks. According to a five-year (1976–1981) plan, the educational system would offer twelve instead of thirteen years of schooling for all children. More classroom hours would be required, however. Under the new plan, the state guaranteed children one year of kindergarten. Additionally, primary and secondary cycles of schooling were reorganized to offer two stages. In the first stage, grades one through four were in self-contained classrooms (cycle 1), with children staying with the same teacher for all four years to benefit from continuous support and instruction from a teacher who knew them well, thus equipping the children for the years to come (Leiner 1985). In the second stage, grades five and six (cycle 2), "special subjects" were offered and the students moved on to new teachers each year. Cycle 2 was followed by three years of junior high school and three years of senior high school. In this way the teachers hoped to "inculcate a love for study and to contribute to the ideological and integral formation of the pupils" (MINED 1977, 122). During the 1970s only a sixth-grade education was compulsory.

According to the design of the Poder Popular, textbooks, curriculum, and methodological norms were to remain uniform throughout the island, with little in the way of an elective system (Leiner 1985). Max Figueroa, minister of education, at the First Party Congress addressed the issue of political education: "the school needed to be able to respond to the demands of socialist society . . . it is the responsibility of all school subjects" (Figueroa 1975, 4). New generations of students were to be immersed in school subjects based directly on Marxist philosophy. These included "Vida política y mi patria" (Political Life and My Homeland) in fourth grade, "Fundamentos de los conocimientos políticos" (Fundamentals of Political Knowledge) in ninth grade, and "Fundamentos del Marxismo-Leninismo" (Fundamentals of Marxism-Leninism) in eleventh and twelfth grades (*Educación* 1990).

As part of the educational reform, testing procedures were altered, affecting most dramatically student performance in the pre-university schools, rural vocational schools, the school to the countryside program, and adult education. MINED devised exit tests, which were administered at the end of sixth, ninth, and twelfth grades. These tests became a controversial issue because of the poor performance of students. In addition, assessments such as quarterly and final examinations and the percent of students promoted, starting in fifth grade, were used to measure the success of the schools and student achievement (Leiner 1985). The pressure for students to perform well on examinations led to an increase in fraud and cheating, as Castro acknowledged on a number of occasions (e.g., Castro 1978).

Although testing existed with regard to subject matter and grade-level completion, intelligence testing and ability grouping were not used in Cuba's elementary and secondary schools. One teacher explained that such "segregation within the school would contradict socialist principles of our society" (cited in Leiner 1985). Exceptions to this educational equity included the special scientific vocational institutes and other specialized schools, such as the ones for art or sports.

The vocational institutes, such as the Lenin School for Exact Sciences, became enclaves for the intellectually elite. Enrollment and dropout rates— a sign of inefficiency—were to be reduced by admitting students who were likely to finish their studies. In purely economic terms, selectivity could help avoid wasted resources. The Lenin School, located outside Havana, was an example of the specialization and selectivity that were initiated in the 1970s; the idea was to build one such school in each of the provinces. The development of this type of elitist school was an effort to produce an educated elite to become leaders of the country, and if they did not become involved in government, more than likely their jobs would not be in agriculture or manual labor. According to the Cuban government, these special enclaves in each province were dictated by national necessity, the need for a scientific cadre. Education came to be regarded as a tool for promoting development through the training of a skilled and technically proficient population, and for drastically altering the traditionally hostile attitudes toward science, technology, and modern agricultural methods (Leiner 1985; Lutjens 1996).

After ninth grade, students who wanted to go to one of the vocational institutes would take a competitive national examination in math and science. Each municipality was given, on the average, an allotment of two spaces at the vocational institute of the province. In addition, behavior, attitude, academic performance, and class ranking were considered. While the students were expected to carry out the usual maintenance and cleanup responsibilities, they did not participate in the school to the countryside program. This school structure was an exception to the countryside model in Cuban secondary education (Leiner 1985; Lutjens 1996).

The rural vocational and technological schools (especially the agricultural ones), which had so much success in the mid-1960s, lost steam in the seventies. Enrollment dropped dramatically, to the point that some schools were left empty. In 1971, 40 percent more students were enrolled in language schools than in industrial schools or agricultural schools (Mesa-Lago 1978). Castro explained that the idea of moral motivation had failed, and there was a lack of material incentives: "Who wants to go to work in the countryside? [It] is rough, it is poor . . . it doesn't change from one year to the next [and will stay like it is] for years to come" (Castro 1972d, 3).

One response by the Cuban government to stimulate student motivation for working the land was to extend the school to the countryside program to the creation of permanent schools in the countryside, which would provide opportunities for agricultural work year-round. The first Cuban school in the countryside was built in 1971. Each rural boarding school was equipped with dormitories, a library, classrooms, laboratories, a cafeteria, a kitchen, recreational areas, and its own agricultural plot of land for cultivating produce for the school's consumption. Approximately half of the day was set aside for academics and the other half for work. Students and faculty lived, worked, and slept on the premises. One of the results of students participating in agricultural field work on premises is that they see and benefit from the fruits of their labor by consuming what they cultivate. In addition, this combination of schooling with agricultural work offsets much of the school development and maintenance costs.

The Cuban government saw this permanent school in the countryside model as consistent both with Marxist philosophy and with Cuban historical roots. In speaking about the school in the countryside, Fidel Castro noted that it "unites fundamental ideas from two great thinkers: Marx and Martí. Both conceived of a school tied to work, a center where youth are educated for life. . . . [T]his school responds to conceptions about pedagogy, realities, necessities . . . consistent with the development of man—connected to productive and creative work" (Castro 1971a, 13). The permanent school in the countryside was one of many types of new schools (others were new teacher training schools and polytechnical schools) that were created in the 1970s as secondary enrollment increased. From January 1970 to December 1980, 1,577 new school buildings were constructed to accommodate the need for schooling at the junior high level (Miranda 1984).

As a result, from 1975 to 1980 alone, enrollment in junior high countryside schools increased approximately 40 percent. The minister of education at the time, José R. Fernández, said, "These schools are for all students, but those who pass sixth grade and don't have a secondary school near where they live are given priority" (Abascal López 1980). Compulsory education was to be extended beyond the sixth grade to cover the age bracket, 13–17 years, with the highest dropout rate. Moreover, these schoolchildren would be subject to special internment combining work and study (Castro 1972c).

Even as continued efforts were made for schoolchildren to advance beyond sixth grade, similar efforts were being made to keep recent adult literates engaged in education. With the Literacy Campaign as one of the major achievements of the early years of the revolution, the follow-up adult education classes were considered a major accomplishment from 1962 to 1974. More than one-half million adults completed sixth grade in the campaign to win the "Battle for the Sixth Grade."

Under an academic testing program initiated by the Cuban trade union, a longitudinal study was conducted on adult literacy rates. In 1963, of the 1,102,153 workers tested, 81.1 percent tested below the sixth-grade level. Thirteen years later, the 1974 census revealed that 39.9 percent were still reading below the sixth-grade level. In response, at the Thirty-fourth Council of the Cuban Workers Federation, held in February 1975, a new literacy program was proposed. Castro proposed that all workers achieve a minimum of a sixth-grade education by the year 1980. The national commission saw to it that resources were mobilized to achieve this goal, stating, "without this minimum of knowledge [sixth-grade level], it is difficult to participate with efficiency in the process of revolutionary changes and the construction of socialism" (Fernández Perera et al. 1985, 11).

With the active support and cooperation of state agencies and mass organizations, great strides were made in adult education. During the five-year period 1975–1980, 848,812 adults completed sixth grade, whereas 535,100 farmers and workers had graduated during the thirteen years before. A ninth-grade education for all became a national goal (Leiner 1987).

How was this accomplished? Peer teachers with proper training became instructors for pre-service teachers. Thus, in 1976–1977, 53 percent of the 24,200 adult education teachers were workers. Thousands of new texts were created to achieve the advanced literacy goals. Texts on the Spanish language, mathematics, geography, and the natural sciences were revised and flexible calendars were implemented to adjust to individual work conditions (Leiner 1987).

While it continued to be important for girls and boys and men and women to cultivate model citizen behavior, use of the New Man terminology was not as prominent as it was in the 1960s. The concept of the new socialist man had not been abandoned but rather was postponed into the indefinite future. Guevara's writings "by and large disappeared" (Bengelsdorf 1994, 103), although his image remained omnipresent throughout the seventies and his name was evoked daily in day-care centers and schools by children reciting the Pioneer motto, "Seremos como el Che" (We will be like Che).

Some aspects of the Pioneer organization may have stayed the same, but others underwent restructuring. There had been a gap between the terminal age for participating in the Pioneer organization (sixth grade) and the age for selection for membership in the UJP (at the end of ninth grade). To close this gap, the Pioneer organization was extended to include seventh through ninth grades. The Pioneers were also divided into two groups: first through fourth graders were the Moncadistas and fifth through ninth graders were the Martistas, named after José Martí. In uniform, the bandana worn around the neck, blue for Moncadistas and red for Martistas, is the only visibly distinguishing feature (Salva 1977).

Although the New Man concept was not emphasized in the seventies as much as it had been in the sixties, student behavior and revolutionary values continued to be of primary importance. Castro expressed indignation over students' apparent lack of concern for socialist property, such as school textbooks: "There's something wrong when we have to educate our young people in the need to care for socialist property. . . . Loafers, people who don't work, criminals are the ones who destroy" (Castro 1972d, 2–3). MINED reported that 50 percent of the books sent to schools were lost each year (Castilla 1971), an example of the interplay between a concern for proper utilization of resources and the consciousness of the people. Moreover, it was also reported that "residual manifestations" of prostitution and homosexuality were found among the youth (Declaración 1971). In 1967, minors had participated in 41 percent of crimes of all types in the nation; by 1971 the percentage had risen to 50 percent (Castro 1971b).

Castro alleged that the high rate of juvenile delinquency could be laid at the door of exemption from criminal sanctions. Whereas the pre-revolutionary code had called for special treatment for those under age eighteen, in May 1973, the age of legal liability was reduced to age sixteen. In addition, tough sanctions (up to lifetime incarceration) were introduced for crimes against the national economy, abnormal sexual behavior, and other offenses (*Granma* 1973, 1).

The Anti-Loafing Law of 1971 (law no. 1231) addressed the students' prevailing lack of discipline and respect for work, making loafing and parasitism a crime, following the example of Russian labor:

The working class condemns all forms of loafing and considers this as a crime, similar to theft, and repudiates the negative behavior of loafers and demands that severe and effective measures be taken against those who, everyday at all hours, steal the social and material goods created through the efforts of the working people. (Consejos de Ministros 1971)

The law applied to all people physically and mentally able to work, between ages 17 and 60 for men and 55 for women, who were not enrolled in an educational program or who were not incorporated in a work center of any sort. The greatest problems seemed to be skipping school and not showing up for work on a consistent basis (*Granma* 1970a, 2). The law operated at two levels: a first-stage pre-criminal state of loafing and the crime of loafing itself. Both levels of offense could result in house arrest, confinement to a reeducation center, and productive work, which often included agriculture labor. The difference in punishment varied in the time served for each (*Granma* 1970a, 2; Pérez-López 1995).

Probably to avoid any repetition of student rebellion, in a speech at the Second Party Assembly at the University of Havana in 1971, new standards were announced for higher education. Students would be evaluated politically for "the necessary and moral conditions." The right to a university education became "a right for revolutionaries only."

Although many of the measures adopted from 1971 to 1973 proved successful, not all were. Dramatic cuts in the dropout rates were reported in 1973–1974 at all educational levels. By 1974, membership in the UJC had increased to 3.3 times the 1972 membership. However, at the Third UJC Congress in 1974, the congress acknowledged the persistence of old problems, calling again for ideological and political work "against all the imperialists' immoral attempts to pervert [the youth]" (Pérez 1977, 35).

The initiatives undertaken to make the Cuban people feel intimately a part of the revolutionary process had alienated some. And these same measures—especially collective work—were now being used as behavioral correction measures, a move that called into question the motives of both the state and its workers. The communist principle is based on the idea that a worker's conciencia will motivate him or her to work, as he or she learns that such work benefits the entire society. In fact, in communism there is no separation between the workers and society. To construct political unity, those individuals who opted not to participate collectively were incorporated into collective, rural work, with the state hoping they would become reintegrated into the revolution. Thus, the revolution attempted to forge a dynamic equation between productivity and consciousness.

The Early 1980s: Socialism or Growth?

The year 1980 tested the Cuban government as no other had since 1970. In April, 10,000 Cubans flocked to the Peruvian embassy. Between April and September, 125,000 Cubans left Cuba on the Mariel boatlift. The unrealized prospects of the 1970s and the visit of more than 100,000 Cuban Americans in 1979 fueled a tense situation. The government labeled those wanting to leave "scum" who had renounced the ideals of the fatherland for the lures of consumerism. The Communist Party organized meetings to repudiate those leaving in front of their houses. The challenge for the Cuban leaders lay in satisfying basic needs—especially in the supply, diversity, and quality of food and other consumer goods—more efficiently and more effectively. The Mariel exodus, which occurred during the time of the Solidarity movement in Poland, impressed on Cuban leadership the need to reinforce its links with the pueblo cubano (Pérez-Stable 1993).

Castro may have assumed that emigration was a convenient way to eliminate domestic opposition while at the same time unifying the pueblo cubano. However, the economic price was high in terms of manpower and the loss of scarce skills. Although the Mariel boatlift might be viewed as just another emigration of dissatisfied Cubans, certain features are worth recognizing.

This exodus may be telling in young people's transition from school to work. With an overrepresentation of young people, mainly in their twenties, economic rather than political dissatisfactions were particularly strong. When asked, "Why did you decide to leave Cuba now?" almost 65 percent of those under the age of 25 stressed economic burdens, which fell heavily on the young. These reasons included "harder time getting a good job to fit my qualifications" and "too much voluntary labor" (Fernández 1982, 196).

Another report on the Cubans who entered the Peruvian embassy described the young Cubans as "hungry for material rewards not available in the austere economy" in Cuba (*Latin American Weekly Report* 1980, 1). During the summer of 1980, several months before events came to a head, it was noted, from the complaints of "many young people," that "the advances in education have led to the paradox of a large number of young people who are 'overqualified' for available jobs. Understandably, this has been a focus of discontent" (*Latin American Regional Reports (Caribbean)* 1980, 5).

Cuba was not alone in this struggle to appease the loyalty of its people. In the mid-1980s, Soviet and East European countries were confronting the same problems: growing inequality, corruption, an erosion of conciencia, hard-currency debt, trade deficits, domestic inefficiencies, the devaluation of the dollar, falling international prices for sugar and oil—all in the face of the Reagan administration's activities and the ongoing U.S. embargo. Additionally, ten years after the introduction of the new SDPE, which was intended to remedy the serious difficulties of the Cuban economy, Fidel Castro drew a negative assessment of its application. Internally, Cuban reformers cited poor performance of the economic planning and incentive systems that had been developed in the 1970s and 1980s, mistakes made by enterprise managers, and a low level of labor productivity and efficiency. As Cuba's relationship with the socialist countries weakened, the regime sought new ways to improve economic performance. Faced with a crisis of socialism, the Cuban government turned to the tenets of the revolution, presenting new dicta in the Party Congress of 1980 (Azicri 1988; Habel 1989; Pérez-Stable 1993).

During the 1980 congress, bureaucracy was criticized as the cause of inefficiency as well as of political insecurity. Raúl Castro, Fidel's brother, second secretary of the Communist Party and head of Cuban defense, blamed bureaucratic comportment for aggravating the existing situations with the embargo and the sugar harvest disappointment (Habel 1989). The problems ranged from laziness, indifference, and insulation to privileges, cronyism, and corruption. Carlos Rafael Rodríguez, one of Fidel Castro's closest collaborators and a cabinet member, noted that bureaucracy was "one of the permanent risks of socialism." He explained, "These are not the times of the Greek agora where the decisions that had to be adopted were few and relatively simple. . . . [T]he essence of bureaucratism is substituting for the role of the masses in the decision making process" (Rodríguez 1980, 320).

To address bureaucracy and recent market reforms, Castro denounced the heads of state enterprises for becoming apprentice capitalists, and also banned the farmers' markets, which had been legalized in 1980 and operated until 1986, offering a variety of fruits and vegetables to the public. Castro lashed out at the reliance on material bonuses to motivate workers, calling once again for moral incentives to build a better society. Furthermore, he began a campaign against *empleomanía*, or overstaffing. In hospitals and factories across the country, studies were done; then workers, sometimes 30 or 40 percent of staff, were dismissed, shifted to other employment, sent home, or sent to work in the microbrigades. Not even the Communist Party was spared this belt-tightening (Domínguez 1993; Padula 1993).

Another situation affecting production and, consequently, the economy was the deployment of large numbers of Cubans overseas. Cuba had sent troops to fight in Africa: one tranche to Ethiopia and another to Angola. In addition, many reservists were stationed in Grenada at the peak of the U.S. invasion. Given the government's desire to win the wars and to perform well overseas in a military role, some of the best managers, technicians, and workers were taken from the home economy for the overseas army, which contributed to a decline in productivity and efficiency in various sectors from the late seventies on. Although the number of Cuban troops in Ethiopia was sharply reduced in the mid-1980s, more than 50,000 Cuban troops remained in Angola until the war ended in 1988 (Domínguez 1993).

At the international level, the 1980 Party Congress reaffirmed Cuba's strong ties with the Soviet Union, defending such international principles as support for revolutionary movements abroad (with special reference to Grenada and Nicaragua). In the economic sphere, the Cuban government proclaimed the institutionalization of the 1970s and early 1980s as "bad copies" of the Soviet and East European models. Furthermore, the 1980 Party Congress emphasized the need for more state planning, reaffirmed the centrality of the Communist Party, and warned of a possible decline in production and exports because of the world economic situation. With mounting U.S. aggression in the Nicaraguan case, Cuba's international relations provoked new tensions at the outset of the 1980s (Habel 1989; Suchlicki 1997).

Educational Policy of the Early 1980s

Forming the "perfect communist" in the early 1980s was still being addressed through the *perfeccionamiento* educational movement, which had been phased in over the period between 1975–1976 and 1980–1981. The Perfeccionamiento

Plan was expected to give Cuban education a sure foundation for further advancement during the 1980s and beyond. However, between the early and mid-1980s several developments indicated that the political socialization of Cuban youth was failing to meet the objectives of the state. The Mariel boatlift sent a shock wave through the society. The children of the revolution, the new men and women in the making, were abandoning the revolution and heading for the United States.

Even as some Cubans were planning their departure from the island, many of the mass organizations met to plan public reaffirmations of revolutionary loyalty. During this time the Pioneer organization created a new branch called the Explorers. In some ways the Explorers were similar to the Boy Scouts and Girl Scouts of America. The activities of the Explorers were mostly connected with nature, camping, and training for difficult times, including U.S. aggression or possible invasion. The Pioneers, along with the rest of the pueblo cubano, were organized to participate in repudiating those involved in the Mariel boatlift—behavior that included throwing eggs at people's homes and calling them "traitors" and "scum," actions intended to heap public opprobrium on the leavers.

The Explorers were one more channel to keep children involved in understanding and participating in model citizenry. The UJC proposed that a Pioneer Palace be built in each municipality, which would then become a center for stimulating career interests and a place of guided nighttime and weekend activities for the children. Additionally, the UJC planned to create centers in each province for Explorer activities. Both the Pioneer Palaces and the Explorer Centers were a part of the Perfeccionamiento Plan, which sought to sustain revolutionary values as part of the education experience.

Cuba's political and educational leaders realized that the improvements instituted under the aegis of the Perfeccionamiento Plan would need to be monitored, and, where and when necessary, corrective measures would have to be applied. They also recognized that in the years ahead, the quality of education would demand increasing attention and resources. Of particular importance in this regard was the need to improve the theoretical and methodological competence of Cuba's teachers, many of whom continued to rely on a pedagogical style reminiscent of their student days prior to the revolution (Richmond 1990).

Realizing that new patterns of behavior must be presented in an attractive manner to accommodate the youth, Castro began to emphasize the role of teachers in the 1980s. At a teachers' graduation ceremony in July 1981, he observed that it is the teacher who gives concrete substance to the lines drawn by the party, insofar as he/she succeeds in putting into practice study plans, programs, methodological guides, and normative documents. The educator must also be an activist of our party's revolutionary policy, a defender of our ideology, of our morality, of our political convictions. He must therefore be an exemplary revolutionary. (*Granma* 1981, 1)

And as Castro expressed this demand for ideological militancy, the audience sat facing an enormous poster hanging behind him and dominating the scene with one of his maxims: "We cannot stop fighting to raise the quality of education for even one day." Thus we find yet another expression in the educational field of that constant theme of the revolutionary message: relentless striving for improvement.

To advance the revolution, internationalist contingents of students and teachers were created, with some 1,000 members working in Angola and another detachment of some 2,000 teachers sent to Nicaragua. By 1981 there were 3,500 Cuban schoolteachers, professors, and advisers rendering international service in twenty countries (Castro 1981).

However, other deficiencies in the educational system persisted. Minister of Education José Fernández said that one of the most worrisome signs was the occurrence of academic cheating in 34 percent of secondary schools, which was engaged in by both teachers and pupils to meet the target educational goals (Thomas, Fauriol, and Weiss 1984).

At an administrative level, deficiencies took the form of major economic mismanagement and personal pilfering of supplies at local schools. For instance, in early 1982, to end the pilfering of supplies, the authorities launched Operation Vulture in La Habana province and on the Isle of Youth. Those who had access to the food deliveries for the school were swapping the food with *socios,* a relationship in which "tacit associates are engaged in equally tacit deals" (the socialist good ol' boys' network—*sociolismo*) and profiting personally (Hildago 1984). Inspections, audits, and improved supervision were initiated to curtail the corruption of the "vultures," and the investigation became a public matter, as it was reported in *Granma* (1982, 3).

The FMC was called on to assist in consciousness-raising and maintaining the voluntary activity of the Movimiento de Madres Combatientes por la Educación (Movement of Militant Mothers for Education). The Madres group had its beginnings in the late 1960s, with mothers helping in rural schools. Fidel Castro, MINED, and the Communist Party officially recognized the Madres. Membership in the organization had steadily increased since its early days. In 1970, the Madres had 2,681 members; by 1976 they numbered 868,000 and by 1985 1,700,000 (Lutjens 1996, Table 5.1, 137), and it was calculated that approximately 90 percent of the mothers in each school belonged. However, the activism of the Madres Combatientes was not limited to mothers. Some of the women of the Madres movement did not even have children in the schools.

The women of Madres Combatientes organized themselves into brigades that worked with classrooms as units in each school. The FMC discussed and assessed the work of the Madres, and took the suggestions and recommendations of the Madres to the school council. The Madres contributed to the implementation of national policy by using initiative and problem-solving strategies to effect the proper functioning of the classroom. As the FMC's *Boletín* (1982, 4) described,

> This movement offers an effective contribution to the work of the school and also serves as a vehicle for the organization to gain exhaustive knowledge of the daily problems that the school institutions face, with the purpose of analyzing them and helping the Ministry of Education find a solution.

The tasks of the Madres in the schools were numerous. They included promoting regular attendance and punctuality, retention, promotion, educational work, meeting with parents, assisting with Pioneer activities, providing teacher support, organizing special events, and assisting in the work-study programs, such as the school to the countryside program. For example, the Madres would visit homes to promote school retention and set up homes for collective study, called "study houses." They aimed to serve as examples and to encourage the development of personal norms and values in line with Cuba's socialist principles. The success of the Madres Combatientes came from their numbers, volunteerism, commitment, and personal interest, all of which frequently resulted in permanent policy changes (Lutjens 1996).

Although education can indeed contribute to the economic and social development in the long term, concurrent favorable developments elsewhere in the economy must accompany rising educational levels. The overeducation problem was fully manifest in the late 1970s and early 1980s, when the government confronted a phenomenal surge in secondary school enrollments, and later when a corresponding demand for higher education began to burden the educational system with high enrollment. The government was forced to institute selective admission policies and to restrict the number of students to the pre-university vocational institutes of exact sciences as well as higher education.

There was no lack of desire for or interest in pursuing further education in the 1970s and early 1980s. However, Cuba was faced with limits in educational expansion and opportunity. The educational, political, and economic engineering espoused by the Cuban leaders, with their idealistic view of the perfectibility of human nature, ran up against material obstacles and insufficient numbers of teaching professionals. In addition, the Cuban youth and state-societal relations were characterized by increased bureaucratization and routinization of power in the 1970s, making the socialist dream more impossible to realize. The faltering of prophecy became one of the root causes of popular disappointment, making it more difficult for the state to sustain popular affection with the people (Fernández 2000). Noting these issues, the Rectification Campaign was launched in 1986. Its social, economic, and political ramifications are discussed in Chapter 4.

1986–2000: Rectification and the Special Period

While the Cuban state tried to appeal to the youth with measures to rejuvenate the Young Communists (UJC) in the early 1980s, the timing collided with the Rectification Campaign. The Rectification Campaign was an austerity program, initiated in 1986, that gave ideology an expanded role in daily life and economic management. This program undid many of the economic reforms of earlier years. As Cuban socialism tried to respond to the concerns of the young people, few economic and political opportunities were available. Moreover, with the dissolution of the Soviet bloc, the revolutionary government had to confront its worst political and economic crisis ever. This chapter examines the intersection of economic and educational measures from the mid-1980s until 2000, providing a backdrop for the ethnographic chapters that follow.

The Rectification Campaign

International and domestic tensions influenced an economic, political and ideological turning point marked by the Third Congress of the Cuban Communist Party in 1986. The second session of the Third Party Congress provided the occasion for the launch of a "process of rectification of the errors and negative tendencies in all spheres of society" that was supposed to resolve the cumulative problems of socialist development (*Granma* 1987b, 3). The economic recession started in 1982–1983 in the United States and other industrialized nations, hitting them hard, and the socialist countries did not escape its negative effects. In contrast to the economic and political liberalization that occurred in other former socialist countries, however, Cuba's

Rectification Campaign took place in the context of centralized planning and a socialist state (Azicri 1988; Lutjens 1996).

The Cuban Rectification Campaign was formally introduced in 1986, almost at the same time that glasnost and perestroika were becoming household words with clear meanings in the Soviet Union. By comparison, the meaning and content of the Rectification Campaign have never been obvious, even for those involved in it.

Some Cubans initially saw the Rectification Campaign as a series of readjustments of the economic mechanisms within the System of Economic Management and Planning (Sistema de Dirección y Planificación de la Economía, SDPE). Some have seen it as a catch-all label for political and economic measures that had to be taken in the aftermath of dramatic decreases in foreign exchange earnings in the mid-1980s. Some have understood it as a mechanism for Castro to weed out technocrats at higher levels. Others, at least in its early days, saw it as a critical point at which the basic structure and workings of the revolution would be reexamined (Bengelsdorf 1994). On the street, Medea Benjamin (1990, 18) reported, the Rectification Campaign came to be labeled the *espera estoica,* the "long stoic wait" (a play on the word *perestroika*).

Part of the basis of the Rectification Campaign was Castro's general critique of the reliance on market forces and motivations—features that were at the heart of Gorbachev's reforms and similar changes in China and in Eastern Europe. These reforms complicated Cuban relations with the USSR. "Perestroika," Fidel asserted, "is another man's wife. I don't want to get involved" (*New York Times* 1989, A1). In partial agreement, Castro, other Cuban officials, and the mass media focused on some commonalities between Gorbachev's reforms and Castro's rectification measures, such as the punishment of corrupt officials (Domínguez 1993).

Castro seemed to think that the deficiencies in socialism required more cadres with a revolutionary consciousness at all levels:

We are not going to the heart of the matter. . . . We are not dealing with our system's—our socialism's—deficiencies. . . . There is a problem of *conciencia*. . . . To what extent do we really manifest political, revolutionary, social *conciencia?* We manifest it often . . . incredibly, admirably, extraordinarily. . . . But, in day-to-day life we are lacking *conciencia.* (Castro 1989, 1)

Conciencia, not autonomous institutions and participation, was the essence of good politics.

How to maintain conciencia and still have the economy functioning with the attributes of central planning was at the heart of Cuba's economic policy planning. The economic mechanisms built into the system in the late 1970s, such as self-financing, enterprise profitability, decentralization, and higher productivity rates, led to abuses and distortions. The problem arose in cases such as the allowance of farmers' markets in 1980, which benefited the consumers and farmers but also caused social dislocation by putting the material resources and monetary profits in the hands of a few. In 1986 these markets were closed, and many other changes were made in policies and personnel to emphasize the need to work for the benefit of the homeland rather than merely for oneself (Azicri 1988; Domínguez 1993; Habel 1989).

Given the dichotomy between the political economy and revolutionary values, the Castro government revived Guevara's economic approach, especially with regard to moral incentives and increased centralization. In 1985 Castro stated, "The mistake with the most pernicious consequences was the belief that only economic mechanisms would insure the construction of socialism" (cited in Jatar-Haussmann 1999, 37). The recourse to material incentives for piecework production had led to earnings that were considered excessive, and trying to fulfill the demand this generated caused difficulties to the overall economy, given the incapacity to keep pace. Economic problems were thought to be a part of a war requiring heroic actions to overcome a prevalent "bourgeois mentality among workers." Castro denounced the self-employed Cubans as "corrupt parasites" on the public sector and condemned what he called the "thousands of wheeler-dealers who cheat, sell, and steal" (37). Consequently, tighter restrictions were implemented affecting private service workers, street vendors, taxi drivers, and those who rented rooms. Castro summarized his sentiment with the following statement:

> In the search for economic efficiency, we have created a heap of evils and deformation, and what is worse, corruption. . . . It is a moral issue, one of principle and dignity not to surrender to commercialism and speculation. (37)

Clearly, the government's about-face in economic policy was politically and ideologically inspired. The driving force behind the policies of this reform project seemed to emulate those of the 1966–1970 period. The political leadership placed "people," not profitability, at the center of their work. The Guevara innovation of volunteerism was revived, with mass participation and the resurrection of production brigades. One's attitude toward work was emphasized to the extent that the route to Communist Party membership began to rely heavily on exemplary worker status (Fuller 1992). In addition, an "affirmative action policy" was installed that was designed to bring more women and Afro-Cubans into the party's leadership ranks (Azcri 1988, 247). Material inducements alone had not led the Cuban people to make the revolution; commitments to *la patria* and social justice had been more central inspirations. The rectification was intended to rescue that élan and incorporate it into the politics of socialism. As a result, the party's role in trying to change workers' attitudes and the organization of work was enhanced under rectification.

The new politics were first evident in the restitution of old forms of labor mobilization. Microbrigades, construction contingents, and volunteer work exemplified the reinforcement to attain economic results. During the early 1970s the microbrigades had been used mainly to build apartment houses. With the establishment of the SDPE in the mid-1970s, planners and managers tended to minimize their importance. By contrast, in the 1980s the microbrigades emphasized socially useful construction, such as day-care centers and clinics; microbrigade workers were mobilized to promote collective well-being. Numbering in the hundreds in the early 1980s, more than 1,200 brigades incorporating more than 117,000 workers were reported to exist in 1985, and the brigades totaled over 2,000 in 1986 (Fitzgerald 1989; *Trabajadores* 1985; Zimbalist 1989).

With the use of the brigades, the Cuban government attempted to democratize production: the brigades were to be involved in more worksite planning, including supervising the organization and distribution of their own work tasks. In turn, participation would awaken a sense of national pride and empowerment in the Cuban people (Pérez-Stable 1993). Although the contribution of the voluntary work brigades cannot be ignored, their ideological aim undoubtedly counted as much as their economic efficiency. As mentioned in *Bohemia:*

> The microbrigades movement represents much more than building buildings. It is a reaffirmation that problems can be solved through the mass line. . . . It is a demonstration that socialism can provide an immediate solution for emergencies of material production, as it has done in the case of education, sport and health. (1988, B22)

With the microbrigades and mobilizations, the Rectification Campaign was trying to revitalize the original spirit or conciencia of the revolution, which the SDPE allegedly had weakened. The Cuban leadership did not accept that, with or without the SDPE, the enthusiasm of the early years could not possibly be the same after thirty years (Pérez-Stable 1993). Appeals to conciencia and mass mobilizations were, nonetheless, the hallmark of the Cuban Revolution, and the ideological campaign was not merely a pretext. Fidel Castro denounced mercenaries for "seeking privileges and profits," as well as those who wanted to "pocket the money they have not earned with their own sweat but through fiddles and speculation. . . . [T]hese technocrats and bureaucrats are infected with a kind of ideological AIDS, a kind of AIDS that was destroying the defense of the revolution" (*Granma Weekly Review* 1986). Despite AIDS being one of the most dubious of metaphors—as is the case with anything related to homosexuality in Cuba—this denunciation strongly conveyed the idea of a battle against a process of division and bureaucratization that could only be fatal for the revolution. As a result, the return to Guevarism in the 1980s tended to be more theoretical than real. The economic and social contexts had changed extensively, and, even more important, the political scene now lacked the climate of ideological mobilization that had characterized the early sixties (Trento 2000).

Unlike Guevara's proposals, the 1986–1990 Rectification Campaign, while striving to lower the cost of production, was based on a strategy of externally based growth. The emphasis was on the creation of nontraditional export sectors and the development of new markets. One of the key elements of this strategy was to attract foreign investment and tourism. Nevertheless, the rectification process resorted to appeals for conciencia and mobilizations, although compulsion often appeared to be a more effective lever (Trento 2000).

Stricter laws were believed to be the means to attain better labor discipline. Penalties were levied against those who persisted in their "mercantile habits." When many enterprises continued to pay excessive salaries, the government created special groups to enforce the policy on wages. People violated the law so extensively that in 1986, the National Assembly president asserted that all laws would from then on be respected. The rectification had evidently not curbed the misuse and neglect of state resources, and the black market continued to flourish. One response was the dismissal of all political cadres, state functionaries, and mass organization leaders who bought stolen merchandise. This measure was defanged, however, when the National Assembly passed a new code that decriminalized many illicit activities and reduced jail sentences for numerous crimes, as well as a regulation that deleted past sanctions from the dossiers of workers who improved their labor discipline (Habel 1989).

Clearly, Castro continued to maintain that individuals, he above all, could overcome obstacles through sacrifice and hard work. The more apparently unreachable the political goal, the more worthy it is of pursuit. Willful political action and tactical boldness shall overcome any obstacles in the long term, even if there are temporary setbacks. This belief had led Castro to attack the Moncada barracks against apparently impossible odds in 1953 and, once in power, to defy the United States. Castro attempted to transform the Cuban people ideologically—first in the late 1960s and again in the late 1980s—committed to revolutionary ideals and untainted by corrupt monetary motivation. In an interview published in *Playboy* magazine, Castro told the interviewer, "Don Quixote's madness and the madness of the revolutionaries are similar . . . the spirit is similar . . . that spirit of the knight-errant, of righting wrongs everywhere, of fighting against giants" (Castro 1985, 183).

The Rectification Process in Schooling:
El Perfeccionamiento Continuo

The policy changes in the early 1980s seemed to be shaped rather than inspired by rectification, considering the criticisms of the mid- to late 1980s. It was agreed that the initial reforms of the Perfeccionamiento Plan had been too ambitious, and that perfecting the system was an ongoing process that had to correspond with the needs of society. For example, course syllabi contained more material than could possibly be covered, and as a result, teachers and students took shortcuts to accomplish the stated goals (Richmond 1990). Quality needed to be addressed, and with the Rectification Campaign of the mid-1980s another phase of educational reform was also initiated in Cuba, called *Perfeccionamiento Continuo* (ongoing improvement). Policies targeted specific dimensions of the organization, content, and administration of the Cuban schools; improvement in the quality of formal education was again the general goal of the reforms (Turner 1987).

At the Third Party Congress in 1986, Castro listed numerous problems ranging from poor administration to *promocionismo* (a fixation on high rates of promotion regardless of actual student performance). For example, according to the *Granma Weekly Review* (1986, 9), in Havana City, only 70 percent of junior high and 76 percent of senior high school students had passed by the end of the 1985–1986 term. Visits to several junior high schools revealed a "poor interpretation of rigorousness" on the part of teachers, students, families, and mass organizations. Other shortcomings included lax examination procedures, poorly prepared classes, inexperienced teachers, a lack of rigor on the part of the teachers, poor study habits among the students, inadequate preparation of university entrants for the demands of their course work, low standards of social conduct among both students and teachers, and the overburdening of teachers with administrative work. Moreover, more than 9,000 teachers had left the profession in the previous school term (Castro 1986). These and other problems were addressed in the Perfeccionamiento Continuo.

The official start of the education reforms was associated with the Eleventh National Seminar for Administrators, Methodologists, and Inspectors, held in February 1987. The seminar was preceded by discussions among the party leadership and by general meetings with educators. The result of the discussions was a plan of 410 specific measures—83 percent of which had been accomplished by the time of the Twelfth Seminar in 1989 (Ministerio de Educación [MINED] 1989).

Beginning with a moderate austerity program, the focus of resources shifted toward social needs, which included a revival of voluntary labor and moral incentives with regard to schools. The construction of new educational facilities with voluntary labor marked the first years of the rectification campaign. Yet limited resources affected intentions and plans, and demands for repairs were not always met. In addition, natural factors, such as Hurricane Kate, destroyed 100 schools in 1985. Moreover, a call for energy conservation and the rational use of resources in education emerged as early as 1985. For instance, there were cautions about wasting electricity in schools, and more attention was given to the methods and rigor with which crops were cultivated in the school to the countryside program and the community school gardens. With a call for the rational use of resources, the Poder Popular continued to take on local school maintenance responsibilities (Lutjens 1996).

Fidel Castro continued to think that human resources could in some way account for the scarcity of material resources. He seemed to fault an overeducated populace for the underutilization of human resources and productive capacity. In the Spanish newspaper *El País*, Castro stated that research and development centers had not been established to "raise wages and produce doctoral candidates, but to resolve problems of production. There are people fresh out of university who work hours and hours preparing to qualify. . . . [T]he proliferation of centers of this kind and the race to qualify are negative phenomena" (*El País* 1987, 2). Therefore, a massive gap existed between the level of education of young people and the available outlets for work, especially for those with university degrees.

As a result of this mismatch between qualifications and available jobs, migration from rural areas to urban areas increased. Demographic trends had also produced a decline in primary and secondary school enrollments, as well as smaller enrollments in rural schools. In addition, pedagogical institutes became more selective, and their retention rates dropped. A new policy in adult education limited access to those ages 17 and older. In 1987, students accounted for 26.1 percent of Cubans ages 12–29, and 9.9 percent were neither studying nor working (Domínguez, Ferrer, and Valdés 1990). The school system was still expected to serve the economy, and the rectification process ushered in significant changes.

Reforms in the curriculum and teaching methods received major attention in the *Perfeccionamiento Continuo*. Attempts in the mid-1970s to inculcate Marxist philosophy starting in the fourth grade were overhauled or "rectified," because "moral dogma" was seen as unfruitful, "not connecting itself with social praxis, not allowing for the optimum fulfillment of the objectives for which they were created" (*Educación* 1990, 102). Modifications in primary school education included a new course in grades first through fourth called The World in Which We Live, the objective of which was "organizing the schooling of the child so that he is familiar with society and nature, proper family, school and social behavior, patriotic preparation, and the understanding of nature" (Turner 1987, 7). In ninth grade, civic education was initiated for the purpose of giving students a deeper knowledge of "civic duties and rights, the organization and function of the State and Communist Party . . . also recognizing social norms of conduct, preparation for family life, and important questions concerning political and moral preparation" (Turner 1987, 11). The aim in secondary education was to eliminate the Marxist theoretical content and to pursue a "more integrated preparation of the student" and a "more panoramic vision of the world" (MINED 1989, 79). The school subjects of art and civic education were both added to the secondary curriculum. In addition, more emphasis was given to practical activity, labor education, and the work-study principle. The foreign language requirement was changed from Russian to English. The number of course subjects taught at both grade levels was diminished by conflating some two-semester courses into one, for example. At the pre-university (high school) level, computer classes would be introduced in tenth through twelfth grades. Along with other curricular changes, the government planned to incorporate these changes during the 1988–1991 school years at all levels (MINED 1989; Turner 1987).

The teaching of the curriculum was as important as the curriculum itself. There was criticism stemming from the gap between teachers' efforts and the results seen in students' work and behavior. MINED perceived the cause to lie in the difference between education and instruction. Teachers were criticized for "traits of formalism, rigidity, and authoritarianism," "difficulties in unifying family and school," and "transmission of information that has a formalistic character in which the students participate only as passive receptacles" (MINED 1989, 132–133). The rhetoric, or *teque*, of the revolution was rejected for a more active and creative learning environment. In 1987 the first visit by Paulo Freire since 1964 signaled the change in perspective as a number of seminars on popular education were hosted in Cuba.

With the renewal of popular education came a renewal in military preparedness on the parts of teachers and students. Active military service became an integral component of teacher preparation in 1986. Schools had been designated as refuges in case of war or U.S. aggression, and the teachers attended classes about once a month for a year to solidify their military preparation and learn how to direct the children in case of an emergency. The classes included practice at a firing range. Initially only male teachers were involved, but by 1987 female teachers too were being strongly encouraged to participate. At the same time, the aim was for the teachers to pass on this patriotic, military, and internationalist education to the students and to remind them of their patriotic duties (*Educación* 1987).

Within the reforms and rectification process of the mid- to late 1980s, the Movimiento de Madres Combatientes was reconceived as the Padres Combatientes (Militant Parents). The modification reflected the greater role assigned to family participation in education and the equal need for attention from the father as well as the mother. However, the change meant a loss of the special regard accorded women's work in the schools. For the most part, it was hard to see any difference between the responsibilities of the school council and the work of the Padres, although the relationship between home and school and the family's responsibility for education continued to be emphasized (Lutjens 1996).

Families, communities, and the state were also concerned about teenage delinquency. In the mid-1980s less than 2 percent of students from ages 13 to 16 neither studied nor worked. These students had opted out of the educational system. Officially, employment was illegal for youth under the age of 17. In response to citizen proposals in La Habana, the Poder Popular established jobs for teenagers, and interest grew rapidly (Beatón et al. 1992; Bunck 1994).

Las escuelas de oficios (trade schools) and *las escuelas-talleres* (school-workshops) emerged as a response to the teenage delinquency situation. It was determined that factors contributing to the increased dropout rate among 13- to 16-year-olds included an unstable home, inadequate pedagogy and methodology in the schools, and the parents' cultural level. The dropouts were called *los desvinculados*, "the disconnected ones," understood as those not incorporated into or participating in the revolutionary project. Thus, the goal was to enroll these students in the new vocational-type schools, which would give them a productive and useful trade with which to participate in society. Those students who showed aptitude and interest could possibly continue their studies at polytechnical centers or institutes afterward.

The *escuelas de oficios* started in 1987 at both the primary and secondary level. Those who were problem students in class or dropouts were given schooling in the simplest labor activities and basic curriculum according to their grade of education, responding to the demands of the local community. The industries in the community dictated the type of trades offered at the school. Three plans existed for the different grade levels. The first was for those who had not finished elementary school. For this primary level, schooling at the escuela de oficio would consist of three and a half years, focusing on a trade but also giving students the basic course work for this level. The second plan was for students who had finished some secondary school but had not graduated from ninth grade. Their education would consist of two years of learning trades along with the basic curriculum of junior high school, guaranteeing continuation in either a polytechnical institute or a return to the track of a general pre-university school (high school) (Roig Izaguirre 1987).

In another attempt to retain *los desvinculados* in the school system, a passing score was lowered from seventy to sixty in 1986. As a result of this new evaluation, Havana province ended the 1986–1987 school year with a promotion rate of 97 percent, but around 15 percent of those students held an average score between sixty and seventy (*El Militante Communista* 1987). If this measure had not been passed, the promotion rate would have been 82 percent—much lower than in previous years. With this new measure, José Ramón Balaguer, member of the Central Committee Secretariat, stated that the statistics "reflect reality more" (ibid., 23). Balaguer indicated that rigor would not be lost as a result of this change. In fact, only students with an average score of ninety or higher could compete for a college education in Cuba anyway. The real difference would be "fewer students in the street susceptible to delinquency or idleness" (ibid., 23).

Eschewing another radical, large-scale reform of the Cuban educational system, the leadership decided to make selective adaptations and minor modifications within an ongoing framework of providing education that was responsive to new needs and the changing circumstances of society at large. Municipalities were allowed to make changes in course syllabi, textbooks, and teachers' manuals in tune with their own stages of *perfeccionamiento continuo*, continual improvement, although links to the "backbone" of MINED were to be maintained (Richmond 1990).

The 1990s: The Special Period

Cuba's fortunes started to change in the late 1980s and early 1990s. The economic recession remained. One reason for the recession was the decline in labor productivity as Cuban workers responded adversely to the policies of rectification announced in 1986 that sought to deemphasize the role of material incentives for work. Personal spending slowed and unemployment increased. The foreign debt crisis and lack of access to the world's financial markets took their toll on the Cuban economy. In addition, the sudden drop-off in aid from the Soviet Union and Eastern Europe, which in 1987 still absorbed close to 90 percent of Cuba's external commerce (Trento 2000), contributed to the negative direction of the economy. Beginning in 1989, Cuba began to feel the full decomposition of the communist regimes in Eastern Europe. In 1990, 40 percent of all food consumed in Cuba originated in the Soviet Union, yet the Soviet Union initiated drastic cuts. For example, from 1989 to 1991, Cuban imports of petroleum products from the Soviet Union dropped by two-thirds, forcing severe rationing throughout Cuba's economy (Domínguez 1993, 4; Moses 2000; Trento 2000).

The heightened economic austerity caused a sharp decline in living standards. In 1991, in response to the new circumstances, Castro declared the beginning of the "Special Period in Time of Peace." The Special Period strategy consisted of a web of austerity measures to conserve energy and raw materials, increase food production, expand markets for exports and imports, attract foreign investment, increase voluntary labor, and introduce some management and selective structural reforms (Pérez-López 1995).

The effects of the economic depression were reminiscent of wartime. Street lighting was reduced or eliminated, gas was rationed, and, because of the scarcity of petroleum, transportation was virtually paralyzed. To counter this breakdown in transportation, Chinese bicycles were imported and popularized. *Apagones* (interruptions of electricity), introduced in 1992, were scheduled for as much as eighteen hours a day. Ox-drawn carts reappeared in the countryside, replacing tractors and other farming equipment.

The international changes had not only an economic impact in Cuba, there were political and ideological repercussions as well. With the end of the Cold War and the collapse of the Soviet Union, as well as Cuban battlefield successes, Cuban troops returned home. Cuba had successfully advised the Sandinista government in Nicaragua, prevented Somalia's takeover of Ogaden, stopped the South African military invasion of Angola, and withdrawn from Ethiopia prior to the collapse of its government. In addition, Castro openly admitted that Cuba had supported armed violence against both the Chilean and Salvadorian governments, both of which came to a formal end in the early 1990s. Whether as a result of battlefield victories that no longer required a Cuban military presence or at the request of governments resulting from the course of international negotiations, the return of Cuban troops to their homeland in the early 1990s marked the end to a remarkable chapter in Cuba's international relations history and influence in the world. Cuba was once again just an island in the sun. The island's policy makers now put aside the impulse to export the revolution as in the 1960s.

The changes in domestic politics in the late 1980s and early 1990s were no less momentous. Fidel Castro continued to dismiss officials who did not agree with his domestic politics. Whereas Cuba's top leadership had remained relatively stable from the mid-1960s to the early 1980s, the Communist Party's Political Bureau was totally revamped from the mid-1980s through the early 1990s. Officials were dismissed for alleged corrupt dealings. The state attacked oligarchic tendencies in an effort to streamline the size of the party bureaucracy. The leadership used the opportunity to weed out ineffective and "problem" cadre and to give select and critical constituencies, such as youth, greater representation within the "vanguard" institution (Economic Intelligence Unit [EIU] 1990). At the end of the Fourth Party Congress in October 1991, only five of the Political Bureau's members from 1975 were still in their posts (Domínguez 1993). A nascent party "reformist" faction (in principle, not formally) thereby gained the means for greater influence over internal party matters (Eckstein 1994).

The Castro leadership could not remain passive in the face of the ruling circles' growing moral degradation while demanding daily sacrifices from the people. But the gravity of the economic and moral crisis was in a completely different league. As stated in an editorial in *Granma,* "the problems that have been faced by the country this summer go well beyond the fate of a handful of corrupt and disloyal men" (Castro 1989, 1). And stressing that this was a much more far-reaching stage of rectification, the editorial went on:

> It is necessary to state quite clearly that, in everything that has happened, there has been a series of errors encompassing every institution of the revolution in one way or another. . . . One of the main features of the situation we have been through . . . is that we have not been dealing with the activity of enemy agents, but with people from our own ranks. We have not had to settle a conflict between revolution and counter-revolution. The serious, hard lesson to be drawn from these events is that, without going over to the

enemy, men who have fought for our cause can do us more harm than any counterrevolutionary; and that, in practice, they can serve the aims of imperialism which has not given up on destroying us. . . . What kind of revolutionary is someone who does not respect either the law or morals, and purports to act as if he belonged to a caste above everything else and all others? What socialism and what revolution can one speak of when one has not had the sensitivity to realize that privileges, arbitrariness, abuses and alienation from the masses are the main reasons for the difficulties now convulsing the socialist system—a system whose vocation was precisely to do away with all such calamities of capitalism?

This editorial is startling for several reasons. First, the causes of the difficulties of the "socialist system" were attributed to the existence of a privileged and corrupt bureaucracy. Up until this time, blame was usually placed on the subjective errors of leaders, the damaging effects of market reforms, and the U.S. embargo. In the summer of 1989 the enemy came from within. The Ministry of the Interior had been virtually dismantled. For example, Arnaldo Ochoa, general and decorated Hero of the Republic of Cuba and architect of Cuban military victories in wars in Ethiopia and Angola, was executed (the trial and execution were both publicly televised on Cuban television) for allegedly trafficking in foreign currency and ivory in Angola. Four ministers, including the minister of the interior, were dismissed. Several officials were imprisoned. Five generals were downgraded in rank to colonel or sent into retirement. And Colonel Alvárez Cueto, the head of financial management of the Ministry of the Interior, committed suicide "out of despondency and shame at the situation that the institution is going through" (Habel 1991, 178). Never had historic representatives of the regime been so harshly condemned since the 1959 seizure of power (Habel 1991).

The Ochoa trial had an earthquake effect in Cuba. Ochoa had been among the "hard-core" Castroites at the heart of the state apparatus, those to whom the most difficult and delicate work had been entrusted. The trial failed to clarify the culpability or the motivations of Ochoa and others, setting off a profound disquiet in the Cuban populace. Several Cubans told me that the execution of Ochoa drove a wedge between Castro and most of his people:

Castro had gone too far. . . . Perhaps Ochoa deserved punishment, but not execution. He was a model revolutionary who made a mistake. Everyone loved him. He did heroic things: sacrificed himself for the revolution over and over again. He made a mistake that was only human. We are all human. . . . And especially during the Special Period, when everyone is using the black market. How was he any different than anyone else? The Ochoa trial was a turning point for the relationship of the Cuban government with its people.

The Ochoa trial, like the persecution of those who participated in the Mariel boatlift, was an incident that most Cubans felt was not properly dealt with by the Cuban government. People thought that the repudiation of those who had tried to leave in the Mariel incident and the punishment of Ochoa were far too extreme. One of the effects of the trial was to highlight how a ruling group can grind down even the most talented and committed, and how responsibility may depend on who is best at playing musical chairs. Paradoxically, the trial led to a questioning of the leader himself, which he had undoubtedly not foreseen. For if the declarations were true and the commander in chief was unaware, then this was a terrible indictment of Castro's leadership style, and changes were in order (Habel 1991; Oppenheimer 1992).

Political repression among dissident groups became tougher; the number of "prisoners of conscience" rose. Public opinion polls conducted by the party revealed a rise in disagreement over fundamental policies between government leaders and ordinary citizens, a loss of status by the Communist Party as an institution, and sharp criticism of many government services, as well as of the inadequate supply of goods. The same polls, however, showed considerable public admiration for many of the government's social policies and individual party leaders (Domínguez 1993).

The source of discontent was the contrast between privilege and corruption, on the one hand, and productivist socialism on the other. The situation was met with repeated denunciations and rectifications by Fidel Castro. And perhaps the "cleaning house" measures would have been enough were it not for the changing international situation. The perestroika changes in other countries gave new vigor to Cuba's destabilized apparatus, encouraging hints of opposition shared by a section of the Cuban intelligentsia. For instance, the bold expression of several Cuban painters from the Higher Institute of Arts in Havana led to a withdrawal of many paintings on exhibit there in 1989. One of them had depicted Fidel Castro speaking to himself in La Plaza de la Revolución (Revolutionary Plaza), multiplied in a mirror to thousands of Castro faces (Franqui 1989).

New challenges to the Cuban government surfaced domestically and internationally. Just a few months after the reunification of Germany, in August 1989, the publications *Moscow News, New Times, International Affairs, Pravda,* and *Sputnik* were banned for the first time in Cuba (Azicri 2000; Habel 1991).

These Soviet publications were exercising their newly acquired editorial independence under glasnost and publishing articles critical of Cuba and the policies of the pre-Gorbachev era. The Cuban government saw the Soviet Union and Eastern Europe in a new light—as betrayers of socialism. These enemies of socialism were now part of a *doble bloqueo*—a double blockade; now both the United States and the Soviet Union were at fault for Cuba's economic problems. Ironically, while warnings were issued not to infringe on the Castroite credo, a month earlier, in July 1989, the Cuban priest Monsignor Carlos Manuel de Céspedes had confirmed in an interview in *Granma* (1989, 6) that the pope would visit Cuba in 1991 (a visit that eventually was postponed until 1998). He also announced that the government had authorized the Catholic Church to reopen a printing house to publish catechistic texts and other general teaching pamphlets (Habel 1991).

It would appear that while one partner was being escorted out, a new one was being courted. Perhaps the liberalization of religious publication was intended to foster a degree of ideological pluralism, to show that secular and religious beliefs could coexist in a socialist society. This loosening of the reins in the religious sphere was another attempt to foster an affective bond to create greater revolutionary support. The principal response from the Cuban people to the economic crisis and its accompanying social and political restraints had been disenchantment with public life, resulting in a retreat to the personal, to the informal, and to alternative sources of hope, such as religion (Fernández 2000). Christian morality complemented the revolution's secular morality in the difficult task of uplifting the nation's ethical standards, especially when creeping materialism had been seemingly rampant with the dollarization of the Cuban economy in 1993, the lifting of restrictions on receipt of remittances from abroad, and increased prostitution. Despite its maximalist will, the state was unable to provide all. Noninstitutionalized religions, such as Santería, were the only religions tolerated by the state until the early nineties, because they did not require physical infrastructure and did not challenge the state. Fernández (2000) suggests that as the politics of passion (the lofty ideals of the state) wilted, the informal economy and its networks of affection (personal relations as network capital) started to provide what the state could not: satisfaction of personal, spiritual, and even material needs through greater religious freedom and a flourishing black market.

The informal economy that operated outside the control and legal provisions of the state was a personal network embodied in people. As the Cuban saying goes, *"El que tiene un amigo tiene un peso en el bosillo"* (He who has a friend has a dollar in his pocket). Personal connections became more important as Cuba, a heavily dependent trading nation, lost approximately 70 percent of its imports and exports between 1989 and 1992 (Moses 2000). There was no Band-aid to hold together the widening gap between official discourse, economic policies, and the expectations of the citizenry in the 1990s. The regime's political religion was rendering itself ineffective, so much so that socialism in Cuba came to be referred to as *sociolismo* (buddyism). This term and the maxim above suggest that the politics and economy of affection can equate friendship with monetary value. Since Cuba's political religion was failing in prophecy, people were counting more on their personal networks to deliver the material and spiritual promises.

The younger generation, frustrated by the direction of the economy and public policy, attempted to discuss critical issues. Glasnost and perestroika awoke interest and hope among Cubans, who expected a similar course of reform at home. However, their expectations were dashed. With something to say and no one to listen, the mounting frustration among the Cuban youth led to another major exodus in the early 1990s. More than 75 percent of the over 100,000 *balseros* who left the island on makeshift rafts were under the age of 39 (Rose-Ackerman 1997). Popular discontent became manifest in a desperate wave of migration, and for the first time in decades, a riot erupted in Old Havana in 1994, revealing an emotional infrastructure that might undermine the regime. The riot was soon quelled by Castro's quick arrival on the scene with his discourse of passion: "*¡Socialismo o Muerte! ¡Venceremos!*" In its natural intensity, the politics of passion emerged, embodied in the Líder Máximo, to settle the score between the impersonal and the personal, or the state and its people.

As Fernández explains, the intensity of the politics of passion and affection depends on the political and economic climate of a country:

> At moments of political crisis the politics of passion energize groups to carry forward the moral pursuit of a new and improved national community. . . . During periods of economic scarcity the politics of affection serve as alternative distribution mechanisms in the black market at the grassroots for survival needs. The politics of affection play more than a mere economic role. They have also given Cubans a space to articulate meaning and identity. The rise of the politics of affection in the informal sphere in post-1980 Cuba has challenged the material and ideological bases of Cuban socialism and the operations of the Cuban state. As the politics of passion faded, the politics of affection flared. (Fernández 2000, 61)

Was the state being undermined by economic factors alone or also by political and moral ones? The root cause related more to the clash between the normative frameworks of the regime in theory and its instrumental procedures in practice. The result was a ripping at the seams involving the Cuban people, who found the schizophrenia of living with the *doble moral* too complicated and unsatisfying. The politics of passion, requiring a political religion and Marxism-Leninism in the public arena, while survival requires a moral code other than the politics of passion, at some point become more than one is willing to tolerate.

Survival Measures

In the struggle to resurrect popular affection for the state and to save the economy, the Cuban government took measures that deviated from the socialist path. One measure was implemented in 1993, when the state depenalized the holding of U.S. dollars by Cubans. Island Cubans could legally put to use family remittances. As a result, net current transfers rose from U.S. $18 million in 1991 to U.S. $828 million in 1999. These moneys included not only family remittances sent by exiles and émigrés in the United States and elsewhere but also informal earnings from tourism and official and unofficial donations (EIU 2000).

And to give Cubans a place to spend these newly acquired dollars, the state allowed them access to the special state-owned stores, the *diplotiendas*, which previously had been reserved for foreign diplomats. Spending in the dollar shops increased drastically. The available data suggest that domestic dollar sales increased from around U.S. $50 million in 1994 to U.S. $1 billion by 1999. The retail margin in these outlets is fixed by the state at 240 percent. These stores provide an important source of income for the government. In mid-1999 new shops selling similar goods but in pesos were introduced. Prices in these Cuban peso stores were fixed at levels almost as high as the unofficial exchange rate equivalent of U.S. dollar shop prices (EIU 2000).

Stimulating the circulation of foreign currency was important for the Cuban economy. The government targeted tourism and the export of nickel and nontraditional products (such as biotechnology). In addition, the government encouraged mainly hard currency—generating cooperative or "associated production," agreements, along with joint ventures and marketing deals. Castro continued to say that the revolution would make no concessions on its principles. Capitalists could contribute capital, experience, and markets. The slogan of the day became "Capital yes, capitalism no." One Central Committee member said, "we have to think like capitalists but continue being socialists" (French 1990).

Economic means and political labels aside, producing and distributing food were key preoccupations. The government's intention was to reach nutritional self-sufficiency in a short time and augment agricultural production destined for export. However, the measures adopted failed to improve the agricultural condition of the country, and there was a serious decline in production. Realizing that the country's most important national security issue was feeding its people, Raúl Castro, in an interview prior to the reopening of the free markets in the fall of 1994, said, "Today the political, military and ideological problem is the search for food" (Pérez 1995, 404). Agriculture, in particular achieving self-sufficiency in food production, was given the highest priority with the implementation of the Programa Alimentario, or Food Program. The strategy stressed production of sugarcane and its by-products and the continued expansion of other traditional agricultural exports. Mobilizations for the Programa Alimentario, meanwhile, prompted at least one protest. Some urban pre-university students, angry about being sent to the fields to do agricultural labor, staged a mini-rebellion. They organized a march back to Havana (Eckstein 1994). Recognizing the limits of the Programa Alimentario, the government exhorted city dwellers to set up fruit and vegetable "victory gardens" in residential neighborhoods: in backyards, empty lots, and open spaces. As of mid-1992 there were more than one million such gardens, tended by families, workers, students, and neighborhood groups. City dwellers, in essence, were to help produce their own subsistence needs (Eckstein 1994).

The Fourth Party Congress (1991) also stressed nonagricultural exports, including skilled services (for example, medical services to foreigners in Cuba and abroad) and manufactured goods with a high technological content, such as biotechnology products, the goal for export being to gain foreign currency. Free-market sales of handicrafts and manufactured goods were also allowed (Díaz-Briquets 1993).

The Cuban government began the process of decentralization of state-owned enterprises and joint ventures with foreign enterprises to sell more products to its people and to increase efficiency and local production. However, Cubans not only wanted more goods, they wanted more services. To alleviate hardship and encourage production, the regime awarded hard currency vouchers to workers in basic industry, construction, fishing, and the tobacco industry, giving these workers access to the dollar stores.

Adding to the networks of affection was self-employment, which became an approved measure by the Cuban government when approximately 25 percent of the total labor force was estimated to be underemployed (Azicri 2000). By 1991 the state had issued 200,000 permits for private work. Further, the Institute for Internal Demand estimates that for each person formally authorized to work privately, at least three more were doing unauthorized private work (FBIS 1991b). Self-employment was used to provide what the government could not, including services such as family-owned restaurants, hairdressers, food stand vendors, taxi drivers, book vendors, and room renters. Most of the self-employed also held state jobs in the formal economy and thus conducted their public and private activities concurrently. The government took its cut by charging a flat tax for this small emerging sector, and by 1996, many of those who were self-employed were working for dollars (Azicri 2000; Jatar-Hausmann 1999).

With more opportunities for self-employment, both formal and informal, the changing economic reality had major ideological implications. The new economic policies created social cleavages, causing resentment and political disaffection among those left out of the opportunities offered by capitalist measures (Fernández 2000; Jatar-Hausmann 1999). These measures moved the country away from the egalitarian practices of the preceding three decades.

Premised on the government's lofty effort to, in its own words, "equalize sacrifice," rationing was stepped up, with gradual reductions over time in official allotments (Eckstein 1994). The unintended effect was the inducement of law breaking. With demand so much greater than supply, prices of goods on the black market skyrocketed, and people did not let this opportunity pass them by. Nearly everyone who could, whether party loyalist or regime opponent, bought things illegally. Black market activity hinged on people's pocketbooks and common sense.

Meanwhile, the illegal marketeering was producing more pronounced class divisions. The population was splintering into divisions marked by those with access to dollars through work or remittances from abroad and those dependent solely on wages or pensions paid in the national currency. In addition, the possibility that self-employment and black market sectors might become a political force with its own sectarian agenda was of mounting political concern to the Cuban government.

One noticeable reaction from the Cuban people was heavy migration from rural to urban areas, particularly from the eastern provinces to Havana. As a result, in May 1997 a new law limited the population in the city of Havana, where massive migration was taxing the city beyond its ability to provide needed services. The internal migration law limited housing to those who had come from other regions. The law caused a surge in requests to legalize Havana residence. Otherwise, these people, popularly known as "Palestinians," were to be evicted and sent back to their city of origin.

Many women migrated from the eastern provinces to Havana, one of the prime locations of tourism, using *jineterismo* (Cuban prostitution) to acquire more consumer goods. According to *Granma International* (Elizalde 1996, 8–9), from a survey of thirty-three *jineteras*, they

> appear self-confident, assertive young women, for whom prostitution is not necessarily a means of covering their basic needs, but rather an option that provides them with an above-average standard of living. It is essentially, a means of acquiring—with relatively little effort in their view—the trappings of the good life, as they see it: dollars in their pockets, household appliances, fashionable clothes and shoes. In the company of a foreigner, they can go to restaurants and nightclubs, spend the night in a luxury hotel, and perhaps, last but not least, marry a foreigner, and leave the country in search of "paradise."

The dramatic changes that have taken place since the dissolution of the Soviet bloc have not only brought dislocations to the Cuban labor market, they have also influenced the population socially. To allay the impact of the labor crisis, the Cuban government has undertaken various policy initiatives, easing work regulations and allowing more opportunities for self-employment, shifting urban laborers to agriculture, and giving high priority to the developing tourist sector. The outcomes of education in this context are important, because the development of interests and behaviors associated with the class-forming distinction between manual and mental work is related to qualifications. With the relatively high educational levels in Cuba, many Cuban workers aspire to professional occupations and prefer not to be enrolled in unskilled, blue-collar jobs desired by the state for economic recovery. The class-forming distinction is also inherent in the positions held, and, as Albert and Hahnel (1981, 37) state, with limits on "the relative knowledge that workers have of the economy and their place in it."

Educational Policy in the 1990s

International and domestic policies were the targets of the continuing educational reform process initiated in 1986 and still ongoing in the new millennium—*Perfeccionamiento Continuo*. Even in the midst of the striking gains achieved in education, the policies of *Perfeccionamiento Continuo* have emphasized many shortcomings "contributing to the problem-oriented character of the 'official culture' in education" (Lutjens 1996, 42). For instance, scientific research, which is indispensable for the future of the country, has been directed toward present practical issues, such as agriculture. The difficulty for the Cuban government and its educators lies in finding ways to redirect youth away from university slots and into agricultural careers, with the concomitant danger of a new elitism emerging among secondary school students. Recognition of popular concerns is of vital importance for the state's goals and legitimacy, whether the issue is to provide more public transportation or more subsidized food staples or to improve the conditions for students studying and working in the countryside. The Special Period, with its economic crisis, had a profound effect on schooling at all levels.

The conditions of austerity were apparent in the educational system. Until 1991, the budget for education continued to grow to a high of 1,853 million pesos, at which time the budget started to decline (for example, a sum of 1,443 million pesos was allocated in 1993). However, in the 1992–1993 school year, education still accounted for nearly 23 percent of the national budget (Uriarte 2008). Meanwhile, shortages of U.S. dollar inputs severely affected the availability of materials.

Even though the education minister, Luís Gómez, guaranteed that the 1991–1992 school year would commence with all of the "essential conditions," the schooling conditions worsened. During the summer of 1993 a campaign was waged to secure millions of notebooks and pencils through foreign donations. And while shortages existed, fees were introduced in 1994 for materials and services hitherto supplied without cost, such as foreign language instruction and lunches in the semiboarding schools. In addition, the stipends provided to students of higher education were redefined as student loans (Lutjens 1996).

The teaching profession felt the impact also. In the mid-1990s there was an exodus from the profession, prompted by a sharp fall in teachers' real earnings (although teachers' salaries were still paid). Even under these conditions, in 1998 there were 18.1 teachers per 1,000 inhabitants. In an effort to reduce the exodus, the Cuban government increased teachers' pay by some 30 percent in 1999. Throughout the economic hardship of the 1990s educational standards were largely maintained, and the literacy rate has been reported to be 96.2 percent among the population older than age 10 (EIU 2000).

Despite the economic austerity, decentralization of power remained a primary goal in Cuba's educational system. Decentralization took effect in the area of administration. In 1990, Ministerial Resolution No. 400 gave school principals more freedom to develop their own pedagogical strategy and tailor it more to local characteristics. For example, students were to study where they lived, and certain vocational specialties were emphasized in accordance with the locale. In turn, this decentralization in the regulation and direction of work allowed more flexibility in the planning of the work in the school, methodology, and the hiring and evaluation of teaching personnel (Lutjens 1996).

Although instances of decentralization and local decision making existed, centralization to a certain extent had to be maintained to ensure educational equity. MINED had always maintained a systematized manner of school inspection, with regard to maintenance issues as well as teaching and learning. However, previously an inventory had been taken and causes were addressed. By 1990 the focus of inspections had changed to finding solutions and publicizing accomplishments. By 1993, several schools in each province had been selected as model schools, or "reference centers." At these reference centers, research was conducted and experimental methods were implemented, making these schools showcases for the latest pedagogical practices. The model schools could thus substitute former bureaucratic top-down advice.

The elimination or curtailment of bureaucracy had its counterpart in the administration of education, too. Excessive paperwork was eliminated (it was explained by the paper shortage), and professional development seminars were proposed for all teaching and administration personnel. The seminars were tailored according to interests and needs, replacing the traditional homogeneous curriculum. Education officials, administrators as well as teaching staff, returned to the classroom to learn new trends and share their expertise. However, little emphasis was placed on participatory management techniques (Lutjens 1996).

The pedagogy in higher education was also adjusted to decrease the degree of formalism and bureaucracy in administrative practices. Che Guevara's ideas were revived once again. Guevara's approach to management theory and practice became a topic of discussion in many publications. A three-article series on bureaucratism appeared in the party's theoretical journal, *Cuba Socialista*, tracing the classical understanding of bureaucracy in Lenin, Guevara, and Castro. Furthermore, a faculty for Guevara studies was created at the University of the Oriente in 1992 and at the University of Havana in 1995 (Lutjens 1996).

An attempt to reduce formalism took place not only in administrative practices but also in the curriculum of higher education. Professors noted that students demonstrated a lack of patriotism and that this became an obstacle to learning the subject matter. According to Oscar Loyola, deputy dean of philosophy and history at the University of Havana,

When a student starts his college education he has no patriotic sensibility and is also lacking any motivation for the subject matter, because he sees it as another course he has to pass with no connection to his own problems and objectives. (*Bohemia* 1995, B5)

Another history professor stated, "the classes become a cold chronological recitation of facts and dates, with little appeal" for the students (ibid.). Reinforcing the official discourse became a challenge for teachers.

Issues of pedagogy and planning were intimately tied to ideas of decentralization. Education officials recognized the need to make the curriculum more appealing and relevant to young people. The rethinking of pedagogy was manifest in teacher education, where practical experience was stressed, as well as articles in MINED's journal, *Educación*, with titles such as "How to Contribute to the Development of Thinking During Class" and "Can Creativity Be Learned?" Individual schools, emphasizing the creation of warm and welcoming environments, also employed participatory techniques. In addition, the journal *Pedagogía Cubana* was initiated in 1989 as another channel for publications, reviving the historical traditions of Cuban educators, as well as for research in creativity and intelligence (Lutjens 1996).

Reflections of a more relevant pedagogy were seen in curricular changes in both secondary and higher education. They included a new emphasis on sex education and computer literacy, and more after-school activities and sports in secondary schools, such as karate. The extracurricular patriotic military clubs launched in the 1980s were closed down in the 1990s, with their functions being fulfilled by the mass organizations (Lutjens 1996).

The state walked a tightrope in trying, on the one hand, to accommodate students' interests while, on the other hand, serving society's needs. In addition, starting in the mid-1980s with the rectification process, demographics began colliding with labor dynamics and needs. Already by the late 1980s the government had selectively reduced university enrollment. The demand for jobs suited to the occupational expectations of a better-educated workforce had been outpacing the economy's capacity to create those jobs.

An explicit concern of the Fourth Party Congress (1991) was how to soften the impact of the employment dislocations caused by the economic crisis. It is not possible to estimate the number of workers dislocated by the crisis because data are not available and many displaced workers were shifted to other sectors of the economy. For many, their jobs were no longer their primary source of income. However, Díaz-Briquets claims that the Cuban government has been able to successfully disguise unemployment by artificially creating low-productivity jobs. Thus, "while several emergency measures have kept unemployment rates low, underemployment, Cuba's perennial and intractable problem, has risen greatly" (Díaz-Briquets 1993, 97).

According to a 1994–1995 study by the Center for Youth Studies, among Cuba's unemployed young people, 71 percent said "they felt no economic motivation to work." A specialist from the center explained, "work has lost its values as the fundamental means of livelihood and material well-being." At a time when young people should have been integrating themselves more into society, 79 percent of unemployed young people were surviving on support from their families or on income received from other sources, such as friends or family living abroad. The young people indicated they were comfortable living this way; only 5.9 percent admitted having a difficult time making ends meets economically. The remaining 13.4 percent had found undisclosed forms of employment (Valencia 1997, 8–9). According to government officials, nearly 30 percent of the labor force was working in market-related activities—in other words, out of the socialist scheme (Jatar-Haussman 1999).

In the 1990s, in order to coordinate schooling with declining employment opportunities, the leadership cut back university admissions. Some type of filter had to be created to limit the candidates for a university degree. The title and headlines of a *Granma* article (Jimenez 1991, 3) reflect an official reversal of the earlier commitment to higher education and professional training: "Can we develop without manual laborers? Should we go on turning out tens of thousands of university graduates when we already have over 320,000 professionals? Not everyone should be an engineer, a professional, or an intermediate-level technician." What would be the basis for this new weeding out in education? Minister of Higher Education Fernando Avecino Alegret stated that only Cubans "capable of defending the revolution in the realm of ideas and in the streets" would be permitted to study in the universities (CubaInfo 1994). Ideological commitment, one of the greatest challenges facing the regime, was rewarded with educational opportunity.

The government's strategy to arouse ideological fervor was also seen in the reappearance of voluntary labor and of the microbrigades, particularly in agriculture. A national campaign was launched in 1996 emphasizing moral incentives and encouraging work in agriculture and construction. The UJC got involved in these matters and sought a revision of the Labor Ministry's rules so that unemployed graduates could be hired for jobs outside their region. In addition, the UJC asked that a skilled reserve be created in which unemployed graduates would be eligible for a state subsidy (Azicri 2000). Moreover, to keep surplus and otherwise restless labor busy, the leadership began sponsoring a major military readiness campaign in anticipation of a U.S. invasion. At the center of this effort was the construction by the country's youth of an elaborate system of defense tunnels (FBIS 1992).

Yet Cuba's national culture was also aggravating the education–labor force imbalance. As Castro (1992, 9) acknowledged:

> Education's momentum was so great that, let us say, we ran, we have run, a certain amount of risk. In a way, we have also seen a big exodus from physical activities to intellectual activities. When we talked about universalizing labor, it was because we were also universalizing education. A society cannot be composed of only intellectuals. Such a thing cannot exist. It is terrible that physical work, manual labor, should be looked [at] with disdain. It is terrible. One can see it, the great exodus that occurred from the countryside to the cities. Not only from the countryside to the cities but from certain jobs to other jobs.

Therefore, the attempt now was to strive to enhance the social value of manual occupations to future generations of workers who aspired to white-collar and bureaucratic careers. The Marxist-Leninist work-study principle, which the children of the revolution (now adults) had been schooled in, was very distant from their perceived role in society.

While the official rhetoric continued to emphasize that manual and mental work went hand in hand, in Cuba as in other countries, education was still regarded as a ticket to a better life. The clearest instance was the decline in the rural labor force owing to the exodus of workers to the cities, even with salary differentials set to favor agricultural labor. Of course, the low social recognition accorded many jobs could also have contributed to job instability. According to Carrobello (1990, 4):

> Family upbringing and specific social considerations cause very few to want to be farm workers, construction helpers, lathe operators, pin setters in rolling mills, or dock workers. . . . Young men refuse to be workers and want to become intermediate-level technicians, not for the pay, because some blue-collar jobs pay better, but because they think the general status is higher.

The schools in the countryside, supporting a curriculum that included daily agricultural work, were also used to accommodate the possible economic impacts in relationship to the communist work ethic. For twenty-seven years the schools in the countryside (the permanent boarding schools) had accommodated junior high students (seventh to ninth grades). Meanwhile, tenth to twelfth graders attended the urban pre-universities, taking month-long leave to perform work in the countryside. However, during the 1990–1991 school year, the Cuban government announced a switch in which grade levels would occupy these schools. The soon-to-be tenth graders would henceforth learn in the countryside schools while the junior high students would be schooled in the city. In interviews with MINED officials in 1999, I was told that the switch was done primarily for two reasons. First, by boarding older students in the countryside, it was thought that productivity levels in agricultural labor would increase. The students were stronger physically and sufficiently mature to handle the responsibility of the work. Second, it was thought that the pre-university students were more prone to "ideological contamination"—influences from the outside world—in urban areas. Moreover, material differences were regarded as more pronounced in the city as well. The government felt that the students' ideological foundation would remain more "intact" in the countryside. Faced with the task of maintaining its labor force, the Cuban government did not want to lose its vanguard youth to the lures of a capitalist culture or illegal marketeering, which were more accessible in urban areas. Dropout rates had increased, and the goal was to keep the young in school and continue to solidify the base for the future of socialism.

The switching of students from the city to the countryside was not warmly welcomed. Parents complained about the poor material conditions and deterioration of some schools, the poor food, sexual freedom, and in some cases inadequate supervision of students by their teachers. There was controversy over the boarding schools from the start, regardless of which age group was occupying them. The pope's visit in 1998 aggravated the controversy, for he stressed a family's right to choose the type of education they wanted for their children. The pope's call was more than a demand for the opening of Catholic schools. It was an implicit criticism of a system that, according to the Catholic Church, separated families and causes essential human values to be lost. Cuban officials countered this criticism by reporting that since the 1991 switch of pre-university students from the city to the countryside, the number of students taking university entrance examinations had increased. Minister of Education Luis Gómez said that the students' voices must be heard and that conclusions should not be drawn from the adults, who at one point supported the direction of the Cuban revolution but who "now manifest[ed] certain paternalistic attitudes."

Not all educators supported the official analysis of the state's schooling efforts. For Patricia Ares, a Cuban lecturer in psychology at the University of Havana, "you cannot speak of the family's social importance and then routinely separate youngsters from parents when the latter need to play an educative role" (Acosta 1998a, 2). The disconnect to which she refers came up frequently. In my search for data on the schooling of children in the countryside, officials, teachers, and parents commented that this policy had always been a controversial one and that the economic crisis had only exacerbated it.

In addition to switching the junior high students' location with that of the pre-university students, other changes were put into place. Many new polytechnical institutes were constructed with the vision of creating more intermediate-level technicians. This goal was to be achieved by redirecting the schooling of would-be high school students from pre-universities to poly-technical institutes in the countryside for vocational and technical training. In accordance with this goal, the 1991–1992 school year started with forty-three new polytechnical schools for the preparation of agricultural workers. And, as hoped, enrollments in polytechnical schools increased while enrollments in pre-universities decreased from 60 percent to 40 percent. In addition, students were required to work more hours in the fields as part of "curricular changes that included more hours of labor" (Lutjens 1996, 166). The government also understood the technical degree as being a terminal degree. These changes were implemented in response to the need to produce more agriculturally, and to restrict urban migration.

Some Cuban people understood the government's actions as efforts to deschool and deprofessionalize the population, and responded with opposition. The revolution had raised expectations beyond the state's means, and families tried to circumvent placements that implied downward mobility for their children. Students continued to enroll in polytechnical institutes after ninth grade, to train as intermediate-level technicians, with the possibility of obtaining a university education afterward. However, very few were able to fulfill their university aspirations. The Cuban government's downscaling in schooling ran into popular resistance. With neighborhood organizations unresponsive to the peoples' concerns, resistance efforts occurred informally, through personal networks (Eckstein 1994).

The revolutionary regime relied on the family for support in the schooling changes and to give the children a "proper" orientation. For most children, the values taught in the school, such as honesty and equality, were clashing with the reality at home and in the streets. The end product seemed to be some disorientation in defining their lives. The parents' loyalty to the revolution was a factor. Some parents feared that their children would be ostracized if their teachers discovered they lived in a nonrevolutionary home.

Children tried to resolve their role in school, which included guarding more family information than one might be accustomed to in other cultures or even in Cuba in earlier years. The illegal activities of their parents might include renting a room without paying taxes to the state, selling cigars without a license, buying or selling goods, including food, on the black market, and so on—all very common activities today. In fact, in conversations with dozens of people from all walks of life, including party members, I was told, "there is no one who does not use the black market. . . . [N]o one could survive just on what the state delivers." The secretary of the UJC downtown, Tamara González, explained, "The tourist visits raise temptation for illegal trade and other deviant behavior that we are trying to eliminate" (Regalado and Rosquete 1999, 3). Students hear one message at school and another at home, a situation leading to, at the very least, a struggle to decipher what should be considered right and what wrong.

From my school observations, I heard teachers wanting students to oppose the U.S. government and all it stands for, while some parents were anxious for their family to move to the United States, or at least gain access to U.S. dollars. The common mantra of hope delivered by the teacher was, "The revolution will provide. If we all do our part, then we will all share in its abundance. We must resist the imperialist, unjust measure of the embargo and do our part to combat the scarcity of resources and support the revolution."

The schools solicited the cooperation of the families in leveling apparent material differences seen at school, as I observed while living with a family in 1999. Any novelty, be it food or a trinket, was discouraged on the school grounds. Most students brought a snack sandwich with mayonnaise and tomato; the school asked that students not come to school with sandwiches made with meat or cheese, because not all families had access to these more expensive foods.

Since the beginning of the Special Period, several resolutions have been issued to ease the labor impact of the economic crisis. These include limiting the length of the work week, setting a minimum wage level for dislocated workers, extending the period of time that working mothers may stay home without incurring labor penalties, and shifting surplus labor from the cities for permanent or short-term assignments in the countryside (as in the case of transferring construction microbrigades to agricultural tasks) (Castro 1991). In many cases, students from rural schools were assigned to labor contingents that are rotated into farmwork every fifteen days, and often for longer periods of time ("Special Period" 1991).

The solutions proposed by the Fourth Party Congress to solve this dilemma included a return to voluntary labor, the further manipulation of salary scales to enhance the attractiveness of rural occupations, and a major restructuring of the country's educational system. Díaz-Briquets (1993) predicts that the first two solutions are not likely to be effective in the long run, while the third is prone to cause unrest among the affected youth and their families.

In 1991 MINED announced a major change for students completing ninth grade. Whereas earlier policy had encouraged attending pre-university school (similar to tenth through twelfth grades in U.S. high schools) and academic training over vocational education, now polytechnical (vocational) training was mandated for 60 percent of those graduating from ninth grade and wanting further education (FBIS 1991, 1992). Castro discussed the scope of this shift:

> There are a number of ideas [regarding the conversion of pre-universities to polytechnical schools] because everything conducive to training people for manual work is very important. It was a considerable step forward when 43 pre-university schools in the countryside became technological or polytechnical schools. . . . Another 50 are also going to be converted; . . . there will be 40 percent pre-university schools and 60 percent of other types; . . . 40 percent still seems a high number but, well, it is a change in the ratio. (Castro 1992, 10)

Under the current predicament, the employment slots capable of accommodating the needs or aspirations of the beneficiaries of Cuba's expansive education system are few. High-priority sectors, such as tourism, foreign assembly, and agriculture, are major employers. However, most of these slots involve either manual labor or very little education. Future Cuban workers are in the unenviable position of having to lower their aspirations and contend with the frustration of unsatisfied occupational expectations, with no other choice but to embrace menial occupations with limited social returns. Regardless of the future course of Cuba's economic and political events, its educational system will be one of its lasting legacies. Only time will tell whether Cuba's great achievements in education will strengthen or undermine the long-term political objectives of the aging leadership.

Those who were born in the sixties and who were children when the revolution started are destined to become Cuba's new leaders. This new generation has moved up in the political structure and has been dubbed "yummies" by *Time* magazine writer C. Booth (1993)—"young upwardly mobile Marxists" who are "educated and ambitious, [and] hold the key to Cuba's future." Some already hold high posts in and out of the Cuban government, such as Felipe Pérez Roque, the new foreign minister. Others occupy positions in scientific research institutes, in economic production centers, the media, the arts, and so forth. They represent the first generation to come of age following the generation of the revolution's founding fathers.

Being highly pragmatic,

the yummies want the best of both worlds: the health care and educational advances of Castro's revolution [keeping the socialist system] and a better material life [from opening the economy to more foreign investment]. Seemingly, the word "communist" has disappeared from conversation, yet the ideas of profitmaking and exploitive capitalism seem repugnant to the Cuban people. Cubans seem to be "nationalists first and ideologues second," according to Robert Robaina, former head of the Union of Young Communists and former foreign minister. He continued: "There is [not] only one way or one model. . . . We're living in extremely complex times for which no one has an exact recipe." (Booth 1993)

Robaina, a rising political star at the time, saw the need to accommodate the interests of the young people. Under Robaina, the UJC sponsored outdoor concerts by Cuba's most popular rock groups. He embodied the "new generation" with his informal, outgoing style. According to Eckstein (1993, 118), "He recognized that ideology and politics could in themselves no longer captivate the hearts and minds of youth." The situation is changing, and with it some of those in power. Clearly there has been an ongoing debate between the old guard, who feared experimentation during difficult times, and the reformists, who were pushing for more liberalization.

This accommodation to the young people is a result of changing paradigms. Otto Rivero, first secretary of the UJC, states:

Ten years ago adolescents did not worry fundamentally about what was being sold in the stores. Today with the phenomenon of remittances, which implies conceptual changes, the person who does not need to work appears. We have a greater incidence of delinquency, and the young people who do not work or study are the seed of it. For this reason, it is necessary that the organization [the UJC] work better, and rely on more competent and trained individuals to analyze the phenomena from a broader and more integral perspective. (cited in Regalado and Rosquete 1999, 3)

Carlos Alberto Torres, head of the division of the UJC responsible for young workers, prioritized, during the Seventh UJC Congress, the UJC committees of the emerging sectors of the economy. Torres explained, "There are weaknesses in its functioning. There are places where one asks what is the mission of the base committee and the response is: 'get dollars and fulfill the plans.' Many times the formative task of political and ideological preparation is lost in the UJC" (cited in Regalado and Rosquete 1999, 3).

Education has unwittingly provided the tools for questioning the tenets of the regime and the roles and rules it has established. As Frank Musgrove (1964, 3) concluded after considerable research on youth and social order, "youth will provide an impetus toward social experimentation and change not when they are given power but when they are denied it." The educational, social, and economic reforms were not enacted in a political vacuum.

The party undertook ideological renewal as part of its internal reforms at the Fourth Party Congress in 1991. With its socialist ends and still centralized means, Cuba differs in its rejection of the ideological trend of neoliberalism and in its reluctance to carry out the structural changes associated with other reform efforts around the globe. Stalwart, Cuba pledges a lasting commitment to education (Lutjens 1996).

Education becomes a telling expression of the interface of the old and the new, revealing where issues of power (of the state) and emotion (of the people) have altered policy. The Special Period shows that educational policy in Cuba has not been an automatic reflection of global reordering: long-term domestic issues have also influenced Cuba's present political, economic, and educational situation. The communist conciencia building has been eclipsed by the noncorrespondence of economic measures to the ideology being taught. The proposed restructuring of the national educational system is a particularly interesting development, since it reveals the depth of the leadership's concern that the formal education system and employment opportunities coincide. In trying to forecast economic measures and their progress, the Cuban government recognizes that costly mistakes have been made in both economic planning and education.

The specificity of Cuban reforms requires determining how things work and what education means to students, parents, teachers, and the greater community. Starting in Chapter 5, my focus switches from history and educational policy to ethnographic portrayals of people working and studying at educational centers in the La Flor neighborhood. In Chapter 5 I describe the neighborhood's school community and some of the informal relations that emerge in everyday Cuban school life. Class materials, course content, teaching styles, and school-related events all contribute to overtly socializing students for work in contemporary Cuban society.

CHAPTER 5

Revolutionary Pedagogy in Action

In the initial stages of the revolution, Fidel Castro declared that the island of Cuba would become "one huge school" (1961, 271). He used these words to emphasize the importance of educating the population through every possible medium and activity, not just through formalized schooling. Every aspect of society had to be dedicated to reinforcing the history, values, and principles of the revolution. The initial sights one is confronted with when arriving in Cuba, such as billboards and sides of buildings painted with revolutionary slogans, reflect the Cuban government's intent to cultivate, or at least to represent, a socialist ideological message of *conciencia*. Boundaries became blurred, however, when I tried to identify what would be considered formal as opposed to informal modes of education in Cuban society. Billboards, press, television, radio, films, songs, poetry, school lessons, t-shirts, posters, theatrical plays, as well as periodic mobilizations and marches are just some of the channels of expression used to convey the revolutionary message. The goal was to create and maintain a monolithic ideological unity by attempting to make the individual adopt the same conceptual, cognitive, and emotional world projected by the revolutionary leaders. The totalizing effect of these channels of projection (Medin 1990) as they are used to educate the Cuban citizenry in socialist norms and values is noteworthy (see Appendix 1).[1]

In this chapter I focus specifically on three educational sites in Havana: Granma Junior High School, the Ministry of Education (MINED), and the Pedagogical Institute. I do not presume to offer a comprehensive description or evaluation of these institutions of education. Rather, my goal is to illustrate the distinctiveness of these educational environments and the students'— and, in some cases, officials' and families'—responses to them. Each institution emphasized value formation and the work-study principle. This focus reflects the belief that, in a socialist society, implementing the work-study principle helps cultivate proper values in students (Minister of Education Luis Gómez, cited in Rodríguez 1995, 2).[2] The three sites I discuss afford a glimpse and a measure of the broader social and political mechanisms at work in Cuban society to develop conciencia in citizens. I also provide evidence that, in the process of developing conciencia, the formal mechanisms of the state must contend with local identities and practices, and vice versa. The La Flor neighborhood, where Granma Junior High School is located, became the base from which I pursued further research at institutions of influence, including the Pedagogical Institute and MINED.[3] These last two institutions ultimately had an impact on educational norms and innovations in schools throughout the island. I found that the tensions in the La Flor neighborhood generally and at Granma Junior High School specifically reflected the dynamics between Cuban institutions and society: the negotiation of identity, power, and what *conciencia* means today.

La Flor Neighborhood: The School Location

Lizabet, a former brigadista, current civic education teacher, and a resident of the La Flor neighborhood, met me at the Literacy Museum celebration and invited me to visit her school one day. A tall, slim mulatta in her late fifties, she had short curly gray hair that she tucked behind her ears under a dark green Castrol baseball cap, small eyeglasses with a chip in one corner, and large, colorful, bell-shaped flower dangle earrings. Lizabet had a very self-assured way about her. She told me how much she enjoyed teaching at Granma Junior High School, a local school for seventh to ninth graders, and promoted it as the perfect place for me to observe the process of revolutionary value formation. I pursued the opportunity.

I did not realize until well into my study that La Flor had a reputation throughout Havana as being an unsafe neighborhood. For months I talked about my research location using only the patriotic name of the junior high school, Granma. It was not until I started dropping the neighborhood name into conversation instead of the school name that I heard unsettling remarks from communities near La Flor. People would look at me in shock and ask, "Why La Flor? What good do you expect to find there?" "The Ministry of Education granted you permission to conduct your study La Flor? Why?" The conversation always seemed to end with a warning along the lines of "Be careful! Keep an eye on your possessions while you are there. And don't go there alone at night!" Residents of La Flor and other neighborhoods mentioned La Puente de la Flor, a bridge that joined La Flor and the Alcanza neighborhood.

According to community knowledge, the bridge had been the site of many suicides. A reference to the area surfaced unexpectedly when I was in a taxi full of Cubans on the other side of town, and the taxi driver, not knowing anything about my research, made joking mention of the economic situation, saying, "If it gets any worse, everyone will be jumping off La Puente de La Flor!"

The community itself seemed to have absorbed an identity of danger.[4] One day, as students arrived late to school, Lizabet said to me while we both stood at the entrance, "Well, you know what type of homes these kids come from." Adopting a drill sergeant's tone, she asked the tardy students, "Why were you late today?" She got no answer, and repeated herself. The boys, looking humiliated by the public reprimand, did not respond and stared at the ground. "You were visiting your parents in prison, weren't you?" Lizabet insisted sharply. The students did not move or answer. Then she ushered them into the building with no further attention to the matter.

The La Flor neighborhood was home to many people of color, mostly black and mulatto, but very few white families.[5] It was also known for having a higher crime rate than other, whiter neighborhoods. The principal told me that most of the students came from families with difficult social and economic situations: a family member in prison, a parent who had abandoned the family. Drug dealing and drug abuse, prostitution, and rape were common. These stressors within individual families were in addition to the economic burden of the Special Period that the majority of Cubans shared. In a 1999 issue of the Cuban newspaper *Juventud Rebelde*, La Flor was described as "un barrio de población mayoritariamente obrera, de gente humilde" (a largely working-class neighborhood, of humble people).[6] The junior high school appeared to be demographically representative of La Flor; I never saw more than a handful of white students on the school premises. I was both the first foreigner and the first researcher to visit the school.

Granma Junior High School and Ciudad Libertad

The days I spent at Granma Junior High School always started with a walk from my Cuban host family's house, about a mile away, through La Flor. Students would spot me from their homes and yell out my name until I saw them and waved back. Unlike in the neighborhoods closer to tourism centers in Havana, I rarely saw a car or a tourist in La Flor. I felt like a novelty, but over time I also felt a sense of belonging.

The white concrete junior high school stood out as one of the few two-story structures in the neighborhood. Although there were trees on the school grounds, the neighborhood itself seemed to have little vegetation. There was an almost blinding light when the sun shone and reflected off the paved streets and concrete sidewalks. The rays danced and ricocheted across homes, which were commonly trimmed with metal railings used as fences, window security guards, or entryway gates. People lived much of their daily lives outside — talking to their next-door neighbors while hanging laundry out on the patio, conversing on the front porch, or taking care of daily errands on foot. There were always young people coming and going from the school, which operated a morning session for eighth graders and an afternoon session for seventh graders. Often students returned to school in the late afternoon for Pioneer meetings, martial arts, or athletic practice.[7]

Students often lingered on the school premises. One popular spot was in the upper story of the school, which had a large patio with concrete benches and overlooked the neighborhood. Typically, this space was used for assemblies and daily *matutinos* (morning revolutionary devotionals), but students also chatted there between classes and before and after school. Another popular spot was the sidewalk in front of the school, close to the ice cream vendor. I would often see children in tattered clothes playing soccer in the street or chasing a bicycle wheel with a stick.

Tour groups were more frequently granted visits to schools in Ciudad Libertad, a schooling compound housing several primary and secondary schools. At Ciudad Libertad, up-to-date research findings were being applied to hallmark schools, and facilities, principals, and teaching staff were considered among the best in the city. The students, a mix of white, black, and mulatto, achieved test scores that were among the highest on the island.

The teachers at Ciudad Libertad told me that, unlike in La Flor, where fewer families seemed to have access to U.S. dollars through their jobs or through family connections abroad, the families whose children attended Ciudad Libertad had many more such opportunities. Adela, the Ciudad Libertad teacher with whom I lived, told me that officials at Ciudad Libertad issued a notice that students were not to bring anything to school that might be *llamativo* (attention-getting), such as toys and other items relatives may have sent from the United States. Moreover, parents were to ensure that their children did not attend school with snacks sold in the U.S. dollar stores or sandwiches containing meat or cheese — items usually acquired in the dollar stores or on the black market. Luis Gómez, the minister of education, announced these new working guidelines, which were intended to "strengthen the teaching of values, discipline and citizen responsibility in school" (Acosta 1998b, 2).

A common feature in both neighborhoods and schools was the worn condition of students' uniforms. The ninth-grade boys wore white shirts with dark yellow pants and the girls wore white shirts with dark yellow skirts. Until the mid-1980s, students were sent home if they were not wearing the proper uniform. However, because uniforms were difficult to obtain, the policy was enforced with less frequency thereafter. For example, white t-shirts with other designs became acceptable. The parents told me they could not find new uniforms, and even if they could, no one could afford them; it was more important to buy food. Consequently, school clothes were passed from one child to another and mended as best as possible (if thread was available). The poor condition of these uniforms cannot be overstated. I never saw a uniform with all of its seams still together. In most cases the waistband or zipper was broken and a belt was used to keep the outfit together. Rarely did a uniform fit a child properly; typically, it was too small or too short. Lizabet spoke of one student who did not come to school because he did not have shoes. She said the class made it a project to try to find someone who had an old pair to give him. Having the proper uniform seemed to be a struggle at all the schools, not just in La Flor. Like socialism, the uniform, the great class equalizer, was coming apart at the seams. The material to keep it together was no longer available, and people were doing the best they could.

Although residents of both areas of town struggled to clothe students adequately for school, beyond the appearance another unexpected distinction emerged: the names of the students at the school. I knew Spanish, but I had the hardest time learning the names of the students at Granma, so I asked them to write them down: Zuraikis, Yuslay, Serinay, Ayamey, Liurdis, Vainerys, Ihunaisy, Yaliana. I asked them how they got their names. Some of their answers were: "from a book my mother read," "it's 'Yemaya'"—one of the Orishas in Santería[8]—"backward," and "after a *santo*." I found it unusual that their parents did not have these names, which is the traditional way for children to acquire their names. In addition, when I had the opportunity to visit schools in Ciudad Libertad, I played a game with one classroom where I went down the rows asking the children to say their names and then an animal whose name began with the same letter. None of the names from La Flor surfaced. Instead, the students gave names I was more accustomed to hearing: Clarita, Susana, Diana, Laura, Antonio, Roberto.

That La Flor is a mostly homogeneous community of Afro-Cubans undoubtedly had some influence on the children's names. What I came to understand was that Santería was a common practice in La Flor and had made its presence known not only in names but also in some of the garb and behavior. I saw men and women *santos*[9] dressed all in white from head to toe; the women usually wore white turbans on their heads when they visited their children's teachers at school. In homes, I occasionally overheard conversations regarding the different levels of *santo* and *santero*,[10] for which rituals had to be performed involving the killing of animals. Purchasing these animals was the greatest obstacle, costing more than a hundred dollars. How were these children's parents able to afford their spiritual calling? One *santo* told me, "It is not uncommon for those becoming *santos* or *santeros* to use prostitution as a means. . . . This is not a recent phenomenon because, traditionally, the blacks have been the ones with less economically and this has been the only sure way to fulfill the call."

In the Afro Cuban, darker-skinned communities, where Santería is more prominent, few have been chosen for jobs in the tourist sector that would provide access to U.S. dollars.[11] Moreover, fewer dark-skinned Cubans have relatives abroad (another source of dollars), and if they do, those family members usually are not as gainfully employed as expatriates of a lighter skin color. The children whose parents are spiritual counselors are met with another mixed message: Is prostitution, one of the prominent social ills from pre-revolutionary days, a viable and dignified means of labor? Children at Granma Junior High School brought up this question more than once in classroom discussions.[12]

Inside Granma Junior High School

Granma Junior High School was quite different from what I later witnessed at Ciudad Libertad. Several teachers at Granma mentioned that, historically, the school had a reputation for having discipline and attendance problems. The teacher attrition rate was high. Second-year students from the Pedagogical Institute accounted for more than 50 percent of those teaching. Principals had come and gone at Granma; however, the most recent principal, Oscar, had been there for four years. All the teachers I spoke with said that since Oscar's arrival, discipline problems had diminished, and several measures—most notably home visits by teachers—had been taken to ensure attendance.

Most of my time was spent either in the classroom or alone talking with Lizabet. Lizabet had taught civic education classes since 1992, when it was introduced into the ninth-grade curriculum.[13] The only other time civic education was part of the revolutionary curriculum was in the early 1960s. At the beginning of the revolution and again in the early 1990s, major economic and political transitions had driven the implementation of a curriculum to solidify civic understanding and promote political solidarity in the revolution.

Lizabet seemed to take a lot of pride in having brought me into the school environment. She appeared to enjoy having people see her with me; being responsible for my presence on the school premises (which was the role she assumed, although she was never formally assigned it) seemed to add to her professional and social capital. She showed disdain for my choice to spend time with other teachers, which tended to limit my opportunities for observing other classrooms. She explained that it would not "be good" for me to associate with Irma, whose husband worked in Mexico. And she did not like me talking to Vanesa, because Vanesa's husband was a revolutionary—a member of the Communist Party—which had earned the couple the right to a car and other amenities. Lizabet used a term to describe Vanesa that I had heard other Cubans frequently use to talk about revolutionaries who had a superior attitude: "*prepotente.*" I found Lizabet to be such an impassioned revolutionary herself that one day I asked her why she had never tried to become a party member. Somewhat defensively, she responded indirectly with an analogy: "You don't have to go to church to be a Christian."

Her analogy brought to light my understanding of the political religion (Fernández 2000) I was seeing actively preached in the classroom and the kind of response that was expected from students. Rote responses were frequently solicited, patriotic songs were sung, and it was not uncommon to hear judgmental remarks regarding how tightly a person toed the party line. While a person seemed to be well respected if he or she were "*revolucionario,*" to be "*muy revolucionario*" was an accolade applied to those who were considered extreme in their beliefs or behavior, exhibiting a superior attitude, and who therefore were *prepotente.* In this way, civil society, by creating its own classifications, mirrored the bureaucratic elite that regulated it.

It was also a revolutionary duty to protect and guard the revolutionary values from possible contamination or harm. Those who did not know me often considered me a possible threat. Lizbet monitored me closely. It was hard for me to tell whether Lizabet followed me closely as part of a political security measure, because she wanted my friendship, because she might benefit financially, or for a combination of these reasons.

Each time I went to the school, Lizabet wanted me to meet her in her office upstairs before going to class. Walking up the stairs, I tried to ignore the stench coming from the bathroom next door (no one knew when the plumbing had last functioned properly). Lizabet used her closet-sized office for parent and student conferences. Students loved her like a *tía,* calling her "Profesora Lizabet." They discussed all sorts of situations in their personal lives with her. She counseled them, sometimes sternly, sometimes more affectionately, depending on the situation. When walking home, it was common for her to stop and chat with families along the way. Students and parents told me that they liked Lizabet because "she always shows she cares."

It did not matter whether I was in Lizabet's office or in the classrooms; the noise level at Granma was much louder than at Ciudad Libertad. The acoustics were different and the furniture was more up-to-date at Ciudad Libertad. In Granma, wooden desks and chairs had iron legs, and the constant screeching of the desks or chairs as the students got up or sat down was barely tolerable. And because the school building was mostly concrete, sounds and voices echoed and were magnified in the halls and classrooms. The classrooms did not have windows; rather, the concrete wall in each classroom that faced the outside had a lattice-like design with openings. This allowed street noises, sunlight, and smells to enter the learning environment. The loud noises and echoes interfered with my understanding of what was being said in the classroom. Often I had to take extra time to check with students and teachers outside the school building to see if I had understood situations correctly.

In the Classroom

Lizabet taught two hours of civic education a week to six sections of ninth graders, each section having around forty students. In the dozen times I observed her civic education class, the students' behavior was very similar to what I had witnessed during my teaching experiences in schools in the United States, Mexico, Ecuador, and Chile: students frequently wrote notes to each other, worked on homework for another class, copied someone else's homework, slept, or doodled during the lesson. Their attention seemed to fade in and out. They appeared to be engaged only to the point that would allow them to stay out of trouble.

Lizabet stood in front of the class each day to teach and, in a very authoritarian way, solicited discussion. She periodically asked students rhetorical questions intended to elicit a unison response. It seemed easy for students to be engaged in something else and then to periodically respond. Her discussion was fairly simplistic and structured. For example, she dedicated class time to defining and reviewing revolutionary values such as solidarity, patriotism, honesty, anti-imperialism, and industriousness and asked students to provide examples from their own lives. She reviewed the rights and duties of Cuban citizens. Although few students had a textbook, it did not seem necessary. Lizabet appeared to be fulfilling one of the important goals stated in the teachers' manual of civic education: "to be careful as to not destroy the affective connection and trust between the two [teacher and student]" (Ministerio de Educación [MINED] 1992, 7). The idea seemed to make the lesson personal, which to some extent, either inside or outside the classroom, Lizabet did.

When students were out of line, Lizabet did not hesitate to discipline them. Such was the case with Olvidio, who one day had turned his attention to drawing a picture of Donald Duck. Lizabet took his picture, showed it to the class, and reprimanded him before the others. Olvidio kept his head down and did not respond, and the class returned to its normal pace. Another student, Nimelio, once challenged Lizabet in front of the class on the rights of Cuban citizens. He was taken outside the classroom and, from what I could tell, never backed down, and ended up in the principal's óffice. I later asked Lizabet about the incident, and she explained that with students like Nimelio, who were being claimed by relatives in the United States and would be leaving soon, there was no behavioral remedy. "Internally," she said, "they have already left Cuba." In this case, the role of state affect (Fernández 2000), like glue, had lost its stickiness with some.

I witnessed very different behavior from the students in math, Spanish, and English classes, where the students seemed engaged in learning and the teachers paced the rows and demanded participation. Everyone had a textbook out and was writing in a *libreta*, a small notebook. Rarely would I see a student off task. The reason for this different classroom atmosphere was understandable: to compete for the few spaces in specialized high schools, such as the Lenin School (sciences), Camilitos (military), the gastronomy or economy schools, or the Pedagogical Institute, students would have to obtain high scores on Spanish and math tests. Mastering English had its value, too: many aspired to obtain jobs in the tourist sector, which provided access to U.S. dollars,[14] or to work for foreign joint venture operations on the island.

Keeping English teachers in the schools was a challenging task in the 1990s since they too had the skills for better-paying jobs. I offered to help out by teaching English at the school, but the principal apologized and explained they were not allowed to have teachers from capitalist countries teaching in the schools. "It's not my rule," Oscar, the principal, explained, "but it is believed that this can seriously threaten the revolutionary value formation of the children and contaminate them with capitalist ideas." However, Oscar did encourage me to be available to help the English teachers outside the classroom.

Wanting to observe an English class, I approached Irma, an English teacher for many years, to see when I might audit one of her classes. We had talked outside class often and enjoyed each other's company. She answered with an openness and warmth that reflected our friendship, but at the same time her facial expressions and hand gestures warned me that the content of the lesson today would toe the *teque* ("official harangue"—Fernández 2000) line, criticizing the United States. "If you don't mind listening to a reading about the United States . . . ," she said hesitantly.

I sat in the back of the classroom, leafing through a copy of the students' English reader. It had been published in 1991. I copied the selection in my small notebook while Irma solicited readers for each paragraph.

THE CITY THAT NEVER SLEEPS

That's what they call New York. More than 10,000,000 people live in New York City. It is not the capital of the United States, but it is the largest city in the country. What do the people who live in New York think of this city?

Angelo is Puerto Rican. He's a tough boy with a kind heart. His father always dreamed of living the American style. Angelo came to New York with his family when he was three years old. Four years later, his father was killed in Viet Nam.

Now Angelo cannot go to school. He must help his mother because she doesn't have a job. Sometimes they don't have enough money for food or medicine. Angelo frequently thinks of his country and that someday he will return with his mother. There are many families like Angelo's in the United States. What will become of them?

Angelo and other children will grow up in a society of prostitution, drugs, racial discrimination, and constant violence. But we may find this in many other American cities. So, isn't it better to say that the United States is "The Country That Never Sleeps?"

Irma solicited a response from the class: "Don't you agree?" In unison, the students answered "Yes." Irma read the selection again, then asked other students to take turns reading it before the class, giving her an opportunity to correct their pronunciation. They answered true/false questions from the book in unison, then Irma assigned homework in the workbook.

The students knew me; I had been visiting their classes for several months. I could not help wondering whether my presence in the school had raised questions in their minds about their way of life and mine. The reading selection depicted an oppressive and hopeless situation for those who might choose to immigrate to the United States. However, on many occasions I had been told, "There's no one here in Cuba who does not have a relative in the United States." One dark-skinned Afro Cuban professor explained that the lives that awaited Cubans in the United States often differed vastly according to their skin color. "Usually the blacks who leave the island have a more difficult time working their way up economically in the United States and, consequently, they probably are unable to send as much money to family left behind in Cuba," he said. Even so, the island Cubans possess ideas, images, and material items representing the United States that are not always negative, such as clothes, music, medicine, or money. In fact, I found their notions of the United States quite dreamlike—that the United States was a place where all material needs were satisfied. Some had more contact than others with relatives in the United States. How did their formal education converge with the informal education they received via their tía in the *Yuma* (a term used to refer to the United States)? Throughout my stay in Cuba, people would distinguish their sentiment about the United States in the same vein as the proverbial "Love the sinner, hate the sin": "It's not the people, it's the U.S. government that we have a problem with."

Irma ended the lesson by asking the students to find the dictionary definitions of the words "tough" and "kind," adjectives used to describe Angelo. I asked Irma about her reasoning for this exercise, which was not in the textbook. She told me that she thought they were useful terms for these students. I nodded my head, thinking, "Indeed, they were useful in negotiating their reality(ies)."

Irma's husband worked in other countries and she sometimes waited months to see him. He always brought the family clothes and useful items for the house. By her frank manner with me, she seemed to recognize the distortedness of the message in the reader. It must have been difficult for the teachers to have to promote these ideas whether they fully agreed with them or not. In the classroom, the teachers did not seem to waiver from the teque. However, in their day-to-day lives they appeared to live, like chameleons, between and within distortions, reconciling appearance and reality in each setting.

After class I sat outside on a concrete bench on the upper landing of the school where the students hung out. Students from Irma's English class sat down next to me and asked me about the discrimination, drugs, gangs, and violence in the United States—impressions left over from the story we had read about Angelo in the English class. I told them that these things existed in the United States, but that it varied. They showed concern about my welfare, living in such a place. "Fortunately," I said, "I have not had much experience as a victim of these injustices and social problems." I explained that when a person's language and color are not the dominant one, that person's chances for success are less. I also commented that it was not always easy to leave one's country and enter a new culture. It was difficult for me to say these things to these beautiful, dark, innocent faces.

Even as the anguish of the moment tugged on my heart, Serinay pulled her candy sucker out of her mouth and, with a look of reflection on what I had said, responded, "Denni, everyone knows that the United States has everything, right? You have the most advanced technology and a pill for everything . . . so why don't you just go back there, to your country, and take a pill to become black like us and then come back and live with us?" Serinay's efforts to make sense of a pronounced discrimination in the United States were compelling. Having some understanding of the racial profiling that was a part of U.S. culture, she proposed a solution—a pill—for me to become a member of La Flor, of what she considered a safer and more accepting community. The offering left me speechless.

A student sat on either side of me with arms wrapped around mine. Another played with my hair and mentioned to me that I smelled like his *tía* who sometimes visited him from the Yuma. Soon many students were sniffing my cheeks and arms. "Yeah, when my *tía* comes she has that same smell. It's also a part of everything she owns: *el olor de allá.* Like when she opens the suitcase to give us the things she has brought us from the Yuma," Eusebio mentioned. "But how can I have that smell if I have been living here for six months?" I asked. "I don't wear perfume. I eat the food of the Cuban family I live with and I bathe myself with their soap and wash my clothes with the same detergent."[15] "I don't know, Denni, but I like your smell," Eusebio confirmed. Another student asked, "Do they inject you with something when you arrive there, so you take on a Yuma scent that marks you forever?" Alain asserted, "My *tía* uses Ivory soap. That's it! Denni, will you bring me a bar of Ivory soap when you come again?" I agreed to do so, and walked back to my Cuban home smiling and perplexed at my unmistakable scent, an identity element that it had never occurred to me to explore, and the profound sensibilities of these curious and affectionate students. Their innocence, openness, self-confidence, and affection for one another were what made it such a pleasure to be with them.

I felt nurtured by the school environment inside and outside the classroom. However, I continued to be perplexed by the success of students who had to learn in a materially deprived setting. Although all the classrooms had light sockets, none had light bulbs, and the rooms tended to be very dark. In addition, there was no chalk for the chalkboards. In fact, I had gone to every supply store in Havana, and it was nowhere to be found. Lizabet became a resource for chalk because her best friend worked in a science institute that had received foreign funding. The foreign country provided chalk, and Lizabet traded her ration of rum from the government for the chalk her teacher friend had. Furthermore, the scarcity of paper made it necessary to do more oral than written testing in all subjects. Like the uniforms, the basic educational and material needs were in threads, badly in need of repair.

While witnessing these circumstances and the plumbing conditions, I was reminded of the conditions Jonathan Kozol described in *Savage Inequalities* (1991), and I went to try to sort out my confusion with the assistant principal, Marisol. Her best friend lived in my neighborhood and was a good friend of mine, which lent us to an automatic *confianza*. I was bewildered by the considerable knowledge base of the students despite their limited resources. I asked Marisol, "How is it that these children succeed under these circumstances?" Expecting to hear the details of a professional development program in place, an educational innovation, or some mechanism or method used only in Cuba, I was startled by her unhesitating response. Smiling, she said, "Love. You can't have education without love, can you? And no one can take it away from you, either. That's why the embargo has never nor will ever ruin our quality of education."

Perhaps Marisol's answer should be dismissed as romantic, but under the circumstances it seemed the only plausible response. Despite the severe economic problems Cuba has had, and the even greater weight of those problems in La Flor, students continued to show evidence of a quality education. The secret had to be something that was little affected by the economy. Cubans often say, "Lo importante no es lo material, es lo espiritual." I have also heard Cubans mention that *lo espiritual* is a part of conciencia. "What is *lo espiritual*?" I asked. The children defined *lo espiritual* as "affection," "friends and family," "to be surrounded by those who love you."

In promoting a collective attitude, teachers encourage an affective dimension: student bonding and student-teacher bonding. As Fernández (2000) argues, an emotional infrastructure is presumed, which includes particular feelings such as solidarity, affection for the leaders and others, optimism, and respect for authority. However unwittingly, the revolution has also provided tools for questioning—not only of the topics targeted for revolutionary value inculcation, with assemblies and the analysis encouraged in the classrooms, but also, inevitably, of the Cuban government's established tenets and rules.

The result has been a wrestling of compromises to foster a stronger bond with youth. The struggle for the hearts and minds of young Cubans has been expressed in material and semiotic ways. These appear in a discourse that is more open to discussion and tolerant of different cultural practices (i.e., religion), and in lifestyle (appropriating certain capitalist ways, such as seeking personal gain). Young people had fallen prey to *el teque* in the 1980s, and because of their distaste for its litany-like nature and the noncorrespondence of *el teque* to reality, at the Fifth Congress of the Young Communists in 1992 the organization adopted the slogan *Sin Formalismos* (Without Formalisms) in an effort to set Cuban socialism on a more authentic footing and renew the vital relationship between the state and the young people. The leadership agreed that a reanimated and rejuvenated socialism was needed to bring youth back into the fold.

At the end of the stay, my mentor from the Pedagogical Institute, Nancy, indicated that I needed to administer a classroom survey. She told me I should type it up and give it to her for approval.[16] On each draft she commented that my questions were "inappropriate"; however, she never would provide me with "appropriate" ones. Thus, it became a trial of patience for me to guess what would be acceptable (the different drafts are included in Appendix 2). Cubans who witnessed this process would tell me "te está pateando" (she's putting you off). They explained that officially, no one will tell you no or directly ask you to leave, but it is the Cuban way to make you so frustrated that you give up and go home.

After more than a month of drafting different surveys and having them checked, my questions were finally approved and I was allowed to administer the three questions on paper to Lizabet's class of thirty-nine students, with the requirement that Lizabet be present. I passed out the small pieces of paper and Lizabet read them out loud to the students. After reading the last question, "What do you think are the three most important values for a person to develop?," she went to the chalkboard to write in large letters the seven revolutionary values in a vertical list: Laboriousness, Anti-imperialism, Solidarity, Honor, Honesty, Patriotism, Responsibility. Students stared at the chalkboard and proceeded to copy down their choices.

Between the tactics used by Nancy and Lizabet, I felt frustrated that I could not openly find out what the students' opinions were. Lizabet talked through possible answers for the two other questions and then collected the small pieces of paper. The guidance and structure she imposed on the students to answer in accordance with the official line would justify those with anti-Castro sentiments. However, I did not sense that this directed guidance was the norm, so I decided to seek the advice of Cuban researchers at Centro de Investigación de Psicología y Sociología. I followed their counsel to readminister the survey after first speaking with Lizabet.

Lizabet said that she just wanted my report "to look good." I told her that

I appreciated her concern but that I was going to survey Irma's class so as to start with a fresh group. This time I told Irma in advance that I did not want students to receive any suggestions for answers. Irma was very accommodating; the students had neither lists of values to consult nor any guidance from Irma in answering the other questions.

I tallied the outcomes for both classes. Irma's class had forty students and Lizabet's thirty-nine. In Lizabet's class, 72 percent of the students considered "honesty" the most important value. "Honor" was second, at 56 percent, followed by "laboriousness" at 37 percent and "responsibility" at 36 percent. In Irma's class, "friendship/companionship" and "honesty" tied for being the most important value, each having been selected by 47 percent of the students. Clearly, both groups of students responded to the affective components of holding a pueblo together: honesty and companionship. The question had asked, "What do you think are the three most important values for a person to develop?" The results left me wondering whether the values that students identified were the ones most practiced, and if so, by whom, or if they were the values most in need today. My original question, which I was not permitted to present, was, "What do you think are the three most important values, and why?" The question in that form probably would have resulted in more detailed and thoughtful responses.

Arguably, a gap has existed between the passion and the performance of the Cuban government. The mortar has been the humanizing aspects of schooling and the creation of the school as a moral community (on their own terms) and family with all its strengths and weaknesses, leaving students, at the very least, building networks of affection—through friendship, companionship, and honesty—that will become their most useful tools, regardless of the direction they take in life. The values of leadership, responsibility, solidarity, self-critique, and discipline are honed daily. In the educational socializing process, a keen sense of self seemed to be developing as students tried to understand, appropriate, or resist revolutionary values. Ideological, schooled behavior and discourse can be misleading, in that they embody simultaneously opposing and meaningful everyday values yet at the same time may be devoid of their literal meanings (Yurchak 2005). Olvidio, according to Lizbet, may already have left Cuba internally, but that does not mean he does not embrace revolutionary values or behavior. Students seemed to be in a constant negotiating process of what they sought to be worthy or useful for their future. In addition, I observed a keen sense of belonging and high self-esteem being fostered by constant group interaction, emphasizing the collective or the group more than the individual.

The Pedagogical Institute

The pedagogical institute located in each Cuban province is a site for preparing future teachers (in a five-year program) and facilitating educational research. With both a master's and doctoral program in *pedagogía*, the research conducted by the various institutes frequently serves the national headquarters, the Ministry of Education in Havana. Spending time in both MINED and the Enrique José Varona Pedagogical Institute in Havana allowed me to witness the collaboration between the two institutions. Most of the research was conveniently applied to one or more of the many schools located on the Ciudad Libertad premises, where La Varona, as the Havana pedagogical institute is called, is located. MINED relied on the professors at La Varona for research applicable to contemporary schooling issues.

After spending some time in the archives in La Varona, I noticed one name that was very prominent in recent research on value formation: Nancy Chacón. I sought her out at La Varona to be my mentor. She encouraged me to attend classes at La Varona, which she had preselected for me. My time at La Varona was spent mostly in professional development classes about the work-study principle and value formation. Nancy's classes on value formation consisted mainly of psychological theory related to the development of values. She drew diagrams on the chalkboard for students to copy about how values are formed and altered and how they are affected by globalization. At one point she started talking about "anti-values," which were in conflict with revolutionary values. In her diagram, neoliberal globalization led to sustaining developed countries through technology. However, it also led to the dehumanization of people. With technology always at the forefront of the revolution, how was Cuba to avoid inheriting the dehumanizing aspects that accompany advancing technology? The key, Nancy wrote at the bottom of the diagram, was education. Specifically, by harnessing educational expertise through technological growth and channeling education through the more humane and fundamentally humanist system of socialism, Cuba would not succumb to the dehumanizing phenomenon of other capitalist countries, in particular the United States. Education would make the dialectical assimilation.

Nancy encouraged me to participate in the class discussions. I was a bit intimidated and resisted, saying that I was just there to learn. One day in class, she continued to solicit some type of response from me, so I asked, "Who decides what is a value and what is an 'anti-value?'" Nancy stated that anything that did not correspond with the revolutionary values was an anti-value. She restated her theory about value inculcation in what seemed to be an effort to erase my questioning and to leave her students with intellectual assurance.

After class, some of the students congregated outside. The students asked me what classes I took in teacher preparation to learn my ideology: "We take Marxism and classes about Cuban history emphasizing socialism; what do you take?" I had a hard time convincing the students that pre-service teachers in the United States did not take classes in ideology. "Then how do you learn capitalism?" they asked. "How do you learn to teach it?" I explained that it was embedded throughout the curriculum and that we are taught only the benefits. "There might be more people resistant to the idea if they were aware of how it operated." In response, the students smiled and asked me if I knew the difference between socialism and capitalism. Recognizing the setup for a joke, I said, "What?" "One purports man's exploitation of man. The other is just the reverse."

Back in the classroom at La Varona, most teaching was done in lecture style, and the lectures combined with the heat in the classroom had student teachers nodding off. I had a hard time staying awake as well. Occasionally the teachers asked the professor questions, or vice versa. I remember one occasion on which a teacher challenged the teque, saying, "This is not our reality." The instructor was quick to respond with "It's our duty to work harder. We are not working hard enough." Then, in a crescendo, she belted out with revolutionary spirit: "Did anyone ever say that this was going to be easy? '¡Luchar por un mundo mejor!'" (We must struggle for a better world!). As if she were trying to extinguish any questioning, she repeated luchar a few more times.

Maybe it was acceptable, or at least expected, for instructors to say this to their students, but I could not imagine saying anything more offensive to the Cubans I had met. They always referred to being in "la lucha." People were doing everything they could to get by. The teachers I spoke with conceded that the teque promoting hard work as the solution used to have meaning and hope. However, they said, the years since the beginning of the Special Period had demonstrated that work alone was not the answer, and people were working harder only to find themselves exhausted. The only enduring economic relief had come with the economic change of the early 1990s: U.S. dollar circulation, increased family remittances, foreign joint ventures, and self-owned businesses.[17]

Foreign influence on the economy and the legalization of entrepreneurship in the 1990s created new avenues for economic growth. Consequently, teachers, along with a wide range of Cuban professionals, reapplied their characteristic resourcefulness and keen sense of organization to more lucrative professions, such as opening up a *paladar* (a family-operated restaurant in the home) or making a corner stand for selling pizzas, cookies, or cakes.

In March 1999, while I was there, the state raised teacher salaries for the first time in years, in hopes of preserving as well as increasing the numbers in the teaching profession. I asked teachers how they felt about the pay raise. They agreed that it was needed; however, they complained that a small increment in pesos did not do much to offset the inevitable dollar expenditures they had to make. Fewer and fewer necessities were available via the libreta ration booklet. Referring to the libreta, they pointed out that during the entire preceding year, cooking oil came in only once,[18] sanitary pads twice, body soap four times, and toothpaste and detergent three times. When the product comes in, they explained, "The whole neighborhood knows and it is usually gone within 24 hours. If you want to live with any kind of dignity, you either purchase the items in dollars, which is more than we can afford, or you work the black market." The black market, therefore, becomes a lifeline and hub for social networking. Those who provided for each other, either by selling or by buying, formed alliances. People usually had one such network near their workplace and another in their neighborhood. Between the two places, people managed to get their basic needs met.

While the black market might be more efficient than the state in supplying goods and services that are not readily available, there are costs to the Cuban government. The government's inability to stem the tide of informal economic and social relations not only shows its vulnerability, it also erodes the government's credibility. Meanwhile, the Cuban people are "working harder" in perhaps new ways to "luchar por un mejor mundo," which is forcing them to redefine the revolution—specifically, to redefine conciencia and the constitution of the Hombre Nuevo. The Cuban government continues to hold the reins at the macro-level, while at the micro-level its control seems to have become much more slippery. The concepts and values of the revolution have not disappeared but have been reconfigured to better answer societal needs. Although speaking specifically about artists in the Soviet Union, Haraszti's (1988) comments shed light on how new generations are able to express themselves in ways that never before would have been permitted and how, with the passage of time, nationalized culture can work without the detailed constant prescriptions of the official party line. "This new culture is the result not of raging censorship but of its steady disappearance," he said. "Censorship professes itself to be freedom because it acts, like morality, as the common spirit of both" (Haraszti 1988, 7).

The Ministry of Education

While waiting two months for permission from MINED to do long-term observation in Granma Junior High School, I took advantage of the time by reading the most up-to-date research possible on value formation and the work-study principle. My time was divided between La Varona and MINED. The Documentation Center at MINED was formally closed; however, because one of my dissertation committee members had written a letter to a MINED official, I was given access to the ministry's holdings. I was allowed to come in every day and read and take notes on materials there. The staff spent most of the time without much to do because they had been informed that the Documentation Center, on the bottom floor, and the upper floors of MINED would be moving to a new, undisclosed location. Recognizing another opportunity for profitability, in the fall of 1998 the Cuban government had decided to turn the MINED headquarters into a hotel.

The air conditioning had gone out in the Documentation Center. The exterior walls of the center were made of glass, but they had no windows that could actually be opened. A couple of fans were set up and, while I sat at a table reading, the others sat near the door in a circle each morning reviewing the previous night's episode of the telenovela *Café con aroma de mujer*. This Colombian soap opera serial was a big hit. Many Cubans reported that it had been a couple of years since a soap opera had captivated the Cuban population like this.[19]

What I found interesting were the conversations that ensued as people commented on the previous night's episode. The protagonist in the soap opera, Carolina Olivares, was a beautiful young woman who lived modestly with her mother and tried to support the two of them, at one time as a prostitute in Europe. Carolina had recently returned to Colombia with her mother in the hope of living a better life and reuniting with the man of her dreams, Sebastián, a man she had fallen in love with in Colombia several years ago. In her determination to leave poverty behind, and with little education to market herself for a well-paying job, she invented a résumé and went after an executive secretarial position in a corporation where she hoped to find Sebastián.

One day, I took note of the conversation the staff was having about the soap opera in relation to education and careers in Cuba. A few staff members commented that Carolina had acquired key skills in maneuvering through the corporate world through her economic and social struggles and her contact with the illegal. She knew how to use her assets of beauty and appearance to cover for her lack of knowledge in other areas. The staff agreed that informal education was just as important as, if not more important than, formal education for navigating one's career. Then they laughed, remarking on the work needed to improve formal education and value formation in their own country. "In reality," one said, "it is the informal that will make the difference."

Their commentary reflected the "makeovers" of *conciencia* taking place as priorities are relocated, if not changed completely. For many of the workers, the relocation of MINED was very unsettling. Many of the revolutionary workers at MINED interpreted this change as symbolic of the government's values and its relationship with its people. Some called it another manifestation of *jineterismo* (prostitution), one of the most pronounced side effects of mixed-market measures. Education had always been a priority of the revolutionary Cuban government, but now the government was willing to sell its sacred cow, its revolutionary hallmark, for tourist dollars. Although the government had secured the building for a multifunctional installation in which a new university facility would be sharing space with museums, a cinema, and other facilities, the new location of MINED remained uncertain for months. Many expressed a sense of disbelief and sentimental loss that the national headquarters for education was being abandoned, neglected, and ultimately displaced by facilities for tourists.

The uncertain future of MINED left its personnel grappling not only with sentimental issues but also with a material setback. Who would be their black market contacts in the new work location? They speculated about what area of town MINED might move to and bemoaned the fact that they would have to leave their longtime, secure black market dealers in Old Havana and then carefully stake out reliable providers in another location. As a result, the move to a new work area was very upsetting, in light of the time and effort it took to establish trustworthy *socios* (contacts).

Finding new office space for MINED was not easy. The government saw as the only solution dividing up MINED into two separate buildings about a mile from each other in a different neighborhood, Vedado. This separation further affected the cohesive base of those who associated and worked with one another in the pursuit of educational ideals. Again, the state pursued material goals at the affective expense of the people.

The responses regarding teacher salaries and the displacement of the country's educational headquarters point to issues of identity, interests, and emotion. The value of education has always been at the forefront of the revolution. Those who worked at the country's governing center for education questioned the priorities of a revolutionary government that felt it was more important to cater to tourists than to maintain its national education headquarters. Tourism and education, and the values each represented, were at the nexus of this change. In these two situations regarding education, the people expected more attention based on the expounded revolutionary values. However, the state's contradictory attitude and practice had caused its most loyal followers to question its credibility and to rely on ties that yielded more constancy: friends, family, and *socios*.

The Search for an Answer

Cuba is not unique in its crisis of values. All countries are faced with making children better citizens, and in so doing they run into obstacles. Nevertheless, each country's context is unique, and the situation becomes extremely difficult when the educational system does not correspond with the social reality. Moreover, the Cuban government has not been complacent; it has been continually trying to improve the system and resolve its issues concerning revolutionary value inculcation.

During the months I was in Cuba, the newspapers frequently addressed the values crisis. Headlines included "Forming values is more than a school subject—It is the school assignment" (Rubio 1999, 3), "The value of values" (2), "Bad habits due to the excess of love" (Guerrero Borrego 1999, 2), and "The school should form a more responsible conduct" (Rubio 1999, 2). For the most part the blame was put on parents and on socialism itself. Both had been far too paternalistic. In the case of Cuban socialism, the government was blamed for providing and promising too much in the early days, to such an extent that more was now expected from the government than it could possibly hope to give. As Minister of Education Luis Gómez commented, "It is one of our most difficult tasks, because in capitalism responsibility is formed spontaneously by the rigor of the system, while in socialism we tend to be paternalistic" (Perera and Rosquete 1999, 3; trans. mine).

Parents were accused of taking up the slack when the socialist measures did not come through. As reported in *Juventud Rebelde*, "the parents want their children to be healthy, but they [the parents] are the ones who are making them incapable of adapting to their social milieu" (Guerrero Borrego 1999, 2). This response also surfaced in my interviews with parents and teachers. I asked Irma, "You participated in the school to the countryside program, and you have told me of all the struggles you had growing up with scarcity in the 1970s. You have just told me that in the end it made you a better person. So, why is that you don't want your son to struggle, if this is one of the best ways to learn values?" Irma stared at me speechless, as if this had never crossed her mind, and said, "Honestly, I don't know. I think every parent wants the best for their children and will do whatever is within their means to help them. My parents did too, but the times were different."

I spoke with Dr. Patiño, an official at MINED who had been doing research on the work-study principle since 1964:

"What is this 'love for work'" like in the new generations?"

—"Well, I am not saying that they have lost this 'love for work,' but I will tell you that they have lost a bit of the love for studying. Everyone thinks (and this is appropriate for the situation in which we are living) that the majority think, 'Why should one pursue a university degree, if those who are earning the most are making bread in a cafeteria or are a cashier in a dollar store, where they earn at least a portion of their salary in dollars?' Historically in Cuba, everyone wanted a university degree, and now people are thinking distinctly as they are a product of the situation they are currently living. It is true that the salary of a teacher does not pay for the basic necessities, and that those who work in a bakery end up with more money than a professional. But this is a thing of the moment; everything has to change."

—"Dr. Patiño, I would like to know if you learned from your experiences perhaps something that this generation has not."

—"Yes, I learned a lot. I learned to be separated from my mother, who did not do everything for me. I learned to wash my own sheets and own clothes and I learned to eat what I had in front of me without being able to say that I did not like it or I want something else."

—"Then why is it that these children do not see the same values in their lives?"

—"I think the parents are guilty. Now that the situation (economic) is bad, the parents of today are not the same as before. Before the parents had more *conciencia*."

—"But why is that parents have changed their mentality? They had a difficult situation and learned from that experience. . . ."

—"Denise, I don't know how to answer that."

The conversations with Dr. Patiño and with Irma were characteristic of other interviews I had with people on this topic that ended with "I don't know." How is this response to be interpreted? Is this something that they have never thought about or is it perhaps something they cannot talk about openly? Both Irma and Dr. Patiño mentioned that the current situation is historically different from the 1960s and 1970s. During the revolution, the Cuban people experienced material scarcity and hardship, but perhaps never to the same extent as during the Special Period. Thus, the historical situation is the difference, and how people interpret it determines how they chose to deal with material difficulties. Are the parents doing the work for their children because, unlike in the past, they know that the Cuban economy and its social repercussions will not be resolved by the labor of the pueblo alone? Do they know this from experience? The parents lived and worked hard because they believed in the dream of a socialist utopia. As they try to prepare their children for the future, is their behavior not indicative of a disbelief in the improvement of the historical conditions to ultimately support socialism? Are the parents not living according to their history and logic?

Inevitably, the government, probably knowing how hard it would be to try to alter the parents' mentality, proposed the teacher and the curriculum as the solutions. Several articles in *Granma* and *Juventud Rebelde* published the initiation of more professional development in the area of teaching Cuban history. "If our young people don't know Cuban history, they will not be able to understand values, such as anti-imperialism" (Perera 1999, 2; trans. mine). "The textbooks must be attractive, and without dogmatism. We must not just focus on knowledge, but imply *feelings* of nationality and anti-imperialism that translate into actions and conduct" (Rubio 1999, 2; trans. and italics mine). As a result, many intensive courses were being offered for teachers through La Varona in Havana and at other institutes throughout the country. In addition, the theme of emphasizing more Cuban history in the schools became a prominent issue in youth organization meetings (Mayor, Regalado, and Rodríguez 1999, 2).

In La Flor, one older woman said that the neighborhood watch group, the Committee for the Defense of the Revolution, was calling on all literacy campaign workers from 1961 to meet and discuss ways to help the neighborhood with value inculcation among families. I asked her to take notes for me when she went to the CDR meeting. When I showed up the next day to hear about the meeting, she smiled and said, "I'm sorry, Denni. I really wanted to do this for you, but I just could not keep my eyes open. I can't imagine it being anything different from what you have already heard. I'm sorry."

In some ways I was seeing the *dos caras* (two faces) of Cuba just by alternating days at La Varona or MINED with time in La Flor. How people were living their lives often differed from the teque. I did not think that the people I had met were lacking revolutionary values, although I would not categorize their values as either pro- or counterrevolutionary. Conciencia was indeed evolving with its context and mirroring the overlapping duality that Yurchak (2005) purports. People were neither abandoning socialist ideals nor buying into the rhetoric; rather, they were negotiating and acting on the two constantly, if not simultaneously.

After spending time with Lisset, a 30-year-old *santo* and mother of a child at Granma, she recognized my intense interest in education and appreciation of the La Flor community. She said, "You need to meet Caridad."

Caridad

Caridad was well respected by residents of La Flor, and her history as a schoolteacher in the neighborhood was well-known. Lisset facilitated our encounter near the end of my stay. When I arrived at Lisset's house, I saw she had made space for people to gather on the concrete patio where the laundry was hung out to dry. She arranged some chairs in a circle, and people started to come in one by one. They were all former students of *La escuelita de Caridad* and ranged in age from their thirties to their mid-fifties. Caridad, at 75, was escorted in as if she were royalty, although her disposition was quite open and simple. She was a petite mulatta with short gray curly hair and an effervescent smile. She wore a long, well-worn, faded skirt and a short-sleeved t-shirt, and her eyes twinkled as she introduced herself to me. In the same sentence she said, "and I work in the street" (the black market).

Impressed by her genuine beauty, I asked, "And what do you do to keep yourself looking so good?" Without batting an eye, she said, "Arroz con chícharo" (rice and chickpeas—the standard Cuban peasant food) and smiled. "And sometimes a piece of meat when I can find it!" The people on the patio all chuckled, as they understood the scarcity of meat and shared in her type of lifestyle.

Caridad had been the first teacher of all those present. She had started teaching in 1942 and had converted her living room into a school. She had never had any formal training beyond a sixth-grade education. "What made you think of starting a school?" I asked. Caridad explained softly,

> I never have liked being told what to do, and I was working for a man, and I did not like my work conditions, so I quit my job and said, "I am going to start a school." The man told me that although I spoke well, I did not have what it took to make a school. I told him that he would see. And after three days, I contacted him to see my school. They were difficult times in the

1940s. I charged 25 cents a week per student. I had students who came just for the morning, some just in the afternoon, and some that stayed all day until 8 p.m. I made sure they all ate well, too.

Caridad's voice faded as those who had gathered wanted to give their testimony of her influence on their lives. "Caridad's curriculum included reading, writing, arithmetic, learning how to tell time, spelling, geography, and history. She used to have a stick and would hold it up to threaten us, but she never used it," said Papito. "There was even a song about Caridad's stick," Fermín said, and he began to sing: "What a hard stick Caridad has. . . ." Everyone laughed, and you could tell by Caridad's warm laugh that she was reliving the joy of her past.

Then Yisel recounted her experience of more than forty years ago:

I remember that in the living room, which was the classroom, Caridad had a big impressive altar dedicated to the Virgen of Mercedes. I knew Caridad's mother, Magdalena. She was a well-known *santera*. We used to act up at the school, and sometimes Magdalena would play the maracas and we would sing. We needed something to settle us down because we did not appreciate the serious of the ceremonies that took place before the altar. On the 24th of September, there was always a big celebration at Caridad's house in honor of the Virgen of Mercedes, and no school. I think the whole neighborhood of La Flor paraded throughout the streets. The neighborhood was lit up with lights, and you could smell all of the fresh flowers that students had brought for the altar. The Virgen looked more beautiful than ever.

Papito recounted a memory of when he was six years old and Caridad gave him a pen as a gift. She told the little boy, "When you grow up, Papito, you will graduate from college and people will call you Dr. López." "I was one of the few that went on to college the year I graduated, but Caridad knew, even though we lost contact," Papito said. "I owe a lot to her."

Caridad was revered as a symbol of someone who encouraged and preserved the essential values of La Flor. She had made quite an impact on her students. Together, we calculated that from 1942 through 1969, approximately eighty-five students had spent from one to three years attending *La escuelita de Caridad.*

Hearing how her former students treasured her and their satisfaction with such a personal experience in education, I asked, "So, how did the triumph of the revolution and the nationalization of the schools in 1961 affect the *escuelita?*" Caridad commented:

The neighborhood wanted me to keep teaching. They did not feel that their children were learning enough in the public school. At the very least I complemented the public school education. So I kept teaching, but we were careful to not be overt about what was going on. There was a lot of surveillance in that time, so everything was done quietly . . . until finally we were discovered and I was forced to shut down the school in 1968. The government wanted me to teach in the public schools, but I was stubborn and stopped teaching altogether.

So what changes occurred in La Flor due to the triumph of the revolution?

Fermín answered, "Well, everything continued the same way more or less." At that moment others repeated, "The Revolution never arrived here in La Flor!"

Another, older man named Elier said:

I have been living here for more than forty years and I can say that although the revolution may have done its work in other areas of the island and here in Havana, in La Flor, it never arrived. And I am going to tell you something that is the history of La Flor. Fidel Castro came to this neighborhood and used that house [he pointed to one down the street] as a hideout for a while before the assault on the Moncada barracks in 1953.[20] Agustín Díaz, a black man and author of the 26th of July Hymn, lived there, too. Fidel and those who conspired here were part of a clandestine cell. The hymn of the 26th of July was heard first here in La Flor before it was anywhere else.

This opportunity to speak with Caridad and her former students revealed a history that few outside La Flor knew. The people of La Flor were proud that they had successfully hidden and protected the rebels, which heightens the irony that the neighborhood has been neglected and forgotten by the revolutionary government. Nevertheless, the people of La Flor seemed to have maintained the values Irma emphasized in her English class: tough and kind. Indeed, as Irma pointed out, they are useful terms for all children growing up today, no matter where they live.

The stories Caridad's former students told about La Flor were stories of identity, struggle, hope, and pride. Perhaps where the revolution did not arrive, Santería was there with Caridad, who helped to preserve a hope that remained unfulfilled through her use of a more holistic, culturally relevant curriculum that connected to the students' sense of cubanidad in ways that the government neighborhood school did not. In addition, whether it was her intention or not, she cultivated values compatible with the revolution: responsibility, a sense of history, sacrifice, hard work, patriotism, honesty, and solidarity. They had brought Caridad to meet me because she has been a symbol, both of the history and values that have sustained La Flor and of what a good education and an ideal educator should be.

The streets of La Flor and the sites of Granma Junior High School, the Pedagogical Institute, and MINED reveal cross-sections of sites of education, negotiation, and mediation. At first sight, these may seem to be ineffective mechanisms, yet on a closer look the authoritative, immutable discourse is understood as more permeable by those who live with it. Cubans' everyday lives are "velvet prisons" (Haraszti 1988) whose chambers of constraint are the very context that generates the spontaneous, inventiveness, and creativity that mark cubanidad, conciencia, and the Hombre Nuevo of the twenty-first century. Never static or bounded, identity and ideology are part of a dialectic that is also actively challenging and shifting the evolution of both. In Chapter 6, I look at Granma Junior High School from an official perspective by examining the mass student organization of the Pioneers and the ways in which it is used to organize and monitor official revolutionary value formation on and off campus.

CHAPTER 6

The Cuban Pioneer Student Organization: Who Will Be Like Che?

The Goal of the Pioneer Organization "José Martí"

To contribute to the formation of more humane men and women, more disposed to their multiple social, physical and intellectual capacities, apt and responsible citizens that intervene actively in the work of the revolution as authors of the history of their people and of the world.

COMPENDIO, PRESIDENCIA PROVINCIAL GUANTÁNAMO

The Pioneer organization is one of the primary means at the Cuban state's disposal to modify and regulate student behavior, having a major impact on the day-to-day running of the schools in Cuba. As a mass organization for grades one through nine, the Pioneer organization is overtly used by the Cuban government to socialize schoolchildren to be responsible citizens. In addition, the organization illustrates, according to Theodore MacDonald (1985, 176), "the degree to which doctrinaire shifts in ideological line can be mediated through the school system."

The purpose of this chapter is to illustrate some of the major activities I observed of the Pioneers and the impact this organization seemed to have on the students at that time. The Pioneer organization comes to life through the behavior and feelings it seeks to promote: emulation, solidarity, collective work and sacrifice, patriotism, and self-confidence or esteem. My intention is to show how these behaviors and feelings form the base for cultivating *conciencia,* one of the primary goals of Cuban citizenship. The activities I chose to focus on were the Pioneers' role in schooling and the extracurricular activities of the Pioneers, such as the interest clubs, the interest circles, the Fuerzas de Acción Pioneril, and the Explorers.

The students at Granma Junior High School seemed to have a keen sense of belonging to their school community, of being active and taking part in many different activities. Although at first glance the internal organization was not obvious to me, and the words "student" and "*pionero*" were used interchangeably, in reality the Pioneer organization takes on as much or more responsibility for the education of children as the teachers and administrators do. The Pioneer organization provides an interface that diminishes the authoritarian distance that usually exists between students and teachers. Before addressing the different aspects of the Pioneers, I find it helpful to provide a brief orientation to the organization's existence and structure.[1]

History and Structure

With the triumph of the revolution in 1959, the not-yet-well-defined communist regime needed an avant-garde to spearhead the educational changes. For that purpose the Jóvenes Rebeldes (Young Rebels), later called the Jóvenes Comunistas (Young Communists, or UJC), was created. The organization's motto, "*Estudio, Trabajo, Fusil*" (Study, Work, Rifle), became one of the Cuban school mottos (Castañeda 1973, 145). The UJC, a selective organization, oversees mass youth organizations,[2] with the goal of recruiting only the best leaders, the vanguard, for membership in the UJC. Consequently, the work of the Pioneers is important to the UJC, and each campus usually has a student representative from the UJC who maintains communication between the UJC and the Pioneer organization.

The origin of the Pioneers (the organization has been known under several different names) in Cuba, as with the Pioneers in all other communist countries, may be traced back to the Soviet Union. In 1968 the Pioneers became a mass organization for Cuban children between the ages of 6 and 14 and adopted the slogan, "Pioneers for Communism: We will be like Che!"[3] The Pioneers boast a 98 percent membership rate. All Cuban students from first through ninth grade become Pioneers. This early socialization through a school organization, according to Urie Bonfenbrenner (1970), provides an atmosphere in which students become more group conscious than students in the United States, where individualism is overemphasized.

Although belonging to the Pioneer organization is optional, parents told me it was not really thought of in that way: "All Cuban students are Pioneers except for the children belonging to Jehovah's Witnesses." As one mother, Beatriz, stated, "No one wants to be singled out among their peers." At the same time, parents agreed with what another mother said, too: "There is a lot of good that comes from being a Pioneer. Students learn what it means to be responsible, to work hard, and to be cooperative." Parents also commented that the Pioneers kept students active after school hours in supervised fun or productive activities so that the parents did not have to worry about their safety. The only objection parents seemed to have was the promotion of the political, as voiced by Beatriz: "All of the Che this and Che that and *comunismo* . . . it's not our reality." With its pros and cons, the Pioneer structure is an integral part of the school structure and culture, from the classroom to the school council.

At the simplest level, each classroom (approximately forty students) is called a *destacamento* (a detachment) and each *destacamento* has its *jefe de destacamento*, elected by the students of the classroom. The jefe of each destacamento reports to the Detachment Council, or *Colectivo*, for the entire school. The Colectivo is made up of nine school representatives: the *presidente*, the *jefe de emulación* (emulation), the *jefe de trabajo* (work), the *jefe de cultura* (culture), the *jefe de estudio* (study), the *jefe de deportes* (sports), the *jefe de actividades* (activities), the *jefe de política* (politics), and the *jefe de la escuela* (school). The jefe of each destacamento, or classroom, technically becomes a messenger in this process, giving the jefes on the Colectivo an update, or report, on each of these areas as they pertain to the classroom, and also keeping the Colectivo informed of the problems or needs of the destacamento. The Colectivo in turn disseminates information to the classrooms via the *jefe de destacamento*. The Colectivo then serves on the school council with the school administration, in a position of active decision making.[4]

Before the disintegration of the Soviet bloc, Pioneers from different socialist countries participated in international festivals to share ideas and promote socialist solidarity. With coordination from the local to the national level (and previously the international level), the students felt they were part of a much larger project than a solely school-based one. This multilayered collective identity, which reaches a national level, reflects one of the ways the UJC cultivates nationalism, patriotism, and solidarity.

Emulation is an integral part of socialist education. With the focus on collective competition instead of individual competition, emulation entails motivating the class collectively to reach an ideal. This process is mostly carried out between destacamentos (in the classroom setting or in an extracurricular activity), with the focus being on completing the tasks set, not on beating the other detachments. Ideally, all detachments achieve or win the emulation. Prior to the Special Period, the *estímulo* (moral stimulus) took the form of public recognition and was recognized with a badge, a star, or a certificate. Today, with the economic crisis, the naming of a "vanguard" or "monitor" group—verbal recognition—is the only moral incentive. In all divisions of education, peers evaluate and decide who will receive recognition, while the teacher oversees the process.[5]

The Divisions and Responsibilities of the Jefes

The detachments were well organized and active at Granma. The *jefe de trabajo* encouraged socially useful work, which could take the form of school maintenance projects. While I was there, the jefe of each detachment promoted bringing items from home for recycling: plastic, glass, wood, and metal. Sometimes these items would be used for art class or would be given to the state for recycling. Socially useful work also included the weekly cultivation and maintenance of a neighborhood garden. The jefe directed projects, gave instructions to his or her peers, and motivated them to participate.

We met one Saturday morning at the school to wash the classroom floors, clean the school bathrooms, and pick up trash from the school grounds. The students worked as a team and did a thorough job.[6] Laughter hung in the air as people joked around with one another while working. Because of our numbers—twelve people—the work did not seem very difficult. During this period I asked Lizabet if there was any documentation of who participated. "Of course," she said, in a frustrated tone. She was disappointed that the turnout of students was so small. "They know this will go on their record either way. And by not participating they are limiting their future options."

As students worked, they seemed focused and proud of their accomplishments. They did not complain while cleaning or working in the garden. Some of the reasons for their compliance might include the following: (1) the workload was appropriate for the students, (2) the work crew consisted of their peers, (3) the work was shared equally,(4) the work atmosphere was casual, and students were allowed to chat with one another, (5) their presence and participation would count toward the possibility of future study or career opportunities. These were conditions that the teacher and students confirmed were factors in the effectiveness of the work crews. No one mentioned any connection to the revolution, the basis for the Pioneers and all of their activities.

In the absence of cultivating a political ideology, the program seemed to be encouraging leadership skills. The students' self-esteem appeared to be reinforced because they had been responsible for maintaining their school or providing for their neighborhood, in this case doing cleanup work or cultivating vegetables and fruits. They had a personal investment in making their world a better place, either by collecting materials, painting the school, participating in school maintenance, or growing fruits and vegetables. They were learning how to plan and work together. Students possessed self-efficacy.

This Pioneer system of peer direction and motivation was present in sports and cultural activities, too. The *jefe de deportes* (sports) organized games, kept records and scores, and assisted the coach. In cultural activities the *jefe de cultura* organized musicals, skits, and the recital and performance of literary works. Students elected the jefes based on their talents in these areas. With the emphasis on the accomplishments of the group rather than of the individual, in Cuba, through the Pioneer organization, the outstanding students must learn humility and recognize their role in communicating and sharing their skills with others.

I witnessed these socialist values in action in a cultural presentation at a school when I acted as coordinator for a delegation of education administrators from the United States. The *jefe de cultura* ensured that students were in their proper places for the presentations. At each school we heard simple but beautifully done songs and recitations, either in the school gym or outside the building. There were no fancy sets or costumes, just kids in their uniforms, with well-choreographed movements and hand gestures. After a couple of different songs, the children on the gym floor all stood in a semicircle and invited us to hold hands and sing with them while their music teacher played the piano. The Cuban children were happy and at ease holding hands and singing; however, the U.S. adults were somewhat resistant and seemed to find the idea of holding hands with what they perceived as brainwashed children uncomfortable and awkward. Nevertheless, the Pioneers smiled and shouted again, "Hold hands and sing with us!" Eventually the adults did, and they repeated the words to the song "Love in Any Language," which the children sang in French, Spanish, and English.

This U.S. group of education administrators had shared with me their preconceived notions about Cuban education on the bus, before we arrived at the school. They expected to see stiff, unhappy students being forced to behave in some unreasonable manner. Instead they saw loving, respectful children who wanted to hold hands with each other and their guests and to sing about love. When the adults finally lifted their arms and swayed from side to side with the children, I saw tears in the adults' eyes.

The smiling children, their eyes bright and focused and their chests held high, seemed to have broken through the discriminatory barrier erected by these officials. The U.S. education officials found the students' self-esteem, affection, and openness quite remarkable. They engaged the students in open discussion and found their responses reflective and serious. One official asked, "If you could meet anyone in the United States, who would it be, and why?" A

14-year-old girl answered, "A school principal, because I would like to know how school is organized in the United States and how values are transmitted in a capitalist country."

After experiencing their performance and hearing their thoughtful answers, the U.S. officials were still reluctant to give credit to a government that did not school children "the American way." The U.S. officials concluded that what appeared to be self-esteem was merely a façade, that these were fearful children who had been brainwashed to be soldiers from an early age.

I found the attitude and behavior of the delegation, which seemed to reflect socialization in the United States, very disappointing. We met with top-level Cuban education officials in the Ministry of Education (MINED) conference room. The Cuban officials greeted us in suits and ties. In contrast, most of the U.S. group, with full knowledge of the day's agenda, wore shorts and t-shirts. No one from our group even wanted to make the first step in introducing him- or herself (even though many knew Spanish), so I asserted myself as coordinator. As the Cuban officials invited questions from our group, the only person (besides me) who posed a question was a man who asked, "And how do you differentiate your education from indoctrination?" Originally I had thought that being coordinator for this group would enable me to have greater access or permission to document Cuban schooling. After that question, I thought my research opportunities in Cuba were over.

When I think back on my classroom experiences as a teacher, it seems to me that one reason why U.S. students do not exhibit as much self-esteem is because they have been taught to focus on themselves first and foremost, leaving them ignorant of the value of exploring difference and cultures outside the mainstream. I have often witnessed Americans compensating for their ignorance by criticizing and bullying others. By the end of the trip, I was elated when a Cuban education official approached me and commented on my behavior being quite different from the others'. He tried to figure out why I was with this group. After I explained, he said, "Just watching the behavior of these education leaders from your country helps me understand why there might be problems in your education system."

With the Pioneer infrastructure in the Cuban school system, students are given far more responsibility, voice, and vote than one would usually find in capitalist countries. Students elect leaders, or jefes, and take peer supervision seriously. More often students would resolve arguments or incidents among themselves. The power rarely stood solely with the teacher or administrator. As a result, students exercised responsibility, leadership, and cooperation, and there was an emphasis on collective goals rather than individual ones.

Sometimes the jefes of the different divisions overlapped, as in the case of a political enactment. The *jefes de política* and *cultura* together might coordinate political "*actos*," patriotic presentations to commemorate various days of revolutionary observance, such as the birth of José Martí, the Bay of Pigs Invasion, or the Literacy Campaign. The jefes would meet and discuss ideas and options with the students, such as the logistics for parades or marches or the choices of skits, songs, or choreography. Through this democratic process they set goals and worked to achieve them together.

Cuban students have been groomed from an early age for formal presentation, performing their work both collectively and individually. As I was told by my schoolteacher friend, Adela, with whom I lived, "All Cuban children, even at five years of age, can recite at least half a dozen poems by José Martí." I had living proof from hearing Adela's daughter, Clarita (five years old), not only recite but also sing patriotic songs endlessly as she colored pictures on the dining room table after the evening meal each night.

In fact, the presentation of the work was as important as the content. Students learned the history behind the work they were involved in so they would not merely recite empty words but assign meaning, with appropriate gestures and facial expressions. The outcome was amazing. Each school seemed to have a repertoire of production pieces that included recitation, song, and dance, and on a moment's notice a large number of students could perform the piece.

Academically, the *jefe de estudio* (studies) tried to ensure that students who did not understand the lessons were getting the help they needed to succeed in class. Socialist emulation was intended to be a win-win situation, with the desired outcome being that *all* students succeeded. The point was to draw on a type of learning concept by which those who understood assisted their struggling classmates academically and morally. Also, within the classroom, other students assumed leadership roles as student monitors: in taking attendance, being a teacher's aid in giving individual explanations, checking homework, and assisting others with assignments. Socialist emulation promoted shared excellence, which required the one who excelled to help those who were experiencing difficulty. Outside school, students gathered to study at students' homes. The designated home, or *casa de estudio*, was informally chosen. There, students would meet to do homework collectively.

As illustrated by these many examples, the mission of the Pioneer organization was woven into all student activities, on campus or off: the promotion of revolutionary values, of which conciencia would be the end product.

The same type of honing of revolutionary values was evident in a peer assessment called "*la autocrítica*," which occurred in assemblies. I attended a ninth-grade class's *autocrítica*, for which the class had gathered under a tree outside the school building. The atmosphere was relaxed. One student was asked to stand and reflect out loud on his strengths and weaknesses as a Pioneer. His classmates were then asked by the teacher whether they agreed or not, or whether they wished to add anything. Self-reflection, emulation, and the election of new jefes were the function of *autocrítica*. According to the teachers I spoke with, this type of self and peer critique normally started in first grade. Over the years, this exercise seemed to have prepared students for public critique and to have helped them develop a keen sense of who they were, in respect to strengths and weaknesses, when measured against the revolutionary ideal.

Also in the mid-1990s, to reinforce the revolutionary values, value-formation hour was implemented to provide an unstructured time for discussion between teachers and their students. During one class hour a week, students were encouraged to bring up any topic they wanted to discuss. I attended one discussion on the topic of prostitution. A couple of students spoke about a neighbor who was a prostitute and questioned why it should be morally condemned. The teacher's answers seemed to be insufficient for them. There were no books or script for the teacher, but the teacher responded with the *teque* (official rhetoric) when her reasoning seemed unsatisfactory to the students. Still, the idea that a casual, conversational space at school had been provided to discuss what most concerned the students was an important step in validating students' concerns about and confusion over the difficult reality they lived.

Another program developed during the nineties was the Pioneer Action Forces (Fuerzas de Acción Pioneril, FAPI). The principal objective of FAPI was to organize students for socially useful work in the community, factories, and educational and service centers to "deepen their sentiment for the love for work" (*Orientaciones* 1998, 1). This program involved the Pioneers on a voluntary basis in an organized program of work in the community for one week after final examinations at the end of the school year. The teachers and administration benefited greatly from the students' participation. I watched as students completed an inventory of the school furniture, scraped gum off the undersides of desks, and did a thorough cleaning of the school. About fifteen students from the ninth grade showed up, and, as in all other Pioneer activities, they starting by appointing a jefe and organizing tasks along an assembly line model, which helped them complete the work efficiently and effectively.

The parents of these students were pleased by this opportunity to help out at school because they knew where their children were and that they were being supervised. FAPI reinforced the concepts of being useful to society and being productive, which the parents whole-heartedly supported. The children were with their peers, and they did not seem to mind doing the work. When I asked the students what they thought of the experience, one student said, "I like helping. It's not hard work." Another said, "It's a good thing to do. I like being with my friends." Moreover, the students received credit for their work, as it was documented in their files and, like other work projects, would pay off later when the students tried to secure placement in the university.

Clubs

Clubs are organized on campus according to the hobbies and interests of students. Some examples include stamp or coin collecting, cooking, sewing, aviation, electronics, history, sports, politics, and nature. At Granma Junior High School, the only clubs I was aware of were one on José Martí and another on the judicial system. From what I could tell, the clubs seemed more teacher-generated than student-generated. A couple of students confirmed my observation. A teacher was a part of each club, and students offered ideas to probe or, in the case of the José Martí club, to celebrate. Students were encouraged to be goal-oriented and to decide on a final product for their time spent together.

Lizabet invited me to her club's reading of the trial of those who sailed with Fidel and Che from Mexico to Cuba on the *Granma* in 1953 to overthrow the Batista government. All twenty-five student members of the club participated and showed excitement in dramatizing the Manichean struggle between the accused "heroes" and the judge. After several rehearsals, they arranged to walk to another junior high school nearby to present the play. The students warmly received them.

Lizabet's position as a teacher of civic education and sponsor of *el club jurídico,* I soon learned, was part of an effort on her part to come to terms with her son's death. Almost ten years had passed since her 17-year-old son went out to walk on the *malecón* (seawall) one night with his buddies and stopped to help a woman change her flat tire. While they were changing the tire in the street an army jeep sped by, hitting her son and killing him almost instantly. Witnesses were shocked; the army jeep never returned. Lizabet identified passengers in the jeep by holding her index and middle finger together and tapping her shoulder. She clarified: "military officials who were drunk." She tried to press charges, but the charges were dropped and she was compensated with just enough money to pay for her son's burial in the city cemetery. Her anger and grief could not be contained. She asked me, "Do you think drunken men who kill an innocent person should go unpunished? They never lost status or served time for their crime." She challenged the state relentlessly, seeking justice; however, the men remained "protected."

He had been her only son. She said her husband dealt with it by making a decision to attend the Protestant Church, whereby, as she described his re- solve, "he became a Christian." She had heard what she considered the church teque, which seemed to have minimized or desensitized her husband's pain over the loss. He had chosen not to talk about it anymore. However, Lizabet explained,

> My love and pain for my son cannot be extinguished. There's not a day that goes by that I don't think about him all day. Teaching is the most construc- tive way I can deal with it. Teaching justice, rights and duties to my students. It's the only way to make the world a better place.

Although the loss of her son and the circumstances surrounding it were never openly discussed, students seemed to know about the tragedy, if not from Lizabet herself, then perhaps just from the dynamics of being a commu- nity, which had tried to console her in her grief. It is this aspect of Lizabet's humanness and struggle with the state that has made her the well-respected and well-loved person she is in the La Flor[7] community, especially when teaching civic education and leading the club *jurídico*. Knowing that her struggle is an ongoing one that has no resolution, students know they are not alone in making sense of the world in which they live. Lizabet would confirm that all is not right with the world, but would add that the possibility still existed for people to make it better.

Interest Circles

The clubs met once a week after school, as did the interest circles. Whereas the clubs met on campus, the interest circles for Granma Junior High School met at the Che Guevara Pioneer Palace, about a twenty-minute bus ride from the school. Clubs focused on interests and hobbies, while interest circles ex- plored possible vocations. Both were optional. However, whereas the clubs were open to as many students as were interested, the interest circles were selective.

Granma's scheduled time to go to the Pioneer Palace was from 1:00 to 3:00 p.m. on Tuesdays. About forty of us waited in excitement on the side- walk of the school for the Russian bus to come by and take us to Lenin Park, where the Pioneer Palace was located. Approximately twenty students had been selected from eighth and ninth grades to attend for the spring semester. The Pioneer Palace interest circles seemed to be a vocational honing ground for the vanguard students. Although Lizabet told me that student selection was based on good public behavior, several students and parents informed me that student selection was based on grade average. "Often the students with good behavior are the ones who make high grades," one parent clarified. Perhaps this was the reason for conflicting information regarding the selection process.

Judging from the students' reaction, going to the Pioneer Palace for interest circle time seemed comparable to the idea of taking U.S. students to Disney's Epcot Center for class once a week. The Che Guevara Pioneer Palace was built in 1980 and is an immense complex with stimulating, up-to-date resources and facilities. Prior to this time, interest circles were extracurricular activities, but they were not housed in centers as fancy as the palaces. They used to meet on school premises, and the interest circles met in factories.

In 1980, each province either constructed or converted a building into a Pioneer Palace. Some of the buildings that were converted were pre-revolutionary mansions. In the case of Havana, a new contemporary structure was built that had more than a hundred rooms, a beautiful, Olympic-sized swimming pool, a farm, a bakery, state-of-the art machinery, equipment, and vehicles (a commercial airplane, tractors, a full-size military boat, and cars), and large areas for entertainment, including a basketball court. The bus circled the complex and stopped at four of the primary areas. Students got off at their predetermined stops (they had chosen their interest at the beginning of the semester).

There were seventeen areas: agriculture, construction, health, sugar production, MINIT (state security, offered by the Ministry of the Interior), commerce, communications, food production, radio, television and film, fishing, industry, electronics, tourism, aeronautics, FAR (Fuerzas Armadas Revolucionarias—military), transportation, and teaching. Within each area were specializations, and these specializations became the interest circles. For example, within tourism a student might choose the vocation of baker, beautician, or hotel service, bars and soda fountain service, or food preparation. Within MINIT, students could learn how to be a coast guard or a firefighter, or how to conduct security checks.

In Havana, these interest circles covered more than 150 academic specialties and were tied to twenty-three branches of the economy. Each of the seventeen areas was linked with a government division that provided raw materials and instructors for the Pioneer Palaces. By tying educational experience more closely to the economy, the interest circles performed an important function. A society that supposedly has forgone the use of wage incentives needs an alternative means of encouraging young people to enter occupations in short supply. Thus the interest circles are a means of informing young people about the content of various educational pursuits while at the same time stimulating student interest in careers likely to make a major contribution to national development. The interest circles are the bridge between the school curriculum and a student's future productive activity.

The representative at the Pioneer Palace told me that the areas and interest circles change depending on the needs of the country. She said that tourism was an example of a new area introduced in the early 1990s. "It is important that students learn how to behave in the midst of tourism," she said, "that they don't beg . . . that they are helpful, patriotic, and continue to work hard." However, a tourism interest circle did not seem to be an easy change to adapt to. According to a research document at MINED, "the theme of tourism constitutes, without a doubt, an important challenge from the educational perspective, for those who pursue value inculcation" (McPherson Sayu 1994, 2). The author's findings show that a focus on a natural setting—that is, a return to the countryside and community service—helps offset "the tourist culture."

Approximately eight students participated in each interest circle, which was directed by a professional who volunteered his or her time at the Pioneer Palace on a weekly basis. The adult volunteer gives students a hands-on experience of what the profession is like. In the health area, I went to the surgery interest circle. A doctor showed and explained the equipment to the students. She focused on the heart and explained its function in detail while pointing to the different arteries on the anatomy chart. The doctor spoke from her own experiences with heart transplants, and the students listened intently and asked questions, intensely engaged all the while. Afterward all the students had a chance to practice the heart transplant on the plastic dummy.

Another time I went to the veterinary clinic in the area of agriculture. The veterinarian showed us photographs of different farm animals and explained their biological development. On our second visit he took us outside to the pigpens and demonstrated how to castrate a pig. Then, following the veterinarian's directions, all of the students castrated pigs. I took pictures. Although the students encouraged me to do the same, claiming that I had been through the same training they had, I excused myself and jokingly told them I could not because I did not have the same conciencia that they had. They laughed but still insisted on my participation. Finally, to quiet them, I stated my only compromise: to hold a baby goat and let them take my picture.

It was clear to me that attending interest circles was a highlight of these children's lives. There was no homework and no grades were taken, and there were many novelties with which they could experiment. In addition, there was a fifteen-minute break from the interest circles, and students could then go to a recess area and play ball and be served ice cream. They saw something authentic, even though they did not live on a farm and few students had parents who were doctors. Seeing and touching equipment and animals undoubtedly stimulated them to learn more.

At the end of each semester, those who had been meeting in each interest circle collectively created a presentation for the others. In this way the students not only shared what they had learned but also stimulated interest among the others for when they would make their choices for the next semester. At the Pioneer Palace, students enjoyed making the presentations because they had access to costumes and all the materials they could think of to make a poster or a construction of some sort.

My only concern was how these children internalized the material contrast between their neighborhood reality and the Pioneer Palace. Students assumed the roles of stewards and stewardesses on an authentic Cubana jet. They served me and other students drinks and snacks, and practiced their English. How did this mesh with their future reality? How did students feel about learning auto and bike mechanics on new cars and fancy road bikes? The children from La Flor learned to ride a bicycle for the first time at the Pioneer Palace, and they were learning to repair the bicycles with specialized tools they had never seen before. These were not even the standard Chinese Flying Pigeon bicycles seen in Cuba. I was told that the sporty eye-catching bikes at the Pioneer Palace had been donated by another country. How did students negotiate their neighborhood surroundings of "*no hay*" ("there isn't any," an expression often heard when going to the bodega for one's ration) and "*inventos cubanos*" (a makeshift way or thing to substitute for what does not work) with the fantasy of the Pioneer Palace?

One day when I visited the quality control interest circle, the eight ninth-grade students and I sat at a table while the teacher showed us Cuban magazine advertisements (another novelty; few Cubans can afford to buy a magazine) promoting the national brand of toiletries, Suchel. One ad had a picture of Sandra Bullock (or a look-alike) lying on her side in a skimpy jungle outfit advertising Suchel deodorant. In a toothpaste advertisement there were five blond-haired, blue-eyed smiling men and women with interlocked arms running from waves breaking on a beach. The students recognized that in both advertisements, the models were advertising Cuban products but were not Cuban. When the teacher left the room briefly, the students joked about the "hidden script" in these images, wanting me to understand how crazy the learning experience was for them. They dared each other to confront the teacher (and the teque), and one did when she returned. "Teacher, is that Sandra Bullock in that ad?" "Of course not," she answered. "She is a Cuban woman." "Are you sure, teacher?" The teacher held her stand. Then the students asked, "Are those Cubans in the beach scene?" "Yes, of course." Taking the point one step further, a boy asked, "Then why are they portraying Cuban culture as all white? Why aren't there any blacks or mulattos, only blue eyes and blond hair?" She retorted, "You know Cubans come in all colors. There are Cubans with blond hair and blue eyes." The students went no further but gave me a confirming stare that said, "See what we mean? The teachers know, and they know that we know, but discussions about reality can only go so far."

As these circles inform students about the content of various professions, what messages are they giving the students about the mode of operation and the social relations of production in promoting products, in recognizing fashion, and in knowing how to repair cars or late-model bicycles, which the majority of the population do not have? With Cuba being known for its medical training and performance, how do students reconcile the absence of medical equipment and supplies for Cubans while fully equipped hospitals exist for foreigners? Likewise, with the history of Cuba's sugar production, why is it that the residents of La Flor did not receive their standard monthly ration of sugar while dollar stores were well stocked with the product? Finally, how do students make meaning of the promotion of quality national products (such as the Suchel brand) sold in dollars but not available for purchase in Cuban pesos?

Whether students posed these questions internally or externally, I was curious as to how the students understood the obvious difference in resources and teaching between their home community and this fantasy park. When I asked a couple of students about this difference, one said, "Maybe this can be our future?" They aspired to "be someone" and to "make a difference in this world." The vocational interest circles certainly stimulated their thinking about a future profession and staying in school.[8] The Pioneer Palace modeled a technologically advanced society, a longstanding goal of the revolution. How long will the hopes of this generation of students hold out?

While most schools around Havana have a scheduled time to go to the Pioneer Palace each week, Ciudad Libertad,[9] a large educational compound made up of many schools (and ones deemed better than most city schools), did not. Apparently, this was a way to equalize differences between neighborhoods, and with the economic crisis, the cost of gasoline to transport all schoolchildren to the outskirts of town would be prohibitive. Therefore, Ciudad Libertad had its own small building where five different interest circles met. These interest circles did not have the same amount or quality of supplies as were available at the Pioneer Palace, but certainly sufficient to give exposure to the target professions. I attended the teaching interest circle, where the teacher was showing the students how to repair school books, and I went to the construction interest circle, where students were asked to draw plans for cabañas at a tourist resort. The students in both interest circles were working hard and were very engaged in their projects. One teacher told me they did not go to the Pioneer Palace because Ciudad Libertad accommodated students on premises. From what I could ascertain, student and adult interest was not as high at this location, and the interest circles had been canceled twice, once because the adult volunteers did not come and once because the students did not come. Was this modest version of interest circles insufficient as an *estímulo?*

Cuban educators see the interest circles as an important link between the curriculum and the students' ultimate vocational choice. The circles are vital in guiding students into areas of needed labor in their changing society. In Havana, it was evident that various campaigns were in place to direct students into the teaching profession, including the promotion of teaching interest circles. Substantiating these campaigns, Cuba's education minister, Luis Ignacio Gómez, praised a new contingent (cohort) of teachers for helping compensate for "the lack of educators island-wide" (Radio Havana, 2000). Seven years later, after the implementation of additional teacher recruiting campaigns, numbers were still low: "The number of teachers and their quality of preparation is insufficient. There is not enough enrollment in teacher education programs to meet our needs" (Mayor Lorán 2007, 6). By 2009, Fidel stated "the most serious problem is not having sufficient teachers. . . . The success of our Revolution, the security of our future, the success of our socialism will depend in large part on the ability to recruit and train Cubans for the teaching profession." He affirmed that "education is the most powerful weapon . . . to create consciousness" (Mayor Lorán 2009, 4). The scarcity of personnel continues to reveal a chronic questioning if not critique of the usefulness and relevance of institutionalized schooling in Cuba. In a personal interview with two teachers, they commented: "Parents do not encourage their children to go into the profession." They explained that the only people who could afford to be teachers are those who have a spouse or family member making money outside of Cuba or in tourism. In addition, the two teachers spoke of the disconnect between trying to speak of the heartfelt rewards of teaching and the virtues of hard work for the betterment of society, when their basic material needs were not being met.

While I was at Granma Junior High School, the teachers were asked to promote their profession and give public testimonies at an assembly in February. In March the ninth-grade students were asked to submit their plans for their future vocation and schooling, including which school they would attend for tenth through twelfth grades—a regular *pre en el campo* or a more specialized school. None of the 174 ninth-grade students chose teaching. I asked students about this, and their replies were all similar: "There's no money in teaching. You work harder and longer than at any other state job, and you don't earn enough to eat." "Other professions have some type of 'perk' from the state. You may receive *una jaba* [a bag] of supplies from that industry, like detergent or paper, but what do we have access to materially in this profession? Not even chalk or an eraser." "'Love for teaching?' I call it martyrdom for the state." "My parents would not let me even if I wanted to. Our profession needs to be a rational decision." The administrative efforts to guide students into the teaching profession at Granma Junior High did not seem to alter the students' choices.

The principal called a faculty meeting and encouraged the teachers to "approach students personally" and do everything in their power to get a commitment from at least one student. By the end of the week, one meek girl quietly committed to teacher training. At a school assembly she was presented before the student body as if she were a heroine. Flooding her with attention, the faculty and administration deemed her service to her country to be of the highest moral code. They mentioned that she was truly a model revolutionary. However, after the many accolades and a call for more to serve the revolution through the teaching profession, the students remained silent. The routine mechanisms had failed. With different formal educational mechanisms at work to direct students' career choices in service to the state, ultimately, the students seemed to be guided by economic logic and personal interests.

The Explorers

Together with vocational orientation, students are given orientation in military defense and outdoor survival from grades one through nine in the Explorers, a division of the Pioneers.[10] In the Explorers, students learn outdoor survival skills and defense skills in case of war. *La Ley del Movimiento de Exploradores* (the Law of the Movement of the Explorers) reads: "*Conoce y cuida la naturaleza. Aprende a valerse de ella y se prepara para la Guerra de todo el pueblo*" (To know about and take care of nature. To learn to appreciate it and to prepare oneself for all-out war) (*Compendio* 1995, 84).

The Explorers organization was created at the time of the Mariel boatlift (1980), when the Pioneers were called on to participate, together with the rest of the *pueblo,* in meetings to condemn those who were leaving the country. The Pioneers organized "*actos de reafirmación revolucionaria*" that demonstrated their enthusiasm and combative disposition (Ferrer 1987, 141). With this incident, the Pioneer organization was broadened to include the Explorers, in order to better prepare children for "difficult situations" politically or while living in a more rustic setting (Ferrer 1987).

The focus is survival. In learning about nature, students learn the names of different plants and insects, how to tie knots, how to build a fire, outdoor cooking skills, first aid, signs and symbols, how to make a backpack from a shirt, and how to hang a hammock. In case of war, students also learn maneuvers for protecting themselves: shooting a gun, the proper use of a gas mask, and defense procedures.

The Explorers met every Friday after school for one hour and dedicated this time to learning survival skills. Occasionally I would see students practicing their knots. Finally, I saw the culmination of their work in a *concurso* (contest) against another junior high school, where all events were timed and judged. Students were put on teams and had to run fifty feet, where there was a rope on the ground and they had to quickly pick up the rope and tie a certain type of knot, which the jefe would shout out to the competing groups. The same procedure went for starting a fire. But because it would be difficult to determine who built a fire the fastest, the end point of the competition was extended: a string was stretched between two sticks (three feet high), one on either side of the firepit, and the first group whose fire broke through the string was the winner. In the final relay students had to run a short distance, put on a gas mask, then run back to the group. To top off the competition, each group had to create an original nutritional dish that reflected nature and patriotism. This seemed to be quite a challenge. Leaves that spelled "Martí" topped one casserole dish made of garbanzo beans. Someone tore up a piece of cardboard to use as plates and served casserole on each piece. Another small piece of cardboard served as an eating utensil. Everyone tasted the unusual food. Although their faces confirmed its strangeness, there were no complaints.

Each grade level had at least one camping experience a year. In addition, there were sometimes sleepovers at a school gym or in a public park close by. One Saturday I accompanied the ninth grade on an excursion to ITM (Instituto Tecnológico Militar, the military school in Havana). The school was gated, and we had to pass through a security kiosk. Uniformed military officials at the school met us on the grounds and gave us an orientation to the training that went on at the school. Then we sat outside in a big grassy area surrounded by the school buildings while the men told us about the school's history and mission. The principal introduced me to the officials and explained my presence. They allowed me to stay, but I was not allowed to take notes, record anything, or take pictures.

After the talk, some students built a fire. Everyone brought a vegetable and added it to the cauldron, and we made a big stew. While it was cooking, some students played volleyball and others relaxed on the grass in small groups and talked. The atmosphere was conducive to solidifying friendships. The focus on work, ideology, and responsibilities was minimal; the goal seemed to be to bond the school community outside the school environment.

In the same vein, we had another excursion at night to a large public swimming pool near the *malecón*. Salsa music played from the speakers, and students were given coupons for ice cream. Some chatted in groups while others danced. The teachers stayed together and kept an eye on the students from a distance while they talked about good shopping bargains and family life, including me in their conversations.

The excursion to the military school and the one to the swimming pool, according to the teachers, were examples of one of the ways the Pioneer organization operated to make the school community more cohesive: "to foster a bond of affection that would lead to an allegiance to the rehearsed revolutionary values and build *conciencia*." By occupying additional after-school hours, the "government also hoped that students would become more interested in staying in school and attending extracurricular activities where they had strong friendship bonds and positive memories."

Interestingly, both the Pioneer Palaces and the Explorers were initiated at the end of 1980, after the Mariel boatlift. Designated camping areas specifically for the Explorers were constructed and Pioneer Palaces were erected. Sometimes dances would be organized at the Pioneer Palaces too. These entertainment measures seemed to ensure that the children's activities would be supervised by the state. With many Pioneer activities planned off-campus, together with encouraging participation and leadership in the Pioneers on campus, this mass organization was a channel for state control of the socialization of young people.

Through the Explorer activities the state could revive the "codes of passion" (Fernández 2000), such as militarism and living in rugged conditions in the out-of-doors, prominent in the Sierra Maestra guerrilla experience and intended to cultivate revolutionary conciencia.[11] Students learned war defense and survival skills, hiking, and primitive camping. Moreover, by learning war preparation, students were reacquainted with imperialism's threat to society and the consequent need for militarization. In 1990, at the beginning of the Special Period, in part a manifestation of the government's strategy to arouse ideological fervor and in part to keep surplus labor busy, the leadership sponsored a major military readiness campaign in anticipation of a potential U.S. invasion. At the center of this effort was the construction of an elaborate system of defense tunnels by the country's youth (FBIS 1992b). The tunnels can be interpreted as an example of the way the hegemonic state looks back to the innovations of the sixties to try to regulate the life of subordinate groups, in this case the youth.

This tunnel work project of the youth corresponds to other projected images alerting the pueblo that they are under attack. With *"refugio"* signs in public buildings, escape maps on the backs of doors in case of war, and underground tunnels in many of the schoolyards, the message was clear: the pueblo must be ready for defense. War drills happen on a regular basis. I heard sirens from my Cuban home for *"día de la defensa."* The community in which I lived marched to Ciudad Libertad. There, children and their parents practiced shooting and the use of the tunnel if under attack.

New After-school Activities

In the late 1990s, the scheduling of Pioneer after-school activities started to come into conflict with a new interest: church activities. An evangelical Protestant church had just been constructed two blocks from the school. The Cuban church had a sister church in the United States, and donations were arriving continuously. As I sat on the sidewalk with Yuneisy, she told me about the cute summer outfit she got in a plastic bag. "And it's new, not used!" She exclaimed.

Yuneisy was a *militante* (leader) in the UJC. To be in the UJC, a student had to pass a very rigorous scrutinizing by both peers and teachers; students were carefully selected. The *militantes* and the other members were announced at the end of the ninth-grade school year. Watching Yuneisy examine her new outfit in its plastic bag, I asked her,

"Do you attend this church, Yuneisy?"

"Sometimes."

"Do you believe in what they are teaching in the church?"

"I don't have a problem with it. The people are nice and they are very generous. But I can't participate in the youth activities there because I have to make my UJC meetings and that has to take priority. But the church has fun things too. . . ."

"Do they offer donations often?"

"Yes." She smiled and giggled, a little embarrassed.

Donations attracted attention, partly because Cubans felt that the government usually diverted them from their final destination. Adela, the woman with whom I lived, told me that the frequent donations of used clothing and medicine from foreign organizations usually were rerouted for sale in the Cuban peso stores. With churches offering new or even used clothes to congregations at no cost, one is left to wonder whether increased church attendance has more to do with religious freedom or access to material items.

However, people in the neighborhood talked quite a bit about the Protestant Church—a sign that the church's organizational mechanisms might be successful in their mission to lead people spiritually. Alain, a 13-year-old boy, told me he had been given the opportunity to play the piano for services and sing. He loved serving the church. Finally, near the end of my stay, three Protestant churches, including the one in La Flor, organized a festival of Christian music outdoors in a wide street at the edge of the La Flor neighborhood. They brought out risers and had families parading down the street for a mile. Adela and her children participated too. She estimated that at least a couple of thousand people attended. She commented that she had never seen such a large turnout for anything other than at the Revolutionary Plaza for a revolutionary event.

International events, such as the pope's visit, as well as developments in Cuban socialism, filtered through a personal affective prism, contributing to the creation of other independent organizations as well as increased attention on keeping the Pioneer organization up to date with social, economic, and political trends. The liveliness of the Catholic and Protestant religious communities, as evidenced by increased church attendance and a growing number of church publications, is unprecedented (Fernández 2000). Moreover, churches are well positioned to spearhead the revival of civil society, building on moral capital and the uncertainty of the Special Period—a time when people typically seek answers to existential questions and the affective solace of religion.

These new civil developments (such as churches, self-employment, joint ventures, and NGOs) are negotiating a public space for themselves within the existing structure. Since the late 1990s these programs, institutions, and organizations have been presenting Cubans with new options. One way these "outside" influences have affected the Pioneer organization has been in the way students define "Pioneer."

¡Seremos como el Che!

To illustrate perhaps a generational evolution or dissolution in the internalization of revolutionary values that constitute conciencia, I juxtapose the conversation that Karen Wald (1978, 183–184) had with a dozen Pioneers in first grade in the mid-1970s with survey responses I collected from thirty-nine ninth graders in 1999. Here is Wald's interview:

"What does it mean to be a *Pionero?*" I asked one little girl. She blushed shyly, looking down at her toes.

"It means to be a communist," offered one of the other children. "It means to be like Che."

"Are you all communists?" I asked them. "Do you all want to be like Che?" They nodded their heads enthusiastically.

"I'm gonna be like Tania," chimed in a little girl.

I smiled. "Who was Tania?" I asked.

"She fought in Bolivia with Che," several voices told me.

"She was a guerrilla. An internationalist."

In the survey I administered to thirty-nine students about revolutionary values, I asked, "¿Qué significa ser Pionero?" (What does it mean to be a Pioneer?) Whereas in Wald's study, the students answered with revolutionary terms, such as "communism," "Che," and "Tania," the responses I received on my ninth-grade survey yielded much less emphasis on revolutionary terminology. The answers varied tremendously, with most answers (43 percent) including a phrase about being proud or honorable people. In contrast to Wald's study, in my survey only seven of the thirty-nine students used revolutionary terminology (two used "revolution," four "patriotic," and one made reference to José Martí) in their answers. The more common phrases were "It means a lot." "It's something very important." "It means to be a good student." "It means to work hard and be useful." Ironically, with the Pioneer motto "Pioneros por comunismo, seremos como el Che," not a single student used "Che" or "communism" in defining the significance of being a Pioneer.

At Ciudad Libertad I was not granted permission to conduct the same survey[12]; however, I was allowed a short audiotaped conversational session alone with a group of twelve ninth-grade students who were waiting outside a school building for rehearsal. Although these students were enthusiastic about being interviewed, they did not seem to exhibit the same enthusiasm in their answers that Wald noted in her study. When I asked them the meaning of being a Pioneer, they all told me that to be a Pioneer was "to be a Cuban student." I questioned the whole group: "No one disagrees or has anything to add?" They all seemed a bit confused, trying to think about what else I might have been expecting. Then a student added, "It means to work hard and study." I probed a bit deeper, "What then is the difference between a Pioneer and a student in another country, say, Mexico?" The students all showed signs of supporting the answer of the vanguard student who became the spokesperson: "The difference is that in Mexico, they call their students one thing and in Cuba we call our students 'Pioneers.'"

Perhaps one could say that my survey and oral interview were just circumstantial. But after spending time with revolutionaries, including men who had served in the Sierra Maestra and men and women who had participated in the Literacy Campaign, I believed these people concurred that Che Guevara was no longer talked about as much as he used to be. They told me that Che had been a model for a set of different political and historical circumstances. He had spearheaded the command economy and advocated the use of moral incentives exclusively. He promoted the "new socialist man," one who would be exhorted to labor for society without personal gain, out of a sense of moral commitment. Apparently, at present, Che's economic platform had little relevance for a mixed-market economy with accompanying conflicting values.

There were times I was tempted to ask, in the context of a mixed-market economy and a value crisis, "What would Che do?" However, I realized from the looks of these revolutionaries regarding my "'Che' questions" that they thought I was caught in a time warp or a nostalgic idealism, and that they were ready to move on to another topic. In a society where people were struggling to get enough to eat, the idea of working without remuneration seemed crazy. Abundant material incentives were now being used in industries, from cigar factories to *agropecuarios* (produce markets). In addition, self-owned businesses, joint ventures, and tourism were becoming more popular. Perhaps the name "Che," along with the word "communism,"[13] is heard less today than in the early seventies because of its lack of relevance. The aspired communist utopia of the sixties has resulted in something vastly different than anyone ever dreamed of.

As I spoke individually with these revolutionaries who had either participated in the Sierra Maestra campaigns or taught in the Literacy Campaign, I would ask them to recount their stories from that time.[14] Inevitably these 58- to 70-year-old people would get tears in their eyes while talking about the past. I was not sure what my role was or what I had unleashed with my curiosity. These experiences became very emotional for me: to hear about people's faithfulness to the revolution, their sacrifices and hard work, as they believed with all their hearts that their service would pay off with a future of material abundance that everyone could enjoy. Understanding the emotional tie that older generations had to the revolution, communism, and Che and how they might feel, knowing their dreams would be unfulfilled, was to me key in understanding what values they might pass on to their children and grandchildren.

The state has struggled to sustain the revolution in terms that would make sense to generations far removed from the revolutionary events of the 1960s. The state attempted to draw on what the leadership saw as relevant themes, such as justice and anti-imperialism (in events such as the Gulf War, the embargo, the battle for custody of Elián, and the U.S. presence in Afghanistan), in mass rallies and in school.

If the motto of the Pioneers no longer coincides with the understanding of the organization students have internalized, what meaning, then, does the omnipresent image of Che, seen on billboards, postcards, posters, t-shirts, lighters, and key chains, have? Even berets with Che's famous star have been mass-produced in Cuba to be sold in tourist areas.

Having fought in the Sierra Maestra with Che, one revolutionary saw the pictures of my dog, Fefa, dressed as different world leaders, and made a suggestion for another picture. He gave me his beret from the Sierra Maestra and a cloth hanging of Che so that I might dress up Fefa as Che, take her picture, and send it to him. When I returned, I brought him a copy of the picture, and I placed it as the opening photograph in my small photo album of Fefa.

The reaction to the picture of Fefa as Che was very interesting. Fefa, a large black mixed-breed dog, sat in an olive green t-shirt with an authentic matching revolutionary beret. In the background hung the cloth wall hanging of Che. Cubans remarked that Fefa had the same steely stare as this image of Che. The Cuban people I showed it to (even MINED officials) were so amused by my dog as Che that they would borrow the album to show it to others. My key contact in Cuba told me that this photo album would be crucial to my gaining access to interviews. Therefore, as I followed her advice, nearly every Cuban laughed, then warned me I should take out the photo of Che because it might cause me problems (Blum 2001).

What do these events tell of the canonized revolutionary hero? Che aligned himself with the socialist vision, in which man would not be alienated from his labor or ultimately commodified, as in capitalism. Ironically, from beach towels to lighters, Che's emblazoned image has become one of the hottest selling items[15] in Cuba for tourists. If the Pioneers motto is "We will be like Che," and if even my dog could be like Che, or any tourist who purchased Che paraphernalia, it seems only logical that the Pioneers would remain detached

Fefa como el Che (my dog Fefa as Che Guevara).

from a historical image that not only came from a different time period but has been transformed into a commodity by the socialist leadership that is removed from its original sacredness. The image of Che has been emptied.

Borrowing from Jean Baudrillard, we can speculate that the commodification of Cuban life during the 1990s has changed not only daily meanings but also the process by which we acquire meaning. While "signs" and their referents used to be more closely related to each other, now commodification mediates the relationship between sign and referent and destroys their immediacy. The sign, the image, comes unbound and can be interpreted according to a broad range of possibilities, according to the logical limits of the code that encloses it (Baudrillard 1983). The image devalues the original by concealing and hiding it. The current images of Che have distorted the referent, just as the images of Che have become more removed from the historical context in which Che lived and died. As Baudrillard (1983, 9) points out, "it is dangerous to unmask images, since they dissimulate the fact that there is nothing behind them." So, for now, Pioneers will continue to repeat their motto, "Seremos como el Che," yet as time passes, I imagine Che's image too will reveal nothing behind it.

The Pioneer organization, with its emphasis on the collective, may continue to give these children moral strength, aptitude, and friendship in the days to come. On countless school projects, students are learning responsibility, cooperation, hard work, emulation, and solidarity. In honing the revolutionary values for citizenship in a socialist society, the mass organizations, including the Pioneers, are facing the challenge of making Cuban politicization and socialization purposeful and revolutionary values relevant in an evolving socialist system.

When push comes to shove, individuals are motivated by economic, affective, and normative convictions, such as career choices. One of the conundrums of Cuba is that it is caught between competing demands: the need to craft an affective attachment to and among the citizenry and the need for technocratic performance and efficiency. Within the Pioneer organization this challenge was met with contrasting images between the politics of passion, or the official discourse, and the politics of affection, a logic or instrumentality used to meet basic needs (Fernández 2000).

Value-formation hour, the interest circles, and vocational clubs were some of the occasions on which the value dissonance became evident. Within these contexts, however, the personal dimension seemed to be the glue that kept the students connected to the structure: the authentic ways in which the students and teachers knew one another, the silent discourse when the teque did not suffice (as in the case of some of the Pioneer Palace interest circles). This affective rationality seemed to be collectively affirmed, whether with articulated words or with behavior.

The Pioneer organization has adjusted its activities to bring them more in line with a changing economic reality. Some of these changes in the mid-1990s included the creation of the value-formation hour, the FAPI, and new interest circles. Nevertheless, with the introduction of these new spaces, which either allow discussion, such as value-formation hour, regarding new capitalist measures and their accompanying values or simply allow students to toy with the novelties presented in interest circles, what kind of conciencia is being taught or internalized?

If Che's veneration and image as the model New Man become consumer products for tourists, what does this tell us of the evolution of Cuban citizenship, and of Cuba's future citizens? Will Cubans consistently have to sell out their revolutionary values of honesty and honor through black marketing, prostitution, and so forth to survive, or have these values been appropriated in new ways? These were the deeper questions I found underlying Cuban schooling, making the modeling of conciencia a strange event, sometimes producing overlapping dualities (Yurchak 2005), as in the case of bitter but patriotic revolutionaries and Lizabet's situation of working through the loss of her son by teaching civic education. What remains is a revolutionary principle that all the money in the world cannot quell, yet has all but deteriorated. Shifts and stability in socialist ideology remain, producing both loyalty and betrayal.

The greatest challenge rests with the teacher who must teach children about the life before them. While in the classroom, Lizabet and other teachers for the most part restricted their dialogue to the curriculum and executed their roles as expected. Off-stage, off-campus, they were quite candid about the difficulty of living and teaching the "hidden transcript," the *doble moral* (dual morality). In essence, they taught what they lived: the norm of simultaneous contradictions. Working with older teachers, such as Lizabet, I noticed their skill in tacking back and forth through the historical shifts of revolutionary experience: reconciling lived experience with *el teque* and one's unrequited belief in socialist values.

The Pioneer organization was a source of affection and personal affirmation for students, and for the most part its structure and activities seemed to be appreciated by teachers, students, and parents alike. The work projects around the school and in the community garden, the Pioneer interest circles, and the Explorers all lent themselves to character building and expanded networks of friendship. The revolutionary values of responsibility, leadership, solidarity, cooperation, patriotism, hard work, and self-government were all being exercised as children maintained the school, weeded the garden, did their homework, and planned further projects together. However, students were aware of the boundaries of formal schooling, where a form of democracy existed with student-run projects and meetings.

The students showed active engagement in the Pioneer activities and displayed a revolutionary-like behavior; however, ironically, none of the students I interviewed connected their Pioneer identity to the revolution, communism, or Che Guevara. The fundamental historical precepts on which the Pioneer organization was founded no longer seemed to be internalized by Cuban young people, who nevertheless repeat the Pioneer motto, "Pioneros por comunismo, seremos como el Che." The disconnect is reflected in the evolution of the symbol of Che Guevara. Che, the model New Man of communism, has now been marketed in the form of key chains and cigarette lighters sold for U.S. dollars in the tourist markets. The disconnect between the symbol and its referent is indicative of a disconnect between behaviors and attitudes, the revolutionary precepts colliding with daily reality. In Vallengrande, fifty yards from where Che's remains were found is a summation written on the wall of the post office: "Che, alive as they never wanted you to be." Paul Theroux (1989, 352) noted, ". . . his intentions were forgotten, but his style was taken up by boutique owners. There is no faster way of destroying a man, or mocking his ideas, than making him fashionable." A comprehensive and tragic death indeed, generating a "new commodified man."

Adherence to a program of self-formation, such as the New Man, requires a real potential for improvement. Are the conditions present today (or were they ever) in Cuba to produce a citizen without personal interests, one who is not motivated by material profit but by moral incentives alone? In revolutionary Cuba, as the Pioneer organization tries to ensure revolutionary commitment in youth, the disconnect resulting from shifts in doctrine continues to present a challenge to educators and those being educated under the current system.

In the school to the countryside program, described in the next chapter, an intense honing of revolutionary values and conciencia is practiced. As the Pioneers went to the countryside, they took on responsibilities collectively, this time as work brigades. When an opportunity arose for me to attend the school to the countryside program, I eagerly packed my suitcase and took my seat on the bus.

CHAPTER 7

Cuba's School to the Countryside Program

Conciencia as Policy

Cuba's school to the countryside program (Escuela al Campo, EAC) mobilizes thousands of urban junior high school students each year to the countryside for approximately one month of agricultural labor, politicization, and socialization. The EAC context not only separates the children from their parents, it also places them in unknown territory and requires them to make sense of it and to carry on. Notwithstanding, the EAC was purposely created as a space in which to secure revolutionary values at a time in life—adolescence—when students are "searching for their individual identity as a person" (Ministerio de Educación [MINED] 1992, 1).

The Cuban Ministry of Education, or MINED, calls the EAC "an incubator for revolutionary commitment," instilling the revolutionary citizenship values of hard work, sacrifice, patriotism, equality, anti-imperialism, responsibility, collectivism, and solidarity with the proletariat, thus creating *conciencia*. The EAC presents an uncommon milieu for analyzing the ways behavioral norms and affective attachments exist in Cuban society. This chapter investigates the link between school and society, focusing specifically on the EAC and its socializing role in creating conciencia in new generations of cubanos.

Cuban young people, the projected vanguard of revolutionary progress, have become ever more removed from the 1959 revolutionary triumph. As a result, major schooling initiatives have emerged to maintain or recreate the revolutionary values, fervor, and commitment necessary to sustain the hegemonic structure.

The idea of the EAC was conceived based on previous successes in using mobilization to and militarization in the countryside to raise consciousness. The government knew that revolutionary consciousness "could not be developed merely by means of propaganda or indoctrination but must arise fundamentally from revolutionary praxis" (Medin 1990, 6), such as through armed struggle or participation in mass actions and mobilizations. In the 1950s the Rebel Army in the Sierra Maestra gained the military support of the *campesinos* (rural farmers) by teaching them literacy skills. The 1961 Literacy Campaign followed, sending more than 100,000 urban young people, clad in olive green uniforms, to some of the most remote regions of the island to teach reading and writing and to impart a new understanding of Cuban history and its future. Conciencia resulted, not only in the emotional and axiological spheres (Fernández 2000) but also ideologically, at a cognitive level, as noted in the writings of Cuban intellectual José Antonio Portuondo (1980, 17): "The young literacy teachers discovered their country, and in a year of direct experience, of immediate contact with the oppressed of country and city, they earned their degrees as revolutionaries and were ready to effect a radical transformation in the unjust social order." The New Left was familiar with this "bodily" process of becoming politically conscious (that is, transformative learning) and termed it "politicization" or "*concientization.*" Paulo Freire (1970) also calls it "*concientization.*" The Cubans called it "*conciencia.*"

By 1966 the EAC had become a major part of Cuban educational policy, and all urban junior high school students were expected to spend time in the countryside. The social aims of the EAC experiment were clearly defined. It was to produce a new kind of man, imbued with love for his country, ready for reform and desirous of increasing the wealth of the community, realizing the value of labor and prizing it, honorable, devoted, and steadfast. More specifically, the aims of the EAC program were to remove the disparity between urban and rural, to establish close links between school and life, to educate the rising generation for work by actually working, and, in line with a common objective, to demand the highest possible standards while respecting the personality of the pupils (Araujo 1976, 12).

The classroom curriculum in many ways prepares students for participation in the EAC program. For example, in the mathematics textbooks, word problems use the agricultural context for learning arithmetic. In the civic education textbook,[1] *el amor al trabajo* (the love of work) is a prominent theme; young people are portrayed as heroes in different types of work, including daily life—defending *la patria* (the fatherland), working in construction, engaging in sports, education, and culture. One photograph shows a teenager aiming an AK-47; others show young people active in the fields. In one, Che Guevara is cutting cane. The captions to these photographs read, "The defense of the socialist patria is the greatest honor and the supreme duty of every citizen," "Work in socialist society is a right, a duty and a motive of honor for every citizen," "Voluntary work, the cornerstone of our society," and "Che: The impulse for voluntary work in Cuba."

With the legalization of the U.S. dollar in 1993 and the increase in flow of family remittances to Cuba, material differences among the Cuban people began adding a new challenge to social equality. When I saw my neighbor, Clarita, at the grocery store where items are sold in U.S. dollars, she took a deep breath, saying,

> With the *escuela al campo* you feel the pinch in your pocket. This cooking oil is to cook extra chicken and to buy some cans of milk and other things that he likes. I know it is not much, but at least this weekend he will have some food with seasoning.

Clarita's food preparation for her son seemed to be the rule rather than the exception. Whereas in the past, students would take only one suitcase, because the state provided much more, since the 1990s two suitcases have been standard, with one suitcase carrying only food. This guarantees some variety to the common daily lunch and dinner, which typically consist of one helping of lentils, rice, and one sweet potato. Families meet after school to strategize ways to help each other out with the items needed for the EAC. In survival mode, the affective network of friends and family fills in the material gap and provides the basics, as the state provides fewer goods than ever before.

With the dissolution of the Soviet bloc in 1989, Cuban society entered the Special Period, from 1996 to 2004. According to Cuban Communist Party officials, the Special Period was a time of extreme material scarcity and market experimentation that ended in 2004. The Special Period did, however, usher in a new notion of the ideal citizen with a socialist conciencia, "*el Hombre Novísimo.*"

El Hombre Novísimo: The Even Newer Socialist Man

During the revolutionary period, from 1959 through the 1970s, the ideal Cuban citizen was a person with the humility and stamina of the campesino yet who also had urban savvy, a classical education, and instruction in Marxist-Leninist ideology. During the Special Period the party began to idealize a new kind of Cuban citizen, the Hombre Novísimo (Even Newer Man)[2]—the focus being on urban man with campesino morals and a campesino soul. This Newer Man was still communist in his modesty and loyalty but was less aligned with a political party and more inspired by the philosophy of José Martí. The Hombre Novísimo had an even stronger sense of national patriotism and unity with all—Marxist and non-Marxist—Latin American struggles against imperial domination (Frederik 2005).

At issue in this debate over the ideal socialist citizen is what is authentically Cuban. The economic crisis of the Special Period forced the Cuban state to market Cuban folklore and Che souvenirs, as well as U.S. consumer items such as Coca-Cola and Nike shoes. These new forms of consumer capitalism have threatened the Hombre Nuevo ideal of the campesino, who has a distinctly Cuban cultural identity, what Frederik (2005) calls *"pura cepa"* (pure stock). Consequently, for many cubanos living in the Special Period, the New Man ideal symbolized Marxist-Leninist notions of a now irrelevant past and irrelevant hero. The public display of *cubanidad* (cubanness) has become increasingly diverse as restrictions on individual expression and religion are relaxed. Wanting to rescue its citizenry from the growing threat of a capitalist "pseudo-culture" of consumerism, the state culture-keepers have been intent on resurrecting the authentic *alma* (soul) of Cuba (Frederik 2005). This means reemphasizing the *pura cepa* ideal of the countryside and campesinos. The state's efforts to revive these ideals make study of the school program, the EAC, especially timely.

Although many American Marxist scholars would emphasize that schools reproduce rigid class inequalities, this chapter explores whether the Cuban Communist Party has been able to mediate the reproduction of class inequalities through educational programs like the EAC. Given the challenges of encroaching consumer capitalism, what type of citizen is the EAC program helping to produce? Is it able to transmit the Hombre Nuevo or the Hombre Novísimo ideals of Cuban identity?

To answer these questions, I look at the historical purpose and context of the EAC based on archival research and review my lived experience with one class of ninth graders from Granma Junior High School in the EAC program. This experience provided me with countless hours of direct observation of and informal conversation with students and teacher.[3]

One of the principal methodologies I used in this interpretive study was to "read" daily discourse through a historical lens. This approach revealed a variety of discrepancies and shades of meaning, and stands in contrast to conventional Western-centered theories, filled with binarisms, which often conceptualize a person or self as a bounded, autonomous individual. Alessandro Duranti argues that it is a mistake to understand meaning in discourse as a "psychological state" that is "fully defined in the speaker's mind before the act of speaking" (1993, 25). Consequently, discursive events tend to be evaluated for their "truth condition" as either true or false.

Echoing Duranti, Saba Mahmood contends that owing to the historical and cultural specificity of a particular discursive formation, "its meaning and sense cannot be fixed a priori" (2001, 212). This suggests that any reading of everyday discourse must always take into account the historical context. Susan Gal and Gail Klingman (2000) expand on this point by emphasizing that discourse embedded in state-controlled societies is particularly susceptible to the larger ideological context. Consequently, any outside observer must learn to interpret everyday talk as a complex negotiation between the state and the ways individual citizens interpret their reality.

The dynamic conception of knowledge as always already partial, situated, and actively produced (Haraway 1988) accounts not only for the semantic (literal) meanings for which ideological discourse stands but also for the pragmatic meanings that emerge in discourse as situated activity. That is, the acts of copying the precise forms of ideological representations become more meaningfully constitutive of everyday life than adherence to the literal meanings (Yurchak 2005). These were some of the fundamental premises that guided the way I "read" or interpreted everyday discourse. As I was to discover, what many Cuban parents and youth say about the EAC program and what they actually do may be at odds. A nuanced reading of everyday attitudes and practices may therefore seem utterly contradictory to non-Cubans.

Preparing for Rural Living: Some Parental Views of the EAC Program

Thirty-five-year-old mother and Communist Party member Vivian recalls her EAC experiences of some twenty years ago. "It was very difficult, but I feel that it made me who I am," she says as she hangs the laundry on the patio. Her daughter's rite of passage is soon to come. But Vivian wants something different for her daughter:

> Thanks to the work I had to do, overall, the first years, I learned to value myself, to persevere in whatever task, to discipline my work habits, including fulfilling the quotas, and to participate in competition among friends. . . . That was very useful later when I had to confront the working world, once I graduated. Now with the young people, like my daughter Elvira, I don't want her to go, and I will get her a medical certificate from the family doctor indicating that she has chronic asthma.

With her affable smile, Vivian admits, "Many times parents with over-protective attitudes are the ones who inhibit their children's spiritual growth by preventing their children from going to the *escuela al campo*." "But if you recognize the value it had in your own life, then why are you reluctant to enforce it with Elvira?" I asked. "The times are different. Every parent wants the best for her or his child."

This short dialogue demonstrates the conflicting and contradictory feelings and actions of parents and their children in respect to the EAC. Vivian is a Communist Party member who uses her party status to negotiate her daughter's absence from the educational system's compulsory and inherently political practice. Vivian explains that the doctor conspires for a small monetary tip or a coveted consumable item, such as beans, cigarettes, fresh fruit, cooking oil, or soap, to produce a medical excuse for her daughter.

Vivian was not alone in opting her daughter out of the program. I surveyed a ninth-grade class of forty students and found that 49 percent did not attend the EAC "for health reasons." This one-class survey, I found, was indicative of the entire ninth-grade class of 279 students, out of which only 50 percent of the students participated.[4] The relationship between work and economy is important, because if the parents or their children do not find this type of education useful in some way, and especially in relation to the labor market, then the state must contend with people's possible disaffection. Although it is tempting to understand Elvira's mother's decision to not have her daughter participate and the bribes accepted by the doctor as acts of political dissent against the state, that would be a mistake. The words of Elvira's mother and her doctor's actions should not be registered in the political and moral categories of a Western democracy. Many living under socialism, like Vivian and her family, genuinely support its fundamental values and ideals, although their everyday practices may appear duplicitous, because they routinely transgress the norms and rules represented in official Cuban ideology.

In a state-controlled discursive environment such as Cuba, the act of copying the precise forms of ideological representations may become more meaningfully constitutive of everyday life than adherence to their literal meanings. The front pages of the newspapers *Granma* and *Juventud Rebelde* (a publication of the communist Pioneers organization) periodically announce that thousands of young people are fulfilling their patriotic duty and demonstrating their love for their country by participating in the work brigades in the countryside. Although Vivian demonstrates her loyal patronage to the Communist Party, she, like many other parents, obtains a medical excuse for her daughter, recognizing the irrelevance of EAC participation in preparing young people for present-day circumstances. She also laments the cost of sending children to the countryside when her daughter could be helping at home or earning money. Vivian admits, "It does not have the same relevance it had for us when we were young."

Parents commonly pointed to a different historical time. As one father explained, "In my time, there was no need to emphasize the service requirement as a means to a career; everyone wanted to go. We were doing our part for our country. It was a way that we, as young people, could contribute to the Revolution." Nonetheless, his wife pointed out,

> Economic conditions were different and we had what we needed then: work clothes, shoes, toilet paper, soap, shampoo, toothpaste, and good food. These were not luxuries back then. There were even shower curtains over the stalls. You won't find these at the campsites anymore. Now the parents must provide what the state does not, so that children can fulfill a duty that will affect their career.

Parents described a time of emotional attachment to the paternalistic state, a time when Cubans believed in the state's promises and served more selflessly. By comparison, currently that belief and service have been eroded by unfulfilled promises, in this case, the substandard conditions at the EAC camps.

Some Student Views of EAC

The young people I interviewed offered some views different from their parents', and often more favorable. What parents often did not seem to fully realize is the social disconnect their children may feel by not going through the EAC program. During the program, one ninth-grade girl explained, "We have fun. We have a chance to be more independent from our families and learn what work is. I am lazy at home and, besides, everyone is going and you don't want to miss out on all of the stories. Everyone comes back with stories." I also asked a mixed group of boys and girls what they found most enjoyable in this program. "I liked best what we did after working." Another ninth-grade girl said, "We would play music and play games . . . dance." "What else did you like?" I asked. "In the EAC, friendship and camaraderie are what I get most out of it. Friendships get deeper. For example, I shared a bunk bed with one girl in the barracks and we became good friends. We were sharing everything." A ninth-grade boy offered, "It's not like at school, where the one who gets the highest grades gets the most attention. I made friends with people that I would not have thought about before because the emphasis is different here. It's on manual work rather than schoolwork. That changes things." Another ninth-grade girl interjected,

> We have to be honest with why we all come. We came to the EAC because it is a school duty, but overall, because it helps us in our career. If in the files where it asks if you fulfilled your duty with the activities offered, that's where this would go, and then you can have whatever career you want.

I probed this a bit deeper: "If your attendance in this program did not affect your future career, would you come?" All of the girls responded with an emphatic "Of course not!" The boys' opinions, however, leaned more on participation, regardless of the possible career incentive. I pondered the answers of these teenage boys, wondering whether they thought they would be seen as less manly if, in this circle of male peers before a woman (me), their answers had expressed distaste for hard work. The students generally recognized this sort of service as part of the immutable discourse reflecting the authority and stability of the Cuban government. The agricultural labor and the recording of one's service or nonservice is predictable and formulaic; one can expect the stereotypical media photographs of young people working in the fields alongside the headlines of "reported" large numbers mobilized.

Citizens often ritually participate in state-sponsored and state-controlled activities like the EAC program because nonparticipation could impede one's career if the family has no party connections. People also simultaneously participate in less formalized spheres of dating, establishing new friendships, and indulging in various small acts of deviating from official norms. This duality of spheres is evident in the previous testimonies of the parents and students about the EAC program, and it is also evident in the everyday practices of the program.

The Wooden Suitcase as Cultural Symbol

Despite the material scarcity, the lack of sufficient food and clothing, the one item of consistency, the one item that no one was without, was the handmade wooden suitcase. MINED officials told me that this type of suitcase went into production specifically to serve the EAC in 1966. No new ones had been made in many years. Nevertheless, each student had one because family members who participated in the 1960s had passed their suitcase down, with each generation giving it a new coat of paint and making sure the family's name or initials and the name of the camp location were well displayed near the handle.

The suitcase's generic exterior gave no hint as to its interior decor. Photographs and magazine illustrations from different generations were pasted on the inside lid. Some showed treasured, far-away family and friends, while other, black-and-white snapshots chronicled the new camaraderie that blossomed at the EAC and a family history of participation in the program. Intermingled with the photographs were magazine illustrations of trendy icons and forbidden USO candy wrappers, offering a taste of fads from different eras. Even though the state sought to provide the necessary luggage for everyone, it attempted to do so in a way that would mask or even suppress individual differences and competition. Nevertheless, individual identity and sentimentality sprouted on the inside of the suitcase lid like wild weeds on a recently tilled field. The unexpected personal markers of identity and resistance mocked the impersonal, classless, utilitarian appearance of the suitcase exterior that was repainted year after year. To what degree did this *maleta de palo* ("stick" or "wood" suitcase, as it was called, because of its simple rudimentary appearance) symbolize the actions and effects of the state in its attempts to mold revolutionary citizens?

Aside from the décor or lack thereof, the other contents revealed a cultural and historical identity as well. Typically, each student packed two suitcases. One suitcase was dedicated to a snack reserve, with such items as crackers, mayonnaise, guayaba paste, toast, and bread pudding (most of which came from the U.S. dollar stores and was bought at high prices). The other suitcase was even more telling of the camp lifestyle, with tattered clothes for working in the fields, toiletries, bed linens, a towel, a bandana, a hat, a spoon, a cup, and a used soda bottle to serve as a water bottle during work in the fields.

Even though the state might not be able to provide the provisions for the *maletas de palo* as it had in the past, during the program's almost forty years of mobilizations, the wooden suitcase still stood, a romantic symbol of educational and generational continuity. It represented the state's attempts to graft the values of collective sacrifice and heroism, solidarity, hard work, responsibility, and leadership onto an identity that it hoped would evolve from an individual one to a collective one. The *maleta de palo* represented the legacy of generations subscribing to the authoritative discourse and also personalizing it for their own use. The EAC ritual and the suitcase's rudimentary appearance were part of the normalization and standardization of Cuban culture. Its longevity gave way to the performative dimension, which began to play a greater role than its constative dimension (reified in various forms as students and their parents found ways to avoid the EAC, to improve their meals by bringing snacks from home in a second suitcase, and to avoid working in the fields.

We loaded the suitcases on two Chevy trucks from the 1950s and boarded the old Russian school buses for our journey to Güines, a *pueblito* (town) in the countryside. The families of the eighth and ninth graders said their last good-byes, many with tears in their eyes. Yuneisy wiped her eyes, saying, "It is hard to think about being away from family. . . . I love them so much." Others told me they looked forward to being just with their friends. However, the toll seemed to be more on the parents than on their children, as reflected by what one mother shared:

> The cost of sending our kids to the *escuela al campo* is more than most of us can afford: the cost of supplementing them with snack food because the food out there is so awful, the cost of paying for the bus ride to go out on Sundays to bring them more food, clean clothes, etc. And, of course, if you don't show up on Sundays, your child really feels let down and you feel like a terrible parent, and others notice you did not make the effort. The conditions of this program are different nowadays; the facilities are not up to par. The state doesn't provide like it used to, and the burden falls on the parents.

Economic conditions, especially since the start of the Special Period, were making parents question how practical this "revolutionary" experience really was and to what degree it was inculcating values in their children that would serve them in the future. It must be noted, however, that such a critique of the role of the state does not reflect dissident ideology. Rather, it reflects different practices that coexist and overlap in the same context. Many parents reported that they did more sacrificing to make this event possible than the state or their children did. The resentment they expressed speaks to the unmet promises of the state, not to the ideals themselves. A dialogical and hybrid quality (Bakhtin 1981) is present in the way parents and youth think about and rationalize the EAC experience. They carry on an internal dialogue over the EAC program being at once meaningful and important and meaningless and unimportant. They harbor anger and resentment that the state does not provide the necessary resources for them to participate in the program even as the state spins "empty promises" that "hard work will bring material abundance for all." Nevertheless, many come to accept the program while finding "personalized" ways to help their children survive the rigors of the countryside.

As the bus pulled away, family members and the departing children waved to each other with both tears of sadness and happy faces. Once we were on the road, the teachers initiated the singing of patriotic Cuban songs, and we swayed from side to side in our seats as we sang. On the one-lane road into the country, blankets of green fields with rows of potatoes, sweet potatoes, and other vegetables welcomed us. In less than two hours we crossed the urban-rural culture boundary. Even after this short ride, I had the sense that a new "family" was forming as these children faced the unknown together.

Güines: '79 Primaveras: The Work Camp

We arrived at our work camp, three miles outside the town of Güines, after turning down a dirt road where a piece of wood was lying on the ground with the camp name painted on it: "'79 Primaveras" (in remembrance of Ho Chi Minh). The site consisted of four buildings huddled close together. In the center was an open dining hall without walls and erected on a concrete slab. It was furnished sparsely with long concrete tables and benches. The two separate wood barracks—one for girls and the other for boys—had a small community stand-alone bath divided by sex. It was equipped with latrines and concrete shower stalls, with small scraps of plastic for shower curtains.

The previous school contingent had left wildflowers in empty soda cans on the dining room tables. Daniel, a student, took one look and said, "Looks like a *misa de muerto* [mass for a dead person]." Everyone laughed, recognizing the obvious connection to Santería.[5] Anxious to get settled at the campsite, the students unloaded their suitcases from the trucks and went to the barracks. The girls' and boys' barracks were basic wooden shelters holding two rows of twenty bunk beds. The barracks were each illuminated by a single light-bulb hanging from the ceiling. The metal-framed bunk beds were well-worn. An old two-inch piece of foam rubber sat on top of a quarter-inch piece of warped wood, supported by the few springs that remained. The toothpaste graffiti of names and dates on the inside walls marked the legacy of former residents.

As students chose their bunk beds and put the linens on their beds, the dynamics of community, cooperation, and collective *resolver* (making do) started to form. Because of the paper shortage, students shared old copies of the *Granma* newspaper for toilet paper. The acute lack of basic necessities did not hit me until an eighth grader, Liliana, asked me, "Can I wear one of your panties during the *campo* [camp]? I don't have any." Liliana then proceeded to show me how to secure my mosquito netting, while another girl, Eulaydis, came over to my bunk bed and tied a red ribbon around my bedpost. She said, with disarming confidence, "The ribbon will protect you from *mal de ojo* [all harm]." Serinay opened a small bag of chips and had only one chip left for herself after offering it around. Students were aware of who had less materially, and they shared what they could of clothing, toothpaste, soap, and toilet paper. At the same time, there were always items stolen and arguments over who owned what items. Necessity drew us together, much as it does in everyday Cuba, in the act of *resolver.*

Without a ceiling fan, the barracks became hot and moist. While we were getting ready for bed, the mosquitoes became so fierce that we started swatting them with our towels. Finally, I initiated dancing with our towels to ward off the mosquitoes. The girls picked up their towels and started swatting them around their waists with dance movements. We added insect puns and exhausted ourselves dancing and laughing until we fell asleep. From that moment on, I became known for my *baile de mosquito* (mosquito dance).

For the first couple of days, not many students showed up for the meals. They relied solely on the supplemental snacks they had packed. Unaware of this practice of packing alternative food for a week, I was the only one who came without a food reserve. I had the idea that I would be like the teachers and just eat what was provided. To my surprise, the teachers had brought their stash of snacks and seasonings from home. Like curious spectators, the students peered out from their barracks and commented in disbelief, "How can you eat that stuff?" With time and consistent, rigorous physical labor, the number of students in the dining hall increased. They realized that their bodies could not survive on snack food alone.

The Work-Study Principle in Action

As the work began, I observed hierarchical values being substituted for collective ones, such as proletarianism, equality, and group responsibility. Students became leaders, interacting with the farmers to set goals and to learn effective agricultural techniques. For efficiency, accountability, and collective work purposes, brigades were formed according to gender, with approximately ten students in each. Brigade work was recognized and rewarded through a system of moral stimuli and emulation of excellence as opposed to material incentives. For example, on a daily basis the brigades that reached their work quota were publicly recognized after dinner. Teachers kept running tallies of the students' work in order to give vanguard recognition for the best brigades at the end of each week on Sunday, during the parents' visitation and family picnic.

Each boys' and girls' barracks selected its vanguard student, whose responsibility was to make sure that every student was out of bed at 5:00 a.m. They also made sure that floors were swept, beds made, personal hygiene attended to, and all were dressed for inspection by 5:30 a.m. This never happened without a good deal of grumbling and whining about starting so early. Points and recognition were given daily for the cleanest and most orderly barracks. In the cool morning air, cold and sleepy, the silent students waited in line to receive their rock-hard roll and warm Simulac (baby formula) to soften it. In this early morning ritual, and throughout the day, the students did all types of work, including janitorial work in brigades. Labor served as an equalizer that bridged gender and race, as well as urban and rural life.

Following breakfast, a revolutionary devotional, the 6:00 a.m. *matutino*, exhorted the students to be patriotic and to struggle against imperialism. The sunrise in the countryside was in itself inspirational. The students lined up in rows in military fashion and stood at attention before a large white sculpted bust of José Martí. Each morning one brigade would lead the *matutino*, either simply reading it[6] or making a creative presentation of the message. The atmosphere was reverent, if tinted with sleepiness and exhaustion. After the *matutino* the national anthem was sung, and then the student leaders gave their brigades their duties and work quotas for the day.

Before joining the brigade, the student leaders first met with the campesino who normally was responsible for cultivating this tract of land to set the weekly agricultural quotas or goals for each brigade. The children affectionately called him "*tío*" (uncle), as he oversaw their labor. Then, after meeting with the farmer, the student vanguard of each brigade returned to his or her brigade and encouraged the others in their work, trying to foster enthusiasm, pride, a sense of humor, cooperation, and responsibility using words, chants, or songs while doing the field work. Teachers were members of the brigades in much the same way as the students were, but they were also prepared to step in if disciplinary measures or medical attention were needed.

Students worked from about 6:15 a.m. until noon, with their recycled plastic soda bottle filled with water—their only relief from the heat. The mid-morning snack of the 1960s and 1970s had been discontinued because it was too costly for the state. The girls weeded the rows of sweet potatoes with only a bandana around their heads for protection from the intense sun. Most students dressed in mended tank tops and tattered shorts; hardly anyone had the boots that were necessary for the work. Instead, they wore flip-flops or borrowed shoes, and their feet sank into the rich, red muddy earth. Without gloves, the girls' hands became sore from weeding thorny plants and fending off red ants. In another field the boys worked bare-chested, hoeing the banana fields. Several hours of hoeing left their unprotected hands blistered. The lack of protection from the sun caused some students to get sick; however, most of the students adjusted after the first week.

"Weeding is the hardest labor," the girls told me. Yuneisy directed the brigade: "¡Adelante! ¡Vamos!" Two of us were put on each *surco* (row) of twenty-five meters in the field. We had to finish two rows each day to fulfill our quota. However, I noted that no one finished even one row a day the first week. We were constantly told we were behind and needed to work harder. Most of the girls whined, and a few sat down in defiance. The two girls next to me said, "I'm tired. I don't want to work anymore!" And for a few minutes some of the students gathered together and just talked. The brigade leader, Yuleydis, allowed the others to rest and relax a bit, although she and I kept working. Yuleydis and I shared our *surcos;* we were partners. She stood on one side, bent over; I stood on the other side, in like posture. I asked her what her plans were after ninth grade.

"I want to go to the Camilitos [military] school."

"Really? Why? What will you become when you finish?"

"I will do what the Revolution asks of me."

"That's very impressive."

She then directed the conversation to religion, asking me about my religious beliefs. Stating her views, she said, "I don't believe in religion. For me the Revolution is all I need. Fidel will provide for us. Those who cling to religion can't be *revolucionario* [revolutionary]. They are not compatible." I acknowledged her pronouncement, and worked quietly. Then Yuleydis broke the silence.

"Do you know who your *santo*[7] is?"

"People here have told me that mine is Regla."

"Really?" she said with interest. "Mine is Ochún."

"Yuleydis, isn't Santería a religion?"

"No!" she responded emphatically. "It's culture."

"I like your culture."

"You do?"

"Yes." We smiled and kept working.

By the second day, Yuleydis felt ill. She went to the camp doctor, who told her that her temperature was fine. He told her it was common for people's body temperature to rise from working in the hot sun. But Yuleydis started feeling worse. Her throat was sore. To understand this event, one must understand that many students fake illness to get out of work. Teachers recounted that since the 1970s, students were constantly finding ways to leave the camp and avoid doing the work. In fact, it was a common practice to place garlic in the armpit to cause a fever. More extreme was the practice of having someone break another's arm. Wrapping an arm in a wet towel first helped ease the pain of breaking it. The camp doctor had the unenviable role of determining who was trying to get out of work and who was really sick. Many of the girls complained of feeling nauseated or having intense headaches. With all the girls coming to him, the doctor was told to let students sit out a half-day of work if they had a fever. In Yuleydis's case, the doctor told the teachers that Yuleydis "was not bad off" and that she should continue working.

Meanwhile, Yuleydis was busy utilizing another common technique to manipulate the system. When Lizabet, a Granma middle school teacher, came out for a surprise visit, Yuleydis made sure Lizabet told her mother that Yuleydis was feeling terrible.[8] The next day her mother showed up at the camp and became angry at the teachers and doctors for making Yuleydis work. She used the ultimate politically correct gambit: "My daughter is *revolucionaria,* and you think she is going to lie?" Back in Havana, with a diagnosis by another doctor, it turned out that the camp doctor had failed to diagnose Yuleydis's strep throat and severe ear infection. Not all attempts to get out of work were bogus, but this incident illustrates the complex pattern of negotiation that goes on in conjunction with the official work norms.

The boys' work generally went much more smoothly and was more varied than the girls' labor. The boys worked in the banana fields setting up a new irrigation system and hoeing. They were active most of the time. They fulfilled their quota each day and had the added advantage of enjoying some of the produce in their field.

Relief from the morning work came at noon. The sound of metal clanging could be heard from a distance, as lentils and rice and boiled sweet potato were served on compartmented metal serving trays. We stood in the serving line with our own cups and utensils from home. We scraped our trays when we were done, then stacked them for cleaning. Students who had sun and skin allergies were assigned to kitchen and cleanup duty, which included all aspects of the campsite: kitchen, barracks, latrines, and showers. After lunch we could rest until 2 p.m. One day during this break two tíos came by and asked me if I would like to go for a ride around the fields in their horse-drawn wagon. Sitting at the dining room table with the other teachers, they smiled and encouraged me. The two older men in their tattered working clothes and dirt-encrusted bodies made room for me to sit between them, and our bodies bounced around while the horse circled the field. I asked them about their work and working with the children. One explained:

The produce from the field tends to get wasted because the students either pull the vegetable rather than the weed, or the amount of work that actually gets accomplished is not enough to make a difference. This is merely an educational experience: living together and working together and doing so independently from their parents.

The tíos stopped the wagon, picked some bananas to give me, and dropped me off at the dining hall. As I waved good-bye, I shouted, "I had a great time!" From that day forward they made sure to see me each day and give me bananas. The other teachers were ecstatic that I had made the new contact for daily bananas. They were proud of me for having learned to *aprovechar,* or make the most of a situation, as well as for sharing the payoff—the bananas— with them. These were precisely the kind of collective spirit and "making do" values that the EAC sought to model and instill in the youth.

Once the break was over, the second half of the workday started at 2 p.m., lasting until 5 p.m. Everyone moaned at the idea of having to go back out again. But once we were back out in the field, the final three hours seemed to fly by. After work our values were tested again. All 150 combined teachers and students would stand in line to take an ice-cold three-minute shower (from a pipe that merely dripped water) in one of the ten curtainless concrete stalls. Cleaned up for dinner, we waited in the serving line to receive yet again lentils, rice, and boiled sweet potato—the sole lunch and dinner menu for the entire three weeks.

My body was sorer from the field work than I could ever recall. The students also complained of soreness quite a bit, but I never heard a single teacher complain. Finally I asked the teacher in the bunk below me if her body ached. Mariana whispered, as if it were a secret, "You mean you didn't bring aspirin?" I shook my head. She quietly insisted that I take some of her aspirin. "Our bodies hurt because we are older. The students can handle it because their bodies are more flexible at their age." Generally, however, the teachers did little of the agricultural labor. They were supervisors, so for the most part they spent time as a group to themselves. They saw to it that the meal was prepared by one of the farmers and that the students who were not in the field working were doing something productive. They oversaw situations with sick students and settled student brawls. The teachers were intermediaries in case the student leaders could not manage the brigades on their own.

Most important, the teachers ensured that the students fulfilled their work quotas. Mariana shook her head: "The girls fulfilled the stated quota at only 14 percent in weeding the sweet potatoes and the boys' work in constructing an irrigation system went beyond the norm." As a result, the teachers, together with the campesinos, lowered the quota each week until the girls successfully fulfilled the quota at 100 percent. The official story was that hard-working schoolchildren labored out of love for the state as they acquired the values for which Che stood. It was crucial that the plan be fulfilled successfully at the level of form—in numbers, figures, statistics, and reports—but not necessarily at the level of its "literal" meaning, satisfying the farmer's expectations or the state's economic need. As I was told by an education official, "The original goal was economic, which it is no longer. The most important goal now is educational. Students must learn the values inherent in working and living together in the rustic conditions of the countryside; to valorize the work of the farmer, and to receive ideological instruction."

Nighttime at the EAC

With the setting of the sun, the experience shifted from one of regimented discipline to *tiempo libre* (free time). Students gathered around the television in the dining hall to watch a telenovela together. The air was warm and sticky. The mosquitoes found us and started to feast on every visible piece of skin. "Let's go get our sheets to protect our skin!" Katia shouted. We ran to our barracks and grabbed our sheets from the bunk beds to wrap around our bodies, then resettled into our TV viewing. While most of the students were engaged in the telenovela, some wandered off to be alone with their friends or *novios/novias* (boyfriends/girlfriends).

After the telenovela, students used the dining hall again. With the one lone light bulb hanging from the ceiling, two tall boys brought their wooden suitcases from the barracks, set them on the stone table, and began drumming a conga with their hands. The driving beat summoned the gathering of the rest. Three more boys brought their water bottles and eating utensils to accompany the drumming. Before long a couple of girls started to dance in a trancelike manner, and the students naturally moved to circle around the dancing couple, swaying and clapping to the beat. The music seemed to resonate deeply within all of us. The dance passionately followed the beat, releasing the labor of the day and celebrating a newfound freedom and camaraderie.

They enjoyed the evening's singing, dancing, and dating atmosphere. As might be expected, after a long day of work, there were a few acts of humorous subversion and ridicule of the official symbols of power of the daily chores, which included discussions of pranks to alter quotas and change the wake-up hour, as well as escaping from the camp to steal from a nearby farm or go to the nearest town. While the officialized public sphere was filled with acts of acquiescence to the state's exhortations to be Hombres Nuevos, the personalized public sphere was full of thoughts (and many times deeds) of opportunities that the state did not condone. The mandated labor was carried out, even if it meant that the teachers and campesinos had to constantly lower the state's productive work quotas. Meanwhile, a very lively personalized sphere of singing, dancing, flirting, and general camaraderie filled the night air. And, just as the students did during the workday, they continued to bond together at night, in a more personalized kind of collective struggle.

Knowing that revolutionary values are explicitly taught in Cuban schooling, government officials required me to administer an exit survey to forty ninth graders at the end of the EAC. I had to ask students to name the three values most practiced in the EAC. When I mentioned that more qualitative, anthropological methods might work better, this caused suspicion about my identity and intentions. I was asked to rewrite my questions several times before they became the questions that the camp administrators wanted. Although I do not have a great deal of faith in surveys, it did show that students thought camaraderie (55 percent), responsibility (30 percent), and solidarity (27.5 percent) were the values most practiced in the EAC. Being independent from their parents, the students were responsible for cleaning their bunk area for inspection, being on time for meals and work, and washing their clothes and sheets weekly in the water trough. There were also conspicuous examples of them taking care of each other in the absence of their families. The students highlighted, and I tend to agree, that everything from the agricultural work to eating in the dining room and socializing afterward made them responsible and more collective. Despite all the examples of egalitarianism, some instances of gender privilege slipped into this idyllic, collective world. Frequently a boy was able to persuade a girl to do his laundry or to have his mother bring clean clothes at the time of parental visitation on Sundays. Teachers often defended this example of male privilege by saying, "Some things are just too difficult to enforce." Identity and social norms surfaced in the EAC.

Interestingly, in the 1990s Cuban psychologist Carolina de la Torre conducted a study regarding national identity with 1,432 students, ages 12–26, in the city of Havana. The students were asked, "¿Cómo somos los cubanos? Contesta dibujando" (Who are we as Cubans? Answer by drawing.). Students were told they could draw one or more people and include text if they wished. The most important part was that the drawing reflect what is most characteristic of Cubans (de la Torre 1995).

In an interview with de la Torre, she mentioned that each age group reflected some distinctions. Most notable, she said, is that among the 13- and 14-year-olds, the ones who customarily go to the EAC, depictions of working in the field emerged with revolutionary slogans.

Examples from "Como Somos" Drawing Survey administered to Havana children.

I asked her how she would interpret the students' drawings. She commented,

> When the incentive is very unstructured, like art, then you don't perceive it although the projection never is a copy of the reality. Anyway, when reality is very structured or very realistic one tends to . . . one copies reality as such in a vulgar way, even though it never is just like that.

She coded the drawings as political and labor, and explained her reasoning:

> The labor aspect is usually a part of the political sphere because work never is so-and-so at his work place. Rather, it is the EAC; work is expressed with the EAC . . . this is the concept of work. What has occurred with the EAC is that in some way it has created for them the concept of work, cooperation, and social utility.
>
> It is true that this is the reality of the EAC but notice that there are no personalized dialogues; they generally repeat the slogans or are shouting at one another to reach the agricultural quotas. This is a part of the "teque," which is the usual symphony of this country. Here, there is an ambiance of a series of words that one says and one repeats and it is not that they are

not true; it is in giving so much energy to all of this, the official discourse is really empty. It becomes something that enters and leaves people because it does not say anything. It's like when suddenly one day someone says "your words moved" me or "I could tell that the words were heartfelt." Why? Because one spoke with his or her own words, and I think that is what is lacking here. The quality of the formal discourse is not that bad; it's just that the drawings are simple and impersonal, as if the children are not mentally retarded but rather identity-retarded. Identity has been transmitted to them as if they were a mirror whose function was to reflect exactly what they are told. The pictures do not reflect a self-appropriated identity, which is a more common behavior for adolescents.

As children grow up there is a time when they start to think for themselves and have their own ideas, and there in the drawings it is evident that that they have not passed through that stage. They are reflecting the slogans and images that they have been given; they are reflecting what is expected of them, and there is where I see that those values are not completely internalized. You see?

Following Yurchak (2005), in these drawings formalized discourse is institutionally repeated and recycled and transmitted into everyday life. It is the state's authoritarian, immutable discourse that allows for creativity. While aspects of the discourse may be personally appropriated, they can be appropriated in ways that differ from the state's intentions. De la Torre mentioned that the personal was absent, leaving one to wonder to what degree the message is a form of parroting or internalization.

The internalization of values is at the heart of conciencia, as well as the questioning of what makes us who we are. To what extent can student value formation be manipulated or influenced? These questions were and are a part of Cuban revolutionary education.

Some Concluding Thoughts

I never really recognized what a polemical topic the EAC was until I was waiting for a bus with a Cuban friend. As we conversed, she urged me to eavesdrop on the conversation of two women in their late fifties who were sitting near us. One woman said that the biggest mistake the Cuban government had made was the implementation of the EAC program: "That was when this country started to lose its values." She added, "It's too early for children to leave home and live in an unsupervised environment." She argued that, contrary to the goal of morally preparing students, the government provided a haven for "loose" living away from the parents. The woman's friend retorted, "And how many 12- and 13-year-olds come back pregnant?" She continued, "Any strong sense of morality and good family values has been lost in the EAC."

Indeed, education officials were quite candid that the EAC program no longer promoted the idea that children were helping the country economically. An official from MINED's Work-Study Division said, "We, as a country, cannot afford to have the children working the fields like before. It sets us back economically. The goal is no longer economic; it is purely educational." He explained that the revolutionary values surrounding collective work and living together were still fostered. However, no official was willing to comment on the incompatibility of the EAC work ethic with the lived reality of increased capitalist measures.

Historically, the students' contribution had the goal of fostering nationalism, patriotism, anti-imperialism, and self-sacrifice. However, with the entrance of foreign investment in the country in the 1990s, the island has not been able to afford the slowdown in agricultural production or the wasted produce caused by the student work program. This is one of the many reasons why the forty-five-day program has been reduced to a twenty-day program. One could make a case that such concessions made during the Special Period have seriously eroded the original consciousness-raising intent of the EAC program.

On the other hand, I have tried to point out how the very structure of the EAC equalizes and inverts the hierarchy. It creates many shared experiences. The collective work also tended to blur social distinctions. Going to the countryside helped erode the academic categories created by the classroom setting, and once outside the classroom, students made friends with children of different skills and backgrounds. Moreover, the students and teachers got to know one another in new ways that made it easier for the teacher to work with the students when they returned to the classroom. Students learned about ways to participate in community service in the countryside, sometimes taking on additional projects to help the farmers. With Freirian ideals of empathy, love, humbleness, and service to and with the campesinos, the EAC context fostered an atmosphere of mutual learning. It was clearly a honing ground for learning revolutionary leadership and for learning to think independently from parents. Students took on leadership roles, including participation in *auto-gobierno* (self-government), became brigade leaders and barracks inspectors. In many instances emulation, a socialist type of competition, existed in most camp activities. Emulation involved not only recognition of exemplary workers but also that exemplariness came from helping others succeed. This intense emotional and physical engagement with and investment in a rural, rugged area were fundamental to building a collective, socialist consciousness. Regardless of the monumental changes that occurred during the Special Period, this powerful affective component remains a part of the present EAC program.

If one acknowledges the rise of a dual consciousness that makes itself distinct in its connection with the dual economies under operation in contemporary Cuba, perhaps we can begin to make sense of the seemingly contradictory attitudes and practices of contemporary Cubans. On the one hand, Cubans still adhere to official ideological messages, and they have a continuing affective attachment to nationalism and to revolutionary leaders such as Fidel Castro. Some observers of the Special Period contend, however, that the excessive expectations of the state for passionate civic commitments may be taking its toll (Fernández 2000). Living a dual life of extolling the Cuban government while buying food and clothing in the capitalist-oriented black market has created contradictions and tensions. Although Fernández questions what it means when the political loses its spontaneous, celebratory quality, falling into a repetitive ritualism, what Cuban young people call *teque* (official rhetoric), his reading is inadequate, because it is the authoritative and immutable rhetoric that provides a haven for the spontaneity and creativity spawned in everyday life.

From my experience living in Cuba, I would say it does not necessarily mean that the political has lost its authority. Cubans are socialized to cooperate with official culture in order to become part of society. "Since the Revolution understands the interests of the people, and since the Revolution stands for the interests of the whole Nation, no one can rightfully argue against it" (Castro 1961a, 14–15). Social critique exists within the limitations of official revolutionary philosophy. As Hungarian writer Miklos Haraszti explains, "Censorship professes itself to be freedom because it acts, like morality, as the common spirit of both the rulers and the ruled" (1987, 7–8). Within the constraints of what Haraszti has termed the "velvet prison," Cubans lead a creative and imaginative life under the prevalent political and therefore social limitations. In some ways, state socialization programs like the EAC are a microcosm of the changing Cuban society. The EAC is an intimate social space that produces networks of friends and horizontal solidarity. As students participate in the ritual of daily agricultural labor and barracks-cleaning routines, they actually ignore the constant exhortations about their low productivity, apathy, nonparticipation, sexualized behavior, and partying. These are the personalized moments when they inject the authoritative, officialized sphere with elements of the imaginative and with unpredictable behavior, which became the new, "normal" life in Cuban socialism during the Special Period.

An excellent example of this inversion of the officialized sphere has to do with food, perhaps the most universal social aspect of all cultures. During the dietary regimen of the EAC program, parents often brought additional store-bought food or electronic entertainment equipment; many parents also washed their children's clothes while visiting them at the camp on Sundays; and students brought clothing for partying to alter the work-oriented camp atmosphere. All of these cultural practices challenged the official socialization regime of hard work, sacrifice, and *chícharos* and rice. In a sense, the exuberant personalized cultural practices of Cubans are slowly changing the officialized sphere. Such practices demand to be acknowledged, and they coexist alongside the heavy emphasis on work and production. It is in this intersection of official and personalized spheres that collectiveness, responsibility, student leadership, friendship, and sacrificing for one another are actually learned. As we have seen, even before arriving at the campsite students begin learning the value of camaraderie by sharing clothing, shoes, and extra food. As they participate in the daily camp routines and fulfill their duties, they continue to develop the practical knowledge needed to survive in a changing Cuban society.

Ultimately, participating in the EAC program helps students learn what I would call a *doble conciencia,* or double consciousness. Such a consciousness bears some resemblance to W.E.B. DuBois's (1990) double consciousness of African Americans. There are, of course, limits to this analogy. When DuBois mentions the "two-ness" of African Americans, it has to do with being both American and black, without forsaking either. Cubans struggle with their own contradictory duality or "two-ness," which if forsaken will make it difficult for them to be a "normal subject" in contemporary Cuba. Thus, in the Cuban case, the *doble conciencia* is tied to a contradictory economic and political reality, demanding different and competing ideological values in order to succeed. The ritualized acts of going to the EAC were meaningful in an "official" sense, because they reinforced the authoritative discourse. At least visually and on paper, and in many cases earnestly, socialist loyalty was reinforced. At the same time, the EAC program was a site of unpredictable and multiple new "personalized" meanings that did not necessarily correspond to the official discourse. This *doble conciencia* is reconciled in Cuba through a nearly ubiquitous *doble moral* (double standard), which exists in many spheres of daily life. As Wirtz (2004) notes, this *doble moral* emerged most prominently during the Special Period.

I draw on the work of Graziella Pogolotti, a renowned Cuban researcher and writer, for insight into the evolution of *doble conciencia* and *doble moral* since the 1959 revolution: "Thereof, what is important is not necessarily the survival of the community in its actual form, but rather the link between Cubans in existence; of its interests, with a wider transforming current" (Pogolotti 1977, 111). Pogolotti recognized the transcendence or transformability of the new Cuban citizen, or Hombre Nuevo, to cultivate through social practice "a permanent deepening of conscience" (Frederik 2005, 427). The ideal citizen of the early period, the Hombre Nuevo has become what Frederik terms the Hombre Novísimo of twenty-first-century Cuba. This "even newer man" is the model for the "authentic" cubano who is truly *revolucionario*, with nostalgia for the countryside (from his or her school to the countryside rite of passage or from being a campesino) and *la patria* (homeland).

The duality I speak of builds on Frederik's Hombre Novísimo, especially in the context of the Special Period, as Cubans look toward Havana for answers to their current economic and political struggles. There is a simultaneous looking toward the past while looking forward to new and novel ways of *resolver;* looking toward the countryside while looking toward the urban in acquiring a futuristic orientation. Since the onset of the revolution and the 1961 Literacy Campaign, the government has been dedicated to having young people immerse themselves in the countryside to learn revolutionary values, such as humbleness, nobleness, hard work, and a collective identity built on putting the homeland and the needs of others before one's own needs. This looking to the countryside has been seen as a way to secure proper value inculcation in urban youth during adolescence, when those values threaten to waver.

The Hombre Novísimo follows the Hombre Nuevo in its very masculine nature; however, its masculine nature feeds off the land—which is often feminized—for its values. The Hombre Novísimo is *"culto,"* cultured in literature and arts, and socially responsible, as Frederik (2005) mentions, but I would add that he is not only nationally but internationally aware, especially in guarding against the contamination of globalization and the possible loss or tainting of the "authentic" cubano. He is in some ways a complicated mix of past and future images.

Ultimately, the EAC plays a pivotal role in cultivating the conciencia of both the Hombre Nuevo and the Hombre Novísimo. On the one hand, the program purposefully removes young people from their urban contexts and provides them with instruction in resisting the temptations of modern society and the accompanying capitalist tendencies (relationships with foreigners, materialism, a resistance to socialist ideology). It also revives the cultural memory of the nation and its people while unwittingly offering an opportunity for the production of new, unofficial personalized norms and practices. On the other hand, the program is a ritualistic incubator of purported revolutionary consciousness, and the seeds of consumerism are present along with the *pura cepa*. The EAC program now serves the Cuban people and the state in ways that were not part of the original plan. As Pogolotti implies, the emergent values will transcend place, because they are based on "a wider transforming current." Time will tell to what extent the Hombre Novísimo will reflect the *pura cepa*, or whether the definition of *pura cepa* will change to reflect new Cuban subjectivities of a growing "pseudo-culture" of capitalist consumption. In light of how slowly culture changes, the complex mix of values and practices that many have conceptualized as a *doble conciencia* and *doble moral* may be expected to characterize Cuban life for some time to come.

Conclusion

Cuba can only be responsible for one thing: for having made a revolution and being willing to carry it to its ultimate consequences.
FIDEL CASTRO, ANNIVERSARY SPEECH, MARCH 13, 1967

Using the Cuban context, I set out to see whether schooling in a communist country might produce a more altruistic, socially responsible citizen than in a capitalist country, and if so, which mechanisms in the educational system influenced this outcome. How Cuban people made sense of their everyday lives was critical to understanding schooling outcomes. At the heart of Cuban citizenship formation has been the model of the New Man and its evolution since its inception in the early 1960s. The educational system as the principle venue of state-controlled socialization has been assigned responsibility for the development of society and of individual personality. In my research I found it important to consider how educational policy related to historical change, and how formal schooling mechanisms were set to respond to contingent political and economic needs. Therefore, I found it useful to chart a periodization of history and educational policy in revolutionary Cuba as the context for the ethnographic portrayals of Cuban citizenship in contemporary Cuba.

Historical, economic, and political conditions alone were not the determining factors; I found that the production of citizenship also relied on the feelings, perceptions, and aspirations of students, teachers, parents, and education officials in relation to their conditions. Emotions illuminate how people relate to the social and the political, what they consider important, and how they express and interpret interests and identities. Although emotions have physical and biological dimensions and thus are personal and individual, they can also be understood as cultural expressions that, while sharing similarities across different contexts, are marked by local specificities. In this book I have highlighted the role of affect throughout contemporary Cuban history to show the confluence of historical situatedness, everyday politics, and education. The revolution both evoked feelings and relied on those feelings to muster support and to survive.

At the time of the 1953 insurrection and the final triumph of the revolution, passion provided the energy to imagine and pursue an alternative future. The politics of passion sowed the seeds for group formation, bonding the leader to the followers and the followers to the leader. (Com)passion drove the revolutionaries in a quest for a moral community and economy, sovereignty, and justice. The vested moral force acted as a catalyst for mobilization and ultimately constituted a source of power. Moreover, the moral imperative rendered the revolution a quasi-religious struggle to "save Cuba" from the imperialism of the United States and the injustices of poverty and the lack of educational opportunities brought on by capitalism. The revolutionaries became "believers" in the new political religion. As part of the moral imperative, the leadership sought the transformation of el pueblo into the idyllic New Man. The New Man would advance socialism, having the proper personality, mentality, or *conciencia* to lead or follow the revolution.

The political religion was reflected in the media and in discourses constructed by the leaders. These were meant to inspire and fuel the Cuban populace with revolutionary zeal. The existence of an external enemy, the United States, served to heighten the need for unity and unanimity and gave legitimacy to political strategies, educational policies, social violence, and coercive authority in the first decade of the revolution. The vital ingredients of Cuba's political religion were the recycling of the guerrilla experience of the Sierra Maestra, the incorporation of an epistemology that relied on Manicheanism, and the belief in the perfectibility of people to become New Men and New Women. Furthermore, children were highly valued by the Communist government because of the fundamental belief that only the young could come to the revolutionary experience uncorrupted and pure enough to become true communists.

One of the most important foci of Cuba's revolution was education—*total* education. To mold the children more perfectly into the revolutionary ideal citizen, it was important for education to incorporate as many aspects of children's lives as possible, so that being a revolutionary was not confined to the school setting but included defense of *la patria*—the fatherland—as well. For example, children were sent to remote areas for several months during the Literacy Campaign in 1961. With total education in mind, the Pioneer organization was created in 1961 to regulate behavior and encourage revolutionary values not only inside the classroom but also outside it, through meetings, work projects, excursions, parades, and other group civic activities.

In addition to the formation of the new generation, the total education policy was targeted toward educating the general population. With it, the government sought democratization and a monolithic ideological unity. With the harnessing of the belief and affection of the pueblo, the sixties became a time of experimentation and innovation in every realm, with *granjas del pueblo* (work farms), *círculos infantiles* (free child care), mass organizations, the Escuela al Campo (school to the countryside) program, the Units for Military and Agricultural Production (rehabilitation work camps), and countless other programs. Implementing one project after another in the 1960s, the state tried a variety of means to inculcate new values and to boost the economy by mobilizing the population into production using moral incentives.

In the 1970s, being economically dependent on the Soviet Union, the Cuban leadership adopted a policy shift that included more centralization and economic rationalization. To achieve greater economic efficiency, there was less reliance on voluntary labor and more emphasis on material incentives. The institutionalizing of the economy had its counterpart in the culture with the 1971 Congress on Education and Culture, which reinforced the overall atmosphere of social rigidity and sought to combat any form of deviation of Cuban youth in order to achieve a monolithic ideological unity. The Padilla affair, which resulted in the imprisonment of Heberto Padilla in 1971, was a sample of this strong arm of ideological control exercised by the Cuban government.

The perfeccionamiento education movement, initiated in 1975, sought to address the formation of "the perfect communist" by restructuring the curriculum and adopting a more rational approach to education for all ages. To address the students' prevailing lack of discipline and respect for work, the Anti-Loafing Law of 1971 was created, making loafing and parasitism punishable crimes. In an effort to maintain the educational momentum of the Literacy Campaign and promises for a better future, follow-up programs were created for newly literate adults, such as the "Battle for the Sixth Grade." Also as a result of the Literacy Campaign and measures for mass education, secondary enrollment increased. The state responded by constructing more permanent schools in the countryside (*escuelas en el campo*) as well as new teacher training schools and polytechnical schools. The permanent schools in the countryside became the model for holistic education and the seed for forming the New Man, with a morning program of agricultural work and an afternoon program of academic classes. Educational measures in the 1970s gave more ideological rigidity and structure to the novelty of the 1960s.

Matters could not continue in this way for very long, however. The rigidity of the system and the reinvigoration of the ideological began to alienate those who had felt intimately bound to the revolutionary process. Many of the collective work measures were being used for correction, which called into question the motives of the state and its institutions. In response to greater regulation and an economy of scarcity, the gap between practice and theory, political promises and social reality, became insurmountable and the politics of affection, *lo informal,* steadily increased, undermining official rules and manifesting alternatives, interests, and identities.

Mounting dissatisfaction, mostly among the Cuban youth, led to the storming of the Peruvian embassy and the Mariel boatlift in 1980. The feeling of devotion to the leadership had eroded and was replaced by sentiments that separated society from the state. Castro blamed bureaucracy and called for a return to moral incentives. Yet with a declining economy, the state found it harder and harder to generate emotional capital. At the time of the Mariel boatlift, student groups were being called on not only to participate in acts of repudiation of the "scum" and "worms" but also to reaffirm their revolutionary loyalty. A new branch of the Pioneers, the Explorers, was created to provide one more channel for youth to participate in model citizenry. For the young, the revolution had fallen prey to *el teque*—official rhetoric—in the 1980s. Young people wanted to infuse Cuban socialism with real meaning, not empty phrases.

As the Young Communists (UJC) tried to address the state's rigidity and formalism by rejuvenating the organization and appealing to the youth, the Rectification Campaign of 1986 introduced an austerity program, which expanded the role of ideological discourse in daily life and economic management. As Cuban socialism started to respond to the young, political opportunities were closing. To make matters worse, the government was about to face its most severe economic and political crisis yet.

The economic tailspin of the late 1980s and early 1990s shook whatever goodwill the government still enjoyed among the young. A harsh new reality emerged in the 1990s, called "The Special Period in Times of Peace." Hopes wilted as promises dissipated. The focus of the Sixth UJC Congress was on *sobrevivencia* and *supervivencia*—resistance in order to survive. The government moved toward greater centralization, leaving the young uncertain and blaming the leadership for its incompetence. Disenchantment with the political religion that failed to deliver the material and spiritual promises it made led to another exodus—the *balseros*—in 1993.

Since 1994 the economy has experienced a sustained recovery, but only with the help of capitalist measures, including the legalization of U.S. dollars, entrepreneurships, increased tourism, joint ventures, and so on. Mixing capitalist measures with socialism has resulted in mixed ideological messages and "tourist apartheid." The contradiction between the two normative ideologies and their resultant frameworks—the public (official norms) and the private (informal norms)—has resulted in rampant dissimulation, as Cubans opt for the *doble moral* (two codes of attitudes or behaviors). The vignettes in Chapters 5-7 illustrate the negotiation and mediation of identities and truths at work, which resulted in the development of a type of conciencia that has a new meaning for the new millennium and for civil society, whose socialist safety net has been sharply reduced. A political formula was adopted involving capitalist measures that undermined the very principles on which socialism stood. This was supposed to be a Band-Aid until the economic wounds healed.

These Band-Aid policies have caused emotional wounds among the old and emotional reactions among the young. The reactions are in response not only to the dire conditions of daily life but also to the clash between the government's normative framework and its instrumental procedures in practice. Although the Cuban people, and youth in particular, have learned how to negotiate the *doble moral,* the application of a differential consciousness does not necessarily indicate an acceptance of it. This widening gap between norms and praxis can lead to what Fernández (2000) calls desocialization, in which people who have rejected the dominant values of the state experience a lack of faith and sentimental loss, losing affective attachment to the status quo. Depending on the degree of contradictory behavior, living the *doble moral* can resemble an accepted form of schizophrenia. And because society as a whole recognizes this phenomenon, a whole new way of life or culture emerges.

The entrance of capitalist measures has led to more class and race distinctions than in previous decades, grafting new identities onto those who had been liberated by the revolution. The difference becomes more pronounced in a predominantly Afro Cuban neighborhood like La Flor. As a result of new foreign influences, some schools have been paired with foreign sponsors or receive visits from foreign delegations more frequently than others. Consequently, these schools receive donations of school supplies and *estímulos* (incentives, such as t-shirts and candy), while other schools receive less or none at all, as in the case of Granma. It makes sense that the government would prefer that outsiders see schools that are racially mixed, which reflects the equality expected under socialism.

Family ties to the United States vary along racial lines, too, with Afro Cubans typically receiving fewer family remittances from abroad. In addition, in the tourist industry and in joint ventures, the tendency has been to hire more lighter-skinned than dark-skinned people. This glass ceiling has lessened the opportunities for Afro-Cubans to gain financial capital and decreased their chances for any kind of social mobility or survival in a mixed-market society.

Surprisingly, in La Flor, the Afro-Cubans did not seem to see themselves as victims of the increasing racist tendencies; rather, they saw themselves as protagonists. Papito spoke with clarity: "We are the ones who will survive the revolution." Because La Flor had suffered from a history of neglect, Papito declared that they knew how to negotiate and mediate circumstances better than those who had lived with more benefits from the revolution.

In La Flor, it was evident that education was provided by the family and the community as well as by the schools. For some students, Santería or the Protestant Church provided hope and optimism in facing the difficult and unknown. Neither religion countered the official dogma, but children did realize that scheduling time for the Protestant Church had to be done prudently in order to remain in good standing with the Pioneer organization or the UJC.

One inevitable juncture was the interplay among Santería, an Afro-Cuban ethnicity, prostitution, and increased tourism. With Afro-Cubans not benefiting as much legally from the growth in tourism, the illegal options became attractive. Mulatta women have been stereotyped as the "best prostitutes." The pay varies, but typically prostitution can be one of the most lucrative professions. Moreover, whether the financial profit is for upgrading life materially or for providing the necessary animals for a Santería ceremony, the rise in prostitution seemed to be generating more questions about its existence, the role of the state, and revolutionary values.

The greatest challenge rests with the teacher, who must teach children about the life before them. Irma, Vanessa, and Lizabet for the most part restricted their dialogue to the curriculum; they acted as if they were on stage and had to play their roles correctly. "Off stage" they were quite candid about the difficulty of living and teaching the "hidden transcript"—another example of the *doble moral*. In essence, they taught what they lived: negotiable identities. Working with older teachers such as Lizabet, I noticed their skill in tacking back and forth through the stormy winds of revolutionary experience, from Lizabet's pride in participating in the Literacy Campaign, the first school to the countryside program, and teaching civic education to political disillusion over the state's response to her son's murder by drunken revolutionary militia. This tacking back and forth was a behavior that students seemed to be learning—tacking between the rhetorical teque and the honesty and affection of what makes a cubano . . . *muy humano*.

The Pioneer organization was a source of affection for students, and for the most part its structure and activities seemed to be appreciated by teachers, students, and parents. Students were aware of the boundaries of formal schooling, and within those boundaries a form of democracy existed with student-run projects and meetings.

The work projects around the school and in the community garden, the methods for making sure students understood the lessons, organizations such as the Pioneers and the Explorers, and work in the countryside all lent themselves to character building and expanded networks of friendship. The revolutionary values of responsibility, leadership, solidarity, cooperation, patriotism, hard work, and self-government were all being exercised as children maintained the school, weeded the garden, did their homework, and planned further projects together.

As students became leaders, and even more so as students went through the schools to the countryside program and experienced a new independence from their parents, manual labor inverted the hierarchical structure typically set by an academic atmosphere. They lived with more social liberation, but they also had to take on more responsibility than at home. Without apron strings to hold on to, many of those from the older generations whom I interviewed said that it was in the schools to the countryside program where they made lasting friendships, which they still held. By providing a communal atmosphere in formal and informal spaces for schooling, these programs facilitated the emergence of networks of affection that proved essential in sustaining the children emotionally, mentally, spiritually, and perhaps in the future, financially.

The students showed active engagement in the Pioneer activities and displayed a revolutionary-like behavior; however, ironically, none of the students I interviewed connected their Pioneer identity to the revolution, communism, or Che Guevara. The fundamental historical precepts on which the Pioneer organization was founded no longer seemed to be internalized by Cuban young people who repeat the Pioneer motto, "Pioneros por comunismo, seremos como el Che." Part of the disconnect may be traced to the evolution of the symbol of Che Guevara. Che, the model New Man of communism, has been marketed in the form of key chains and cigarette lighters for U.S. dollars in the tourist markets. The disconnect between the symbol and its referent is indicative of the disconnect between the state and its people, between revolutionary precepts and daily reality.

Daily news media and research reflected more dialogue about the values crisis than what I witnessed in the schools: perhaps because the government wished to target the adults, the main readers of newspapers, for the solution. The articles, often quoting MINED officials, pointed to the source of the values crisis as excessive paternalism on the part of the state and the parents, as well as the detrimental effects of globalization and neoliberalism in producing what Cuban educators have called "anti-values." The answer has been articulated as better teacher training and a renewed emphasis on Cuban history to instill revolutionary values.

Adherence to a program of self-formation, such as one resulting in the creation of the New Man, works only when there is evident potential for improvement. Are the historical conditions present today in Cuba to produce a citizen without personal interests, who is not motivated by material profit but only by moral incentives? Historically, have these conditions ever existed in Cuba? Communism, based on Marxism, cannot truly operate unless the people's basic needs are provided for. In socialist Cuba, housing, health, and education may have been adequate, but household items, mechanical parts, clothing, and food have always been black market items (and red market items when the Soviet Union was in the picture).

The capitalist measures put in place in the early 1990s only revealed more clearly the distance between the New Man ideal and the human lived reality in Cuba. With the growing separation between the state and its people, the passion and affection of the people were rerouted from full trust in the state to an acceptance of an ongoing negotiated pastiche of socialist ideals within the growing capitalist measures, reflecting both allegiance to and disaffection for the state. Alternative networks have been built between friends and family to compensate for the lack of fulfillment on the part of the state. In turn, this rerouting has been responsible for the emergence of new understandings and meanings of socialism.

If the Cuban people are only half-heartedly responding to the state and its mandates, what is the future of the revolutionary values and conciencia characteristic of the New Man? Cubans have reworked the revolutionary values into their personal networks of family and friends to resolve the material lack (*lo material*) and also to reap spiritual benefits, *lo espiritual*. Friends and family reciprocate sacrifice, hard work, solidarity, responsibility, honesty, and affection.

Personal networks, operating on the revolutionary values of the New Man, have produced a new dialectic, a new relationship to the state. Whether these new identities and interests, based on emotion and reason, achieve the degree of agency that Fernández (2000) predicts and actually provoke a major political change remains to be seen. However, at this stage what does exist is an educational system that unwittingly has reproduced societal behavior, norms, and values. The Cuban educational system has modeled the values it has taught, teaching students ways to negotiate and mediate the doublespeak of Cuban society. The prevalence of this dual discourse is rooted in something deeper, what I have called a *doble conciencia*, an internalized understanding of the powers at work, and the *doble moral*, both of which are necessary for navigating in a mixed-message society.

In every society people negotiate the private and the public; however, in the case of Cuba the essence is ideological and axiologically pronounced, hovering on an almost schizophrenic identity for survival. Conciencia in itself does not imply the superficial; rather, it refers to the internalized motor for social operation. To possess a *doble conciencia*, therefore, is to have internalized ideologically and axiologically the codes, hierarchical and horizontal, of both capitalism and socialism. The networking and affection of friends, family, and teachers seem to provide the buffer and support for children to sort out and learn how to maneuver through the contradictions and disjunctures during this Special Period in Cuban history.

The collapse of the former Soviet Union in 1989 devastated the fragile base of the Cuban economy, producing a catastrophic impact on living standards and threatening social cohesion as economic class differences became more pronounced (Burchardt 2002). The relationship between the state and its people enduring such was tenuous at best. In 1996 a modest economic improvement began and continues, but the ideological fallout was grave. Segments of the youth population turned to crime and underground market activities (Wooden 2004). The number of out-of-school and unemployed disaffected youth and pregnant teenagers increased (Strug 2006).

The Cuban government was desperate for a path to social recovery. The required periodic demonstrations in Revolutionary Plaza to protest the embargo and, in 1998, the incarceration of the "Cuban Five,"[1] although visibly reflecting solidarity, internally, according to those interviewed, served more as a reminder of decades of a routinized public performance without fulfillment on the part of the state. When I interviewed former brigadistas and asked, "What would it take for young people to understand and acquire the values you once learned?" most people just shook their head in silence. However, two people, reminiscing, said, "It will take something like the Literacy Campaign to bring us together again."

Opportunity came knocking in November 1999, when the Cuban boy, Elián González, survived a capsized boat at sea. His rescue and repatriation proved to be the galvanizing fulcrum the Cuban government needed. The government responded to the Miami exile community's question about the quality of life in Cuba by framing the conflict as part of an ideological "*Batalla de Ideas*," in which neoimperialism threatened Cuba's national sovereignty. The question of a child's custody when he has witnessed his mother's death at sea and his father lives in Cuba was a logical one. Few people outside a certain faction of the Cuban exile community argued that the boy should not be with his father. The Battle of Ideas, launched in 2000, was born out of the upsurge of popular mobilization in Cuba to demand the return of Elián.

And it was more. Unlike the marches and protests against the embargo and the Cuban Five, the fate of a child and the logic of his custody were something that even a five-year-old could understand and defend. The Elián episode thenceforth became the emotional glue to secure the disaffected. There were countless *tribunas abiertas* that placed people of all ages and backgrounds on a public platform in front of the microphone declaring their love for their country and its children and condemning the injustice on the part of the United States. Even groups that had been marginalized by the revolution, such as those associated with Santería, entered center stage in the *tribuna abierta*. Finally, the government could redeem itself and fulfill a promise: Elián's return was an attainable goal.

Similarities begin to emerge between the Literacy Campaign and the custody battle over Elián. The Literacy Campaign lasted eight months. The campaign for the return of Elián lasted seven. On one of my visits in 2000, before Elián's return, former brigadistas compared the media use to that of the Literacy Campaign. One woman, with her arm bent and her hand, palm down, in front of her chest, shook her hand from side to side three times, each time saying with an exasperated look, "Elián." She indicated that the propaganda was never-ending: Elián t-shirts, billboards, commercials, TV spots, radio and newspaper stories, *manifestaciones, tribunas abiertas,* and songs. Cuban society was saturated with the Elián cause. With a just cause that successfully resurrected and achieved in the Cuban populace a belief and understanding of the United States as exploiter and enemy, the Elián drama moved the Cuban population closer to ideological unity. It renewed the sense of national unity and a collective identity that recalled the accomplishments of the revolution, especially in education, as cameras turned to the six-year-old's empty school desk and his classmates in their red-and-white Pioneer uniforms calling for his return. What could evoke more emotion than the fate of a child?

It was on the coattails of the euphoria over Elián's successful return in June 2000 that the multipronged campaign, the Battle of Ideas, was initiated, encompassing more than 170 cultural, social, and educational programs to secure and reinforce socialist ideology. One of the programs led to the creation of the School for Social Work in October 2000 in Cojímar, outside Havana, and subsequently three other schools like it.[2] The students who were selected to attend the School for Social Work were primarily school-leavers and unemployed youth who resided in Cuba's poorest neighborhoods. Graduates were assured of social work jobs with good salaries after graduation and were selected by the UJC, with approval by school officials.

The school at Cojímar was created to train social workers for community-based practice with at-risk populations, such as disadvantaged youth, juvenile delinquents, school dropouts, and other vulnerable groups, within their own communities. Students were trained to work collaboratively with representatives of mass organizations and with People's Council members. According to a Cuban psychology professor who participated in curriculum development for the school, "Government leaders were concerned about growing delinquency and alienation among youth and growing socioeconomic divisions in society."[3]

This community-based practice set up to help disaffected youth carries some of the Literacy Campaign overtones as well. In the Literacy Campaign, the brigadistas were not selected for having a strong ideological orientation; rather, they acquired it with experience during the campaign, just as the social workers did. Social work schools, as in the Literacy Campaign, prepared students to become "friends of the family, knocking on doors not touched by the Revolution," according to one social work student (*Rock Around the Blockade Newsletter* 2003). Relationship building was at the heart of imparting and solidifying ideals of the Cuban Revolution. The person-in-the-environment approach follows the work-study principle and the use of affective attachment to build a stronger community and greater national unity. In 2004 Fidel Castro, in a speech before the Cuban National Assembly, praised social work by referring to the graduates as the "true worker's army of the soul" (*Prensa Latina* 2004). Using the word "soul" shows that the state's goal and achievement need to be internalized and heartfelt; this is what will solidify the revolution. As in the Literacy Campaign, the young became heralded heroes and leaders who involved themselves in challenging situations in the name of the revolution.

Also riding on the coattails of the Elián episode in 2000 was the state's charge to the young people to do their part to offset the grave teacher shortage. The desire to become a teacher with state wages at the equivalent of U.S. $20 a month had been eclipsed by jobs related to tourism, where dollar tips supplemented the state salary. The state put its money where its mouth was and offered teacher candidates, *maestros emergentes,* a fast track to becoming professionals: eight months of free, on-the-job teacher training with free room and board in Havana (instead of the traditional five years of pedagogical training), and a monthly stipend. In response to "the putative loss of the teaching vocation among the young" (*Granma* 2002), Castro praised the *maestro emergente* programs to graduate students with only a ninth-grade education as well as incorporating the more than 86,000 unemployed 17- to 29-year-olds from all over the island (*Granma* 2002). These adolescents became class monitors for *teleclases*, the idea being that televised classes would maintain the quality of content and ideology and the *maestros emergentes* could focus on classroom management and follow-up discussion. These young teachers were honored in the media as the brigadistas in the Literacy Campaign were who braved the political, economic, and ideological conditions of the sixties to ensure that everyone's right to education would be realized. In fact, during a speech to ninety graduating teachers, Castro praised them for "recreating the history of the literacy campaign" (*Granma* 2002).

Obviously, it is not the students or teachers who are recreating the history of the Literacy Campaign; it is Castro and his cabinet members who perceive that the constant recreation of missionary zeal evident in the Literacy Campaign and of political passion in activities, programs, mobilizations, *tribunas abiertas*, marches, protests, and putting young people at the forefront will keep the revolutionary fire going. There is a constant looking to the past for answers to the present. Yet nostalgia also induces stagnation.

More than 4,000 retired teachers were called on in the fall of 2008 to return to the classroom to rescue the *maestros emergentes*, who were seen as "not having enough knowledge or maturity" (Grogg 2008). In April 2008, with no forewarning, Raúl Castro dismissed the former minister of education, Luis Ignacio Gómez, a decision that Fidel Castro assumed and wrote about in his column, "*Reflexiones*," arguing that the administrator "habia perdido energía y conciencia revolucionaria" (had lost energy and revolutionary consciousness). Can conciencia, once acquired, be lost? Gómez was Cuba's minister of education for eighteen years. Fidel Castro's diagnosis of the reason for Gómez's dismissal is very telling of the state of the nation's efforts to educate its people.

The rejection of the present plays a major role in the desire to return to a past, however idealized this past may be. One's own mortality is never easy to face, though the revolutionary leader's face has all but disappeared. With death comes new life and vigor, though the present indeed builds on the past. The socialist ideals are not lost or dead, however dormant they may sometimes appear. Conciencia continues to evolve into something less and less fixed than what the state thought it could define in the sixties and seventies. Values vaunted in earlier years—self-sacrifice, solidarity, and the rejection of consumerism—are still instilled in today's youth, but Cuba is increasingly bearing the brunt of globalization and capitalist influences. Its insulation is wearing thin. Tourism, foreign investment, American pop culture, Internet access and visiting Cuban Americans offer young people a different worldview, making the role of schools in teaching ideology perhaps more challenging than in the past. Those termed "disaffected youth" are actually young people who have hopes, dreams, and aspirations and are in search of what is authentic.

The New Man has not and will not exist in the same form of the sixties and seventies. Who is he or she? And what kind of conciencia does he or she embody? I find helpful Laurie Frederik's (2006) description of the Cuban people as "waiting for Godot." In Samuel Beckett's play, the awaited Godot never arrives. The Cuban government's organized activities for mobilization and public demonstration of solidarity and passion for the revolution are juxtaposed with a civil society in which lives are marked by separation from family in the United States and waiting for fulfillment. The Elián episode brought this physical and in some ways psychological and ideological fragmentation to the fore, as Cuban values were reified through the proposed future of the young boy. What does the Cuban Godot embody?

The model of the New Man for the twenty-first century is what Frederik calls the *Hombre Novísimo*, or "even newer man": one who is a complex combination of past and present images, rural and urban values—humility, self-sacrifice, an appreciation for land and hard work (Che Guevara), along with a *martiana* (José Martí) emphasis on being cultured in the arts and letters. He has an interest in both national and international issues, with an acquired skill in creating makeshift inventions, *inventos cubanos*, to respond to scarcities, beat the system, or simply assert his creativeness and share the benefit with others. The Hombre Novísimo is being formed in the wake of waiting and separation.

In the introduction to this book I quoted Eric Hoffer: "the radical has a passionate faith in the infinite perfectibility of human nature." This idea coincides with Castro's utopian vision of Cuban society and his schooling system to achieve the New Man. However, Hoffer thought both radicals and reactionaries would eventually morph into their apparent opposite. To what extent might this apply to the Cuban revolutionary?

Barack Obama's presidency will be telling. He is the first president in almost fifty years to agree to meet with the Cuban president. Obama has already agreed to lift restrictions on U.S. Cuban families visiting the island and restrictions on remittances. Interestingly, the saga of Elián has been revisited as Obama appoints to his administration two attorneys who helped return Elián to Cuba—a selection that angered Cuban Americans. Perhaps reconciliation is near, and Cuban youth will find an authenticity in which they can participate, reconnect with their families abroad, be more participatory in shaping their form of government, and lead their country in a new direction.

The "even newer man" is one who has the maturity and wisdom to reconcile capitalism and socialism on the island, the histories of the United States and Cuba, and to propose a meaningful and productive future for the island and its people. Perhaps the Hombre Novísimo is closer to what Eric Hoffer saw as the "liberal," one who "sees the present as the legitimate offspring of the past and as constantly growing and developing toward an improved future" (1951, 73). Perhaps this is the Godot the Cubans are becoming as they wait.

The evolution of the new socialist citizen involves new literacies, as so blatantly revealed in the tourist sector. Crafted from one of the hotel bath towels, in the center of a wrinkle-free bedspread, sits a beautiful white swan. On the desk near the television is a note in English from housekeeping: "Dear Mrs. Merton, Thank you opportunity [*sic*] to serve you. Griselda." As this was the guest's last night at the hotel, she decided to leave a tip next to the note. Reminiscent of the Literacy Campaign, the "final test" required of the newly literate was a letter to Fidel thanking him for the opportunity to serve the Revolution. Nowadays, Cuba's economic sustainability lies with its socialist citizens who are literate in tourism. In literacy a country creates its future and bears its reputation.

Suitcases, Jump Ropes, and *lo espiritual:* Methodology *a la cubana*

Revolutionary Cuba[1] has been termed a "politically-inspired forbidden research terrain,"[2] one that has dissuaded many social scientists from pursuing research on the island (Fuller 1988, 100). In traveling back and forth to Cuba, suitcase packing and jumping rope become useful metaphors to discuss methodology in this forbidden research terrain. The more I learned from the Cubans, the more I deliberated over which items I would pack—or leave out—to meet the forty-four-pound weight limit for the trip. The suitcase contents changed dramatically after my first visit to Cuba, and what I brought back from Cuba each time evolved too. In this chapter I open my suitcase and unpack what I brought home from the field: new perspectives about research methods in a politically sensitive context, and a better understanding of revolutionary Cuba and myself.

An identity marker of self and other, suitcase packing represents both the traveler and the target culture. In addition, I use the metaphor of jumping rope to show the difficulty of entering and maintaining a connection with new cultural rhythms and practices. Together, these metaphors aid in discussing the intersections of my informants' and my perspectives. Through this discussion I hope to offer new methodological ideas for researchers on Cuba and other politically charged and materially strapped contexts.

Researchers are often discouraged by the established parameters of conventional ideological discourse from adopting novel intellectual perspectives in framing and analyzing their research problems. To navigate the logistical and political obstacles bounded by Castro's ideology, I relied on the guidance of my primary informants. This collaboration yielded new strategies for conducting an ethnographic inquiry about one of Cuba's more sensitive research sites and topics, the school—generator and meter of ideologically explicit values. Following my informants' suggestions, I focused on the historical, highlighting the changing referent, "*antes*" (before) and the operative mechanisms of "*lo material*" and "*lo espiritual*" (spiritual, as in humanitarian) since the beginning of the Special Period. Consequently, our collaboration yielded some novel considerations regarding data collection, reciprocity, identities, and access, as well as data analysis.

My suitcase of stories about the Cuban people and myself is filled with the rich detail and transformational experiences of ethnographic research. Our interaction and learning from and about one another and the subsequent transformation were all part of the phenomenological process of continual co-creation that ethnography offers. Instead of studying people, the ethnographer learns from them. When people are merely studied, observed, and questioned as subjects or respondents, the investigator may be detached. When "subjects" become teachers who are "experts in understanding their own culture, the relationship between investigator and informant becomes quite different. The investigator will ask those who he studies to become his teachers and to instruct him in the ways of life they find meaningful" (Spradley and McCurdy 1972, 12).

Ethnography is a textual genre that can be evocative in a literary sense without sacrificing representational realism. Thus, I chose ethnography to chronicle peoples' feelings, values, and beliefs in everyday life to capture the state of *conciencia* in present-day Cuba. In detailing the investigative process, I use stories from the field to explore the shifting and sometimes contradictory suitcase contents of my research experience.

Images That Led Me to My Research Topic

I was drawn to Cuba because, as a schoolteacher, I had noticed children becoming more self-absorbed and seemingly insatiable consumers. I wondered whether children in a noncapitalist society could truly be socialized to be more altruistic and socially responsible. On my first visit to Cuba, in 1995, I pursued documents and first-person accounts of the 1961 National Literacy Campaign. This campaign was a massive event, which made finding informants a relatively easy endeavor. This project ultimately set me up for dissertation data collection later in 1998–1999.

The process of interviewing the former Literacy Campaign *brigadistas*[3] caused me to reevaluate my identity as a U.S. citizen and the act of conducting social science research in Cuba. During this fieldwork I was not fully aware of what I represented as an Anglo from the United States. Patria, an educational administrator at the municipal level, helped me understand the depths of my own positioning and location.[4]

Patria was an honored revolutionary and, at 55 years of age, a guest speaker at education events. Oddly, she had asked to use a friend's apartment for our meeting. It was just the two of us in a nicely furnished high-rise apartment, sitting in chairs across from each other: face to face. As she seemed to be mustering some kind of strength to converse with me, she said, "I never thought I would ever find myself face-to-face again with a person from the United States." There was a long pause as she stared at me. I felt like an exotic animal that, because of a perceived unpredictability and possible danger, had been safely caged, to be examined carefully before being let loose.

My own schooling had never put me in the position of an oppressor or a participant in a damaged or damaging culture. Now being made acutely aware of this identity, I nervously acknowledged my representation of historical oppressor and asked her why she chose to meet me. She responded, "I want the United States to know the 'truth.'"

After I thanked her for her efforts to meet me, she began to talk a little more easily. For Patria, I was both listener and someone who could retell her story. She described her experience as a teacher during the 1961 Literacy Campaign:

I was nineteen when I taught literacy classes at the Bay of Pigs. Adults who had never learned to sign their name were learning to read and write. Why did your military find that so threatening: people understanding for the first time their own history, which was protected from them by imperialist domination?

She proceeded to give a clear image of the U.S. invasion.

Finally they took us at gunpoint from the bungalow, a makeshift school, to another shelter. They said they had come to liberate us, and I shouted, "And who told you that there was someone here that needed to be liberated?" They took us, the teachers, hostage without food for two days. The soldiers taunted and tortured us, but we maintained our revolutionary beliefs.

She paused again with tears in her eyes.

No amount of torture could have hurt me as much as the scene I returned to inside the school. When we walked back into the school, the students' books and notebooks lay covered in human feces and urine. This experience had such an impact on me that I was flown to Havana for psychological treatment. When I was released a month later and offered work in the capital, against everyone's wishes, I returned to the small town at the Bay of Pigs. I wanted to finish the work I [had] started.

Patria offered to help me with my research, and I was grateful to be in the position of trying to level barriers in my own country and culture with "the truth." She felt the stories would have more impact if authored by a "North American" (her term for me) educator rather than by a Cuban. With this initial acknowledgment of our limitations and privileges, we started our collaboration.

In interviews with other Literacy Campaign participants, inevitably the conversation turned to the challenge of passing on these revolutionary values "from before"— *antes*—to children today. The aged brigadistas acknowledged being transformed by the mass mobilization to the countryside and the cultural exchange that took place there, but they were perplexed about how to solve what they knew as a "values crisis" in Cuba.[5] One person suggested that what was needed was another literacy campaign.

When I reflect on these initial impressions of Cuba and compare them with my impressions after prolonged engagement with Cubans, it reminds me of window-shopping. I was enticed by the novelty of socialism in daily Cuban life, such as free education and health coverage, ration booklets, a sense of community, striving for justice, and collective tasks, from work projects to mass mobilizations. However, looking through a display window allowed me to see things only one-dimensionally, and only what the merchant wanted me to see. The more time I spent in Cuba, however, the more frequently I had an opportunity to "go inside" and examine the "the product" more closely and from different angles. These instances of going inside gave me a better understanding of the acquisition, maintenance, and negotiation of values and patterns of thoughts and the feelings that accompanied the processes and the product.

Fidel's reference to Cuba "as one huge school" resonated with the revolutionary images that greeted me on my arrival to Havana. As the taxi pulled away from the José Martí International Airport, the revolutionary murals and billboards asserted themselves: "*Decididos a seguir siendo libres*" (Decided to continue to be free); "*Por la unidad que defendemos*" (For the unity that we defend); "*Dignidad, patria*" (Dignity, fatherland); "*Creemos en la Revolución*" (We believe in the Revolution); "*Listos para vencer*" (Ready to overcome); "*Luchar por el futuro por un mundo major*" (Struggling for the future for a better world); "*Cuba: Firmeza y coraje*" (Cuba: Steadfastness and courage). This projection of revolutionary messages depicted a national pride and stands in contrast to U.S. commercial advertisements, which not only market jeans, athletic shoes, and SUVs but also objectify women and racial minorities in the process. Indeed, the Cuban government was trying to promote the nonmaterial, *lo espiritual*. In addition to the murals and billboards, many Cubans wore revolutionary t-shirts with images and sayings of Che Guevara and José Martí. These shirts rarely had to be purchased, because various institutions distributed them in celebration of annual commemorations of historical events. I was left wondering to what extent these messages reflected authentic beliefs.

Lo espiritual, Language, and Emerging Trends

My early experiences in Cuba, coupled with the omnipresent revolutionary slogans I saw broadcasted around the city, prompted me to ask people how they came to terms with the material scarcity. In response, Cubans would often say, "lo espiritual es más importante que lo material" (the spiritual is more important than the material). *Lo espiritual* was defined in such terms as *los valores* (values) and *el afecto* (affection, love, attachment, emotion). One Cuban researcher who had traveled to the United States said, "People in the U.S. have pursued the material at the expense of the '*lo espiritual.*' We may have material scarcity here in Cuba, but if I have to chose, I would much rather have the '*lo espiritual*' and enjoy my hardships *with* people than be alone and have all of the material comforts." When I asked people to define conciencia, they told me that it too was "*lo espiritual.*"

"*Lo espiritual*" summed up all of the revolutionary values that harked back to the Literacy Campaign. Those who participated in the Literacy Campaign were emotionally passionate about the experience and what the revolution represented. Inevitably, in the many interviews I conducted, none of the participants kept a dry eye. I asked one of my informants, "Why is it that everyone cries?" One said, "Do you think we did all of that work in the sixties with the idea that we would live the life we do now?" Another said,

> Do you think my husband, who fought in Escambray and obtained a college degree, aspired to make cakes at the age of 58 and sell them on the black market so we would have enough to eat? Not to mention all of the black market activity we must participate in to get all of the ingredients to make the cakes. A vendor surreptitiously passes by my workplace window each day. If I can sell so many *dulces* at my workplace and sneak them in, I will get one for myself. This is illegal. These are not the values we grew up with, but these are the survival values.

Another participant stated, "It's like a marriage gone sour. You have been the committed one in the relationship while your spouse has been the opportunist. At what point do you try to satisfy your own needs? Because if you don't, who will?"

Those who did not participate in the Literacy Campaign usually were unwilling to elaborate on their feelings about it, probably because of the political nature of non-conforming. However, one of my neighbors, knowing my research topic, asserted her views:

> That Literacy Campaign was not all that the Revolution pretends it was. Yeah, it happened. But what actually happened? Children saw and experienced a different lifestyle. The literacy rate didn't improve greatly as a result of these youngsters. They came back pregnant. There was a lot of danger in those remote places because of the counterrevolutionaries. My parents wouldn't let me go because of the danger. . . . And now look at effects of our high literacy rate. Sonia [a 19-year-old neighbor] will get somewhere not because of her formal education, but because she has a voluptuous body and an outgoing personality. My daughter . . . well, she has pretty long blond hair [the woman gives me a look when she says "blond" to indicate its higher value], she doesn't have much of a bust, although otherwise her figure is fine. It's just that she has never had that flirtatious, animated personality like Sonia. She's studying medicine. We'll never have any money. Sonia keeps going to the clubs and meets foreigners. There's the promise of a secure future.

The end of my first visit to the island was the week prior to July 26, a holiday celebrating the attack on the Moncada army barracks in Santiago de Cuba in 1953, which set the stage for the 1959 Cuban Revolution. Joanna, a U.S. researcher, wanted to show her support for the revolution. With black-spooled braids on the left side of her head and red ones on the right, she wore her black Che t-shirt proudly.

Spotting Elena, a librarian in her late forties who had assisted us in our document searches, we expressed our appreciation for her help during our time there. Upon seeing Joanna, her face stiffened and she quickly disappeared into the library stacks. When she returned, the area around her eyes was moist from crying. I asked her if she was okay. She said,

> To see Joanna, a young U.S. woman with such revolutionary fervor . . . when we have trouble getting our own children to appreciate what the Revolution has done for our own country. I, as a black woman, would not have this position as a librarian if it were not for the Revolution. My children don't understand that. They didn't live the struggle that my family did.

Those who feel close to the revolution, either because they participated in it or because they benefited significantly from it, have heartfelt allegiance to the commemorative events organized by the state. As the domestic and external contexts have evolved, contradiction and conflict have been emerging between the expectations set by the revolution and the attitudes of Cuban youth. The recent generations never knew the revolution and "*antes*"—"before"—that their parents and grandparents experienced; they were more familiar with the dual economy and its accompanying *doble moral,* or dual morality. Like chameleons, the Cuban youth take on the colors necessary to negotiate the *teque* (political rhetoric) in their society. The *lucha* (struggle) is multilayered. Signs of the *lucha* are seen in all spheres of society, not just between the state and the pueblo but also between generations of Elena and the youth.

"*Lucha*" and "*antes*" mutually and historically shape one another. The experience of the *lucha* was shaped by the historical conditions. For the generation that experienced the triumph of the revolution, *antes* meant before the Literacy Campaign, socialized medicine, and education accessible to all Cubans. For the younger generations, *antes* marked before the fall of the Soviet bloc and the beginning of the Special Period, which included heightened material scarcity, *apagones* (scheduled blackouts in residential areas to conserve electricity for tourist areas), the legalization of the U.S. dollar, joint ventures, and the surge in tourism and prostitution. Cuba went from material prosperity to scarcity in the twentieth century: for example, Cubans have known and used toilet paper, Kleenex tissues, deodorant, and other hygiene products, but now consider them luxuries. The Cuban government's implementation of a mixed-market economy to rescue the economy after the Soviet Union pulled out has yielded a somewhat mixed ideological message, influencing the ways Cubans negotiate their reality. Obviously, each generation's lived experienced of *antes* would influence their hopes and aspirations of the past, present, and future luchas.

The use of *lucha* was so proliferate that it had become a part of a greeting. When asked "¿Cómo estás?" many Cubans responded with "¡Allá en la lucha!" (There in the struggle!)—sometimes in a tone of fatigue and other times in a tone of conviction, like most encounters, everything seemed to have a *doble sentido* (double meaning). Were people making reference to the material struggle, the ideological struggle, or both? The known understanding of these words was encased within the private world of each individual and seemed to be publicly and purposely expressed with an air of ambiguity. The expression was very telling of the context of the Cuban people in the late 1990s and also of the context of my experience as researcher in the struggle to know how to interpret what I was seeing, hearing, and living.

In the daily factory of conversation, other new codes of reality were being created also. Some examples included the emergence of "*la shopping*" for any store that sold goods in U.S. dollars, and "*paladares*."[6] Also, the term "*jinetera*" became popularized during the Special Period. Literally meaning "jockey," it was slang for "prostitute." Before the revolution, *puta* or *prostituta* was used, with the connotation of "whore." *Jinetera*, however, was not a pejorative term but rather denoted one who, like a rider, was well trained (well educated), in control, "riding" the tourist and the system for material profit. This linguistic mediation is more dense than the simple incorporation of consumer neologisms, such as *videocasetera* or *Nintendo*. This is a learning process that includes a socially determined relation to specific kinds of knowledge.

Older expressions, which had been abandoned, were reappearing to articulate a new subjectivity. This is the case with the recuperation of the word *señor*. Walking down the street with other Cubans, frequently someone would yell to one of the men and ask, "Señor, ¿la hora?" inquiring about the time. In revolutionary Cuba, typically "*compañero/a*" (companion or buddy) would be used in any situation where one might say "Miss," "Ma'am," or "Sir." The men who were with me would comment on this emerging trend of addressing one another. The substitution with *señor/a* might express a reevaluation of discourse at the interpersonal level. This manifestation of pre-revolutionary vocabulary could be interpreted as an indicator of an ideological change or a new set of values. Dignity is being reinvested in a term that was previously devalued for its impersonal implication. At the same time, the term *compañero*, which implies a shared identity, has been laid aside. Perhaps *compañero/a*, like the Che image plastered across billboards and t-shirts, has become a worn-out expression, emptied of its original significance.

These images of language and culture, which seemed to reflect convulsions in the axiological and ideological arenas of informal and formal education, are part of the context that continuously shaped my methodology. With the understanding that schools are the factories charged with producing the values necessary to fulfill a society's intellectual and labor needs, I probed the ways Cuban schooling was adapting its socialization mechanisms to accommodate an evolving economic system. I heard people express dissatisfaction with the current economic situation and compare it to conditions before. I observed the ways economic upheaval caused them to enter into a complex process of juggling revolutionary values with more capitalistic, albeit survival, values. As a result, the value scales for *lo material* and *lo espiritual* were being altered too. As researcher, I also took these material shortages into consideration to understand my own identity, power, positioning, and the emerging cultural norms in contemporary Cuba.

Research Design

Hammersly and Atkinson (1995, 24) comment that "even less than other forms of social research, the course of ethnography can not be predetermined." This does not eliminate the precautions and pre-fieldwork preparations that the fieldworker should take. Moreover, the researcher's work should not be haphazard, simply heeding the path of least resistance. Following Hammersly and Atkinson, I kept an ongoing journal and this research design was an evolving and reflexive process at every stage of the project.

Each time I entered a new situation in Cuba, I was reminded of jumping rope as a kid. The politically sensitive discourse that was in operation became the steady beat of the swinging rope. There was always a thrill in being able to run inside the beating rope and keeping the jumping pace going. However, it was not easy, especially with other people holding the rope; I remember watching closely, moving my hands in a motion to mark the rope's swing. Finally, I would enter with the swing of the rope, closing my eyes tightly for a moment with hopefulness. I would feel more secure once I was in, but the task of maintaining the momentum and coordinating myself with the beat, marked by others, was always a challenge.

Negotiating life, especially in a different culture, like running in the swinging jump rope at the right time, requires intense observation and a type of participation that involves adjusting one's lifestyle or cadence to that of others. Just because one chooses to participate does not mean there is an automatic familiarity with the native culture. Rather, it means one has chosen to make cultural adjustments in order to participate, to be vulnerable. I lived with a Cuban family, participated in household chores, and attended family events.

At the hospital, I supported a Cuban friend going through childbirth alone. I learned that since the Special Period, bedding, soap, towels, toilet paper, and food are no longer provided by the state but rather are the responsibility of the patient and family to provide. While accompanying another woman to a consultation about her infertility problem, she told me that if she did not bring a gift for the doctor, she would be less likely to get the help she needed. This reciprocity for medical care has been coined "*el plan de jaba*" (the bag plan). She said, "Just look when we go in the small room for the consultation." There the doctor had a display of goods on the shelf:

beans, cigarettes, fruits, and vegetables. As she needed x-rays to complete the consultation, our task was to find a black marketer from whom to purchase x-ray film for her next examination.

Over time I began to question whether I could distinguish what research was from what it was not. I was taught that my research was to be "systematic and scientific," and therefore did not know where to place or what to do with the personal and emotional aspects of others' lives and my own. At first I filtered them out in my journal. However, the longer I lived in Cuba, the more difficult it became to separate the value of formal interviews from the value of long journeys by bus and on foot with my friends to do errands. If it were not for my genuine personal investment, my professional outcome might have been vastly different. My engagement was not merely temporal or solely instrumental; it continues today with a handful of Cubans while we are many miles apart.

My formal interviews were conducted with forty participants for twenty to sixty minutes each. Because the sight of documents drew suspicion, I coded the tapes with letters from the alphabet and asked participants to acknowledge their consent on tape using their assigned letter. I had no problem audiotaping people ages 18 and older; these interviews usually took place in the privacy of their homes. The generational interviews that took place in peoples' homes were much more relaxed, but the tape recorder still elicited uneasiness. Many times what I caught on tape was merely a warmup for longer oral histories that people shared after the tape was turned off. Conversely, interviews with Ministry of Education (MINED) officials and Cuban researchers were conducted at their workplace.

The junior high school setting, however, seemed too sensitive for audiotaping. The school had never had a Cuban or foreign researcher visit. The use of a tape recorder seemed to make the principal and the teachers uncomfortable, so I left it at home. In fact, it was not until the end of my study that MINED officials realized they had granted me permission to conduct research in what they termed a "marginalized" school, and quickly arranged for me to observe at Ciudad Libertad, a showcase schooling compound nearby. In addition, qualitative research is virtually unknown in Cuba. School personnel and my Cuban mentor found my methods of prolonged observation, lengthy interviews without programmed questions, and note taking suspicious, and encouraged me to use surveys instead. The closest thing I could compare my research to was *testimonios*, personal historical testimonies used to recycle the revolution. Because of the challenges of trying to tape interviews, I tried to compensate by taking copious notes in a notebook while I was there, then fleshed out the conversations on my laptop computer once I returned to my Cuban home.

Each evening I ate dinner with Alma's, Susana's, or Adela's family. I lived with Adela. Her sister, Alma, lived down the street, and my other contact, Susana, lived about a mile away. The routine was usually the following: everyone came home from school or work and showered before dinner. Children did their homework while the women prepared dinner and recounted the day. Then the entire family would sit and eat together, and the man of the house would often wash the dishes and clean up afterward. Neighbors came by and visited after dinner, or we went to visit friends, and the evening would end with watching a telenovela.

Visitors could interrupt dinner or practically any activity and be given immediate hospitality. However, if anyone were to come to the door during the telenovela, a family member would simply say "Siéntate" (Sit down), while all eyes stayed glued to the TV. This behavior seemed to be the custom, no matter which house I was in. Telenovela time was sacred. It was not only a guaranteed escape but also a meter of reality, a continuous referent in daily conversations. Adapting to the routine of participating in meal preparation, housecleaning, and telenovela conversation seemed to be key to my success as a fieldworker, capturing the beat of the jump rope.

Permission

The Department of Anthropology at the University of Havana was deemed "unnecessary" in the early 1960s and was dissolved by the new government. In addition, Cuba's "forbidden" designation by the United States only heightened the methodological problems in seeking authorization from both governments to carry out research.

As an educational anthropologist, my proposal to conduct research about Cuban schools (the school being one of the best-guarded state institutions) was not a request that was readily answered.[7] A fax from MINED, an overt political instrument of the state, suggested that I not waste my time coming to Cuba because it would take many months for the officials to evaluate my proposal. Later, in Cuba, other Cubans explained that this was the Cuban way of putting people off—"*la burocracia.*" "The Cuban government does not want to be perceived as oppositional to the United States; it is more 'politically correct' to be ambiguous." I, on the other hand, was waiting for a direct no, and decided to continue my inquiry until I was instructed otherwise.

With patience and persistence, at least twice a week I rode my bike many miles across town to wait for MINED to give me an answer. Referring to my acquired knowledge of the city of Havana as a result of my extensive bike rides, one MINED official introduced me to another, saying, "¡Es más cubana que nosotros!" (She is more Cuban than we are!). I offered to help translate documents in MINED while I was there, and after a while I did not feel so foreign and they did not seem so official. We would talk about the previous night's telenovela and the possible outcomes of the characters. I met people's families, and at times I felt like family. I devoted one morning just to listening to the stories of the revolution from Pablo, an 84-year-old parking attendant who watched my bicycle in the *parqueo* of MINED. Other MINED officials said I ought to consider getting my hair cut for free at the MINED beauty shop, since I was "practically an employee." I let go of waiting to start the research and realized that this experience within MINED *was* research.

Like any other tourist, I entered with a one-month renewable (for another month) visa. If at the end of two months I was not granted a research visa, I would have to leave. After one month I was given verbal approval, but no research could be initiated without written authorization. My Cuban "family" told me that I was being "put off," and they doubted I would be granted permission.

Adela explained that, with no major signs of progress, the officials hoped I would become discouraged and leave. I proceeded to divide my time between the José Martí National Library, La Varona Pedagogical Institute, and the Documentation Center at MINED. In addition, my primary contact, Alma, suggested that I continue interviewing participants in the Literacy Campaign to get their perspectives on value formation today. Thus, my typical day was comprised of note taking in one of the research facilities and audiotaping the stories and perceptions of former brigadistas. Meanwhile, Alma, Adela, and Susana took it upon themselves to facilitate my formal authorization to do research in the schools. All three women were married, but unhappily. Being a part of my research project seemed to distract them from the everyday struggles and give them a sense of empowerment.

The women often spoke of their husbands being more loving and respectful before the Special Period. Since that time, they had experienced more spousal arguments and more distance in relating to one another. The man had more difficulty supporting the family economically with just his state salary. With their husbands' economic power diminished, the women assumed a more proactive role in working the black market. In Susana's case, the Italian company for which she worked paid part of her salary in U.S. dollars, and she made cakes to sell on the black market. Alma sold her state-rationed rum on the black market, and Adela, with her musical background, gave private music lessons in her home. Correspondingly, the husbands would use the money their wives had earned to buy meat. However, in each case the women noticed that the men were spending more than what it should cost for meat, which became a source of contention. Household tension mounted as *lo material* eclipsed *lo espiritual*.

In accompanying one another on errands and household chores, the three women and I became a source of support for one another. With the neighborhood CDR,[8] private lives became public very quickly, but I felt they confided in me because I was "safe" as an "outsider." They could sort out their fears, pain, and confusion and know that it would not become neighborhood gossip. In each family, the woman was the one who had more marketable skills or know-how. Susana orchestrated the cake making, Alma the rum trade, and Adela the music lessons. The women suspected that their husbands' resentment was at the root of the emerging domestic violence that they would endure.

My women friends saw a *santero* or a *santo*[9] for assistance in resolving their household conflicts and nurturing *lo espiritual*. They invited me along to consult the spirit world to see whether my research was sanctioned, and if it was, what I should do to ensure authorization from the Cuban government. At the very least, using a Cuban medium provided psychological relief and support. The prescriptive technique inherent in these "readings" became a useful feminist tool for decision making, and in my case for my staying focused, "knowing" where and how far to go, and "knowing" in whom to confide. It provided another way of seeing and knowing, which proved to be very dependable in my fieldwork logistics and methodology. I had my "adviser" to whom I could turn.

Alma and Susana frequented Rosy, a *santo* in the La Flor[10] neighborhood. Our mile walk to Rosy's house became one of our strongest bonding experiences. "Talking while walking," Alma and Susana would tell me, "is the safest way to talk. Staying in motion makes it harder for people to hear." These experiences evoked *lo espiritual* among us because very personal issues arose in the *santo*'s reading of the cards (the medium of the *santo*). After the readings we would chat on Alma's front porch, drinking our *Toki refresco*,[11] reviewing the situations in our lives, and giving one another support for the tasks ahead of us.

At one point the situations in Susana's life and mine became more difficult, and Susana insisted we needed to see the *santero* Bernardo, who lived in Guanabacoa—several miles away, to which there was no direct means of transportation. We met at 4:30 a.m. one morning to catch the first in a series of vehicles, a combination of buses and hitchhiking. It took us several hours, and then we waited our turn in his small living room for about an hour. Bernardo was an 85-year-old *santero*. Susana had been seeing him for years; however, because of the *lucha* to get there, she could only afford to visit him two or three times a year. Bernardo's living room had a beautifully decorated altar, and Susana explained to me the symbolic value of the plastic dolls dressed in different colors, the pictures, and the flowers.

Bernardo performed his readings by tossing *caracoles* (shells) and calculating numbers based on the number of shells that landed face up or down. Susana had her reading first, then it was my turn. Bernardo indicated that one person in particular was making my authorization problematic, and he gave me special tasks to perform. He told me that the arrangement of the shells indicated that the spirits wanted this research to take place, so it was my duty to go forward with my plans and bring him a cow tongue so he could perform a ritual with a machete. He said, "Bring the tongue for the ritual. And in case you are granted permission, a rooster must be brought in fulfillment of the spirits' wishes."

Alma and Adela went with me to get the tongue a couple of weeks later for my follow-up trip with Susana to see Bernardo. My Cuban female friends seemed to be empowered by their knowledge of where to go and what to do to ensure my safety and success. They had written the name of the designated "tongue person" on a small piece of paper, put it in a small glass of water, and put the glass in the freezer. They told me that this way they were "freezing" or putting a stop to any problems this person might cause in relation to my work and me. Confident, they smiled and declared, "Instead of the Campaña de Alfabetización, we are participating in the Campaña de Autorización!"

Bernardo's and Rosy's readings coincided as far as which day would be my most fortuitous in going to MINED. Accordingly, my women friends did everything they knew to pave my way to get the necessary signatures for authorization. They instructed me to dress in my saint's color, blue. In addition, I was to write down the names of people who might be my two greatest hindrances to getting permission on separate pieces of paper and put the paper in my shoes. I was about to fold the pieces of paper before I put them in my shoes when Adela corrected my process. She said, gesturing with her hands, "they must be face up." Then, while I stood in place, she lifted each of my feet in turn and set it down again to put pressure on each piece of paper. "You want to flatten these people," she said. Her husband punctured the top of a pill container so that I could sprinkle on my path the special powder Bernardo had made to keep the evil spirits away from me. He had also made me a perfume for added safety. The perfume smell was so repugnant we all swore it would repel the stray dogs that typically befriended me on my bike route. This communal preparation process felt like a cross between having friends dress me up for Halloween and having squad leaders inspect my weapons before battle. When I finally got my daypack ready, Adela exercised her final blessing with *cascarilla*, a chalklike substance, and used it to draw a white cross on the bottom of each shoe.

The troublemaker in my permission process became subdued, and I got permission in a very dramatic event.[12] I did not know if I should laugh or cry. Was it the power of my saint's color, the pieces of paper in my shoes, the crosses on the shoe soles, or that odorous perfume that I was wearing? Regardless of the reason, the collective effort to obtain this permission made the experience a cathartic one for me. I had tears in my eyes when the MINED official told me this was the first time a foreigner had been granted permission for long-term observation in the Cuban schooling system. I felt honored and considered it a privilege to have obtained this authorization. The ultimate trust on the part of MINED and the struggle and sacrifice of others involved in this process have consequently shaped which stories I tell.

At the end of my stay, I finally found time to buy a live rooster in the market. I repeated the long journey to Guanabacoa with Susana, hitchhiking with the *gallo* in a cloth bag. It moved in the bag and made noises throughout the trip, causing people to look my way and smile. Adela found my participation in Santería rituals comical and said, "¡Cuando tú termines tu doctorado no vas a tener un doctorado de educación, vas a tener un doctorado de las ciencias exactas de brujería!" (When you finish your doctorate, you are not going to have a Ph.D. in education, you are going to have a Ph.D. in the exact sciences of witchcraft!).

Reciprocity and My Identity

I valued the friendships of my informants, and they wanted a continuous report on my research, which I gave without boundaries other than maintaining the anonymity of participants.

Reciprocity was also key to accessing resources that I had never contemplated. For instance, because people had little discretionary money, parties were hardly affordable, but most people seemed to make the sacrifice to buy or make a birthday cake to celebrate family birthdays. Enjoying baking, I wanted to bake a birthday cake from scratch for my Cuban mentor. Susana and her husband made the cakes for supplemental income, and as I came to learn, the ingredients were only affordable on the black market. Getting the flour, eggs, sugar, oil, and chocolate on the black market took most of the day, and Susana told me that I did very well to acquire the goods so quickly. She then coached me through her mental recipe.

The most surprising element of the cake-making process was that this was all done without an oven.[13] Susana used her pressure cooker and one of the two working stove burners to cook one cake layer at a time. She removed the cake in one piece, wiggling it carefully through the half-inch lip on the pressure cooker. She also knew exactly when the icing was at the correct boiling point without a thermometer. The Italians at her workplace had been ordering her homemade cakes, and they also supported her business by bringing her cake decorating supplies from Italy when they were abroad, including food coloring, and sprinkles, items that could not be found in Havana. These added foreign novelties made her cakes in high demand. After I finished decorating Beti's birthday cake, Susana remarked that I had exceeded her expectations in my handwriting and by fitting all of "*Feliz cumpleaños*" across the cake. She immediately requested my decorating talent for Saturday mornings, their biggest delivery day. In return, she offered to photocopy documents for me at her workplace—an unexpected bonus.[14]

I quickly learned that the actual cake making was much easier and less time-consuming than the combination of searching for the ingredients and making the delivery.[15] My family arranged a ride for me on the back of a friend's motorcycle to make the forty-five-minute ride on bumpy roads to deliver the cake to Beti's home. Of course, the motor was turned off as we coasted downhill to conserve gas.

It is not the Cuban custom to put a cake in a box mostly because paper products are in such short supply. Usually cakes are delivered on a piece of sturdy cardboard. I sat on the back of the motorcycle, without a helmet, with both arms out to one side holding an uncovered cake by the edges of the cardboard underneath it. With my left arm pressed against the motorcycle driver's back to steady my balance and hold on to the cake, I hugged the motorcycle tightly with my thighs (in petrified fear) as the bike bounced around on the potholed streets. I was the only one who seemed to think this situation was peculiar or even slightly dangerous. I had seen people walking down the street to deliver a cake, but the other dimensions of cake making and delivering had never occurred to me. This was my initiation into a deeper aspect of Cuban culture that I had only superficially seen — symbolic of other deeper stories that probably existed that few outsiders understood completely. It was hard to imagine how anyone could juggle getting ingredients, making cakes, and delivering them, on top of maintaining a full-time job.

Cake making initiated me into a whole new system of trade. In showing my gratefulness to those who assisted me, it would have been easier and more efficient to just purchase something they needed at the dollar store or to give people money. However, I wanted to acknowledge their ways of giving, which seemed more personal, involved more time and effort, and tapped into what I was now finding so nurturing: *lo espiritual*. So I did my black market deals for the ingredients to create a *guayaba tortica* (a Cuban fruit) cookie. My choice for reciprocity seemed to have defied their expectations of their image of Americans as prone to expediency and impatience. I enjoyed the process of taking more time, effort, and inventiveness — getting the ingredients, creating a recipe in my head, and then trying to bake the cookies in my family's oven, which only had one temperature, 200 degrees. Enjoying the homemade *torticas*, this was another instance where people remarked that I was becoming more *cubana*.

As a dog lover, I also became close friends with the neighborhood widow, Clarita — the de facto veterinarian who walked to Ciudad Libertad to feed stray dogs. She was one of the biggest fans of the pictures of my dog, Fefa. Clarita was a retired teacher of Marxism who loved to talk about Cuban history and pedagogy. I visited Clarita regularly to discuss Cuban politics, history, pedagogy, and to accompany her in bringing leftovers to the stray dogs in Ciudad Libertad. Inside her house the walls were lined with books; she would always open a book or show me a piece of revolutionary memorabilia and retell the past. We spent hours comparing the past and present. She had a firm revolutionary spirit, but she was also willing to enter into a critical discussion of current policy and politics. Throughout, she perceived me to have a revolutionary aura. When she introduced me to other revolutionaries whom she thought I should meet (or that they should meet me), I felt she showed her greatest affection for me by saying, "And the Party sent her."

Clarita and others soon started introducing me with "*es revolucionaria*," and they would usually include, "Show them the pictures of your dog and your permission to do research." I felt odd that my identity in Cuba had been highlighted as revolutionary, and I had never claimed to be pro-revolutionary or an advocate of socialism, not that I was opposed to this label either. I just wondered how I got it. Maybe it came from the ways Cubans interpreted my behavior. Mona Rosendahl (1997) explains "revolutionary" as a term describing one who is participatory and makes sacrifices. To some extent I engaged myself in this way, but perhaps this thought about me also came from my fascination in listening to people's stories about the revolution.

Seeing my interest and willingness to participate in these cultural challenges, my key contacts made another proposition. The law prohibited Cubans from buying and selling beef (punishable by a fine and imprisonment). However, one family knew of a contact for beef. I bought thirteen pounds of raw beef for twenty U.S. dollars and split it among the three families. I was instructed to make the deal at night for greatest safety. The contact gave the raw meat to me in a heavy plastic opaque DHL mailer and briefed me on what I should say if I got stopped. I put the DHL mailer in my daypack and rode home quickly on my bike, feeling a heavy, cool fleshiness against my lower back. Although I was not stopped on my bike, the briefing of precautions frightened me. In addition, another obstacle, not realized until later, was that, with glassless windows, the neighbors would smell the beef while it was being cooked on the stove, and they might inform authorities. The stakes were higher than I had realized, and therefore I refrained from participating in this type of deal again. This jump rope pace was an uneasy one for me, and I quickly opted out of the game.

The Move

My Cuban family suspected that neighbors were jealous of them, perceiving them to be profiting financially from having a foreigner living in their house; *lo material* was disrupting *lo espiritual*. The housing law stipulates that rooms may not be rented without a rental license, which entitles the state to a monthly tax. To avoid the fees for acquiring a license and charging me, the family and I agreed that I would contribute food and household supplies and that no money would change hands. This arrangement lasted for four months, until state security showed up at Adela's and her husband's workplaces. The officials did not interview Adela or her husband but rather, in their absence, spoke with their co-workers. These workers were told to warn Adela and her husband that if I did not leave their house, there would be "consequences." The momentum of our daily life died that day, as if the jump rope had been set down while others took hold of the ends when I arrived home. Few words were exchanged. The routines of cooking and doing homework were impregnated with a silence of uneasiness, sadness, and resentment toward the political boundaries that dictated social mores. My neighborhood was not set up for renting rooms because it was not close to tourist sites. However, Clarita was able to find me a place, which was, unfortunately, far from La Flor.

The next day Adela's husband tied my suitcase to my bike with rope. As I rode my bike across town to the tourist area of Vedado, I felt that I had left Cuba. I landed at a house full of strangers where I would begin my patronage of a new Cuban industry: tourism. In the *casa particular,* the elderly couple was accustomed to tourists that came and went. Their manner with me was distant and seemingly superficial. My desire to share my day or cook with the woman of the house was not readily invited. Although friendly, the family's access to more of *lo material* seemed to erode the communal and *lo espiritual* aspects I had found in my former neighborhood.

While I was trying to adjust to my new home, my friends were also adjusting to new dynamics. They were experiencing increased spousal abuse, which I was unaware of until one day when I visited them on the way home from the nearby school. When I knocked on the door, her son opened the door crying. His younger brother stood trembling and crying as he stared at his beaten mother on the floor.

I looked for ice in the freezer but the only ice was in the glass of water we had previously frozen with the piece of paper inside. The mother took the glass and held it near her swollen eye, and with typical Cuban humor said, "Well, finally this person [referring to the name on the paper] has made herself socially useful!" We laughed, and, then, having become more relaxed through her laughter, she quietly sobbed.

When people came to her door, she smiled explaining that her bruised face was due to a biking accident. The topic of domestic violence, as in many parts of the world, was taboo. She could not let anyone else know. My heart was torn, knowing that while I still lived in the neighborhood, nothing like this had happened. She clarified, "He can get away with it now that you are not here." She told me that I was helpful because I was not judgmental, and she thought this was intrinsic to "the American way." She said that if she were to tell her friends, their answer would be one of toleration: "That's the way men are." "Try to change your habits that get on his nerves." I made a habit of stopping by more often. *Lo espiritual* outweighed my material world; fulfilling my commitments as researcher and friend became a very challenging experience.

Data Collection and Recollection

What I thought would be a cut-and-dried interview became an emotional event steeped in *lo espiritual* for the interviewee and me, something I had not anticipated. Oral histories are "a context in which identity is practiced" (Friedman 1992, 840). In contrast to written narratives, the audience to which the interviewee directs his or her story is immediate and interactive (Errante 2000). Oral history is also "remembering and telling [which] are themselves events, not only descriptions of events" (Portelli 1981, 175). What distinguishes oral histories from other kinds of interviews is that the interviewer-interviewee dynamic "is also and primarily mediated by the nature and context of remembering" (Errante 2000, 17).

I hoped the oral histories would provide an understanding of the daily life of Cuban schools at different historical moments and how students' experiences of schooling might influence the informant's *conciencia*. One Cuban friend suggested, "talk around the topic, do not ask directly what you are looking for . . . and acknowledge history." Accordingly, I started my conversation with older people by asking what their education was like in school before the revolution. Then I would inquire into their role at the time of the triumph of the revolution, why they thought the socialist utopia had remained unfulfilled, and why the revolution was not able to reproduce the values they had acquired in the sixties.

Through trial and error, I discovered there were "watershed questions," questions that opened the floodgates of memory. For those who experienced the 1960s, asking about the Literacy Campaign elicited the recall of emotional bonds with people, values, sacrifice, and meaningful work. For those born in 1955 or later, the school to the countryside program was the rite of passage that, when recalled, brought to the surface emotional connections and disconnections with official discourse and with people in their lives. The interviewees became vulnerable as they amplified important memories; at times their openness took them by surprise. This openness did not occur every time, but when it did, the interviewee and I entered into what Csikszentmihalyi (1990) calls "flow." These were moments of optimal experience when our self-efficacy was heightened and social bonds were strong.

After one teacher spent more than an hour describing her experiences, she asked if I could replay the tape and listen to what she said. We sat quietly while she stared at the floor, listening to her emotional retelling of history. Afterward, she seemed stuck in the past, and it took some time for her to recuperate.

For the most part, negotiating this flow deepened my ability to secure perspectives regarding the socializing role of Cuban education. Kaufman (1974, 570) describes the "interpersonal bridge" as the "emotional bond that ties people together . . . such a bridge involves trust and makes possible experiences of vulnerability and openness. The bridge becomes a vehicle to facilitate mutual understanding, growth and change." With every memory interviewees revealed their humanity, which in turn drew out my own. I found myself listening more to the whole person and less to exactly what they were saying. Interviewees seemed to appreciate having a respectful auditor who recognized their sacrifices and ideals, as well as their recent sense of despondency and betrayal.

For these interviewees, education was not just another life event but a crucial *identifying* experience. They became sad when recalling how the country's sense of euphoria and commitment to socialism had gradually collapsed. Since the onset of the Special Period, people often expressed a sense of loss, and education, the hallmark of the revolution, became a source of grief. Volkan (1988, 6) writes that "it is through mourning that we accept changes within ourselves and within others, and become able to face reality about our unfulfilled hopes and aspirations." The elders I interviewed pursued their education in the name of the revolution, and therefore the revolution, during which the interviewees had had educational experiences, was crucial to their identity. The telling of those educational experiences was an important component of their "impression management" (Goffman 1959)—that is, how they wished me to see them.

Memories, however, can cause us not only to remember but also to forget, and to reinvent certain aspects of our personal and collective pasts. Teski and Climo (1995, 3) write that the "individual and . . . collective memories each [try] to validate the view of the past that has become important . . . in the present. Forgetting or changing memories . . . makes the present meaningful and also supports the present with the past that logically leads to a future that the individual or group now finds acceptable."

Remembering "conditions before" became a way of "forgetting" some of the present the interviewees disliked: material scarcity, prostitution, corruption, bureaucracy, and despair. Remembering a time when hope sprang eternal, the future was bright, and there was a collective sense of purpose and unity that felt good and brought satisfaction. The jokes about hardship marked another collective experience. When interviewing groups, the remembering and telling recreated the context of community and camaraderie over which they had been grieving, generating a "memory pool."

Hearing and seeing signs of the socialist dream deteriorating was painful. Their emotional stories were describing the shifting scales of *lo material* and *lo espiritual* over time and the survival behavior that Cubans have begrudgingly acquired to contend with economic and political inadequacies. By the time I left Cuba, I had grieved with those who felt betrayed by the revolution, with those who felt they had betrayed the revolution, and with those grieving over the ineffectiveness of the revolution they now attributed to their youthful idealism.

Data Analysis and Interpretation

Lo espiritual unexpectedly entered into the transcription and interpretation of my audiotapes. The process became a shared event that evoked another unexpected bonding, excitement, and transformation for a couple of women and myself. When transcribing my tapes in Cuba, I could understand only about 90 percent of what I had taped. When I asked for assistance in making sense of some words, my Cuban buddies said they wanted to transcribe the tapes. At their state jobs, they sat idle all day and wanted to have something to keep them busy. After lengthy discussions about protecting those interviewed and the use of headphones, Alma and her friend and coworker, Marta, transcribed all of my tapes.[16]

Most interesting, this transcribing process had an unpredictable effect on us. Alma and Marta were stimulated by hearing conversations they would not have initiated for fear of being suspected as counterrevolutionaries or unpatriotic. They enjoyed learning about the problematic of value transmission through teachers, researchers, and officials at MINED. When we met to exchange the transcribed tapes for new ones to transcribe, the women were anxious to give their opinions about the content of their tapes.

Their critiques of the dialogue were interesting, and I took notes. When Alma heard Cuban researchers of education deconstruct the problem of value formation in contemporary society, she commented, "I never thought about it this way before." Marta mentioned the way that the interview had been shaped by various dynamics.

They tell you what they *can* tell you or what they *want* to tell you. Part of this has to do with the limitations present in our own society [what they termed "*el control*"], and part of it has to do with using a tape recorder, which changed your identity to representing an authority, or the official discourse. The other part has to do with your way of soliciting information.

As these women seemed interested in my research, we continued our debriefing sessions.

I was surprised by the interest Marta and Alma took in helping me position myself better to get more authentic data. They told me that my approach of directly asking for specific information "caused" my interviewees to be more abstract, skirt questions, and wander off track, using what Retzinger (1991) terms "verbal hiding strategies." Marta and Alma recommended that I listen more carefully to the ways Cubans converse, what is and is not said, and they suggested that I focus more on the verbal and nonverbal cues so that I could enter more sensitively and successfully into conversations. Again, the jump rope image came to mind as I tried to match myself to the cultural patterns of conversation so that I could access more authentic responses.

Much later, Alma commented, "Did you notice how with participant H you beat around the bush? You kept it focused by staking the parameters, but you never asked directly. Did you notice how much more information you got?" Marta followed with excitement, "This person opened the curtain for you! Up to this point, no one had gone this far. Granted, there still exists the step of 'walking through,' but you have come a long way!" Alma explained with her hands raised perpendicular to her chest, side by side, "It's as if your communication is represented by one plane and ours by another. These two planes [i.e., hands] will never become one, but the planes have come closer and closer with your sensitivity, practice, and time spent here." "And your coaching," I added. The highlight of my research experience was the interest and participation of several people in the transcription, data interpretation, and analysis. Value formation and young people were a common conversational topic; people shared their opinions with me, and more frequently and openly when it was not an interview.

In the depths of my collaboration, the human conditions of Cubans shaped my appearance, my interactions with others, and my data collection and analysis, and caused me to be more reflective about my own values. For instance, during a preliminary trip to Cuba in 1995, Cuban women had asked me for sanitary pads as my trip came to a close. I gave what I had left over, then asked Alma to fill me in on how Cuban women handled their menstruation. She explained that a ration of ten feminine pads arrived at the *bodega* approximately every four months and the bag cost them ten pesos (U.S. $0.50). "Women invent ways to *resolver*," she stated.

> I buy raw cotton on the black market and place it in my panties. Sometimes the cotton is not available and then I rely on an old sheet. We have an old sheet that my mother has been using to make white shirts for her grandson's Pioneer uniform [they use to be provided by the state]. From the remnants, I improvise.

The image of Alma placing raw cotton in her panties and trying to walk without losing it—with dignity—has never left my mind, or heart. The next summer a local pharmacy donated maxipads, and I brought them with me. At her house, I showed her that they had "wings," and the jokes followed. As we caught up on our time apart in the rocking chairs on the front porch, I asked Alma if getting what she needed materially had gotten any easier. Coincidentally, at that moment a young woman walked up to the front gate with a large floral bag draped over her shoulder and whispered "psssst" to interrupt us, then softly asked if we wanted to buy feminine pads at a dime each. Alma smiled and shook her head in the direction of the traveling black market saleswoman, then turned to me and said, "There, you have your answer."

As I packed my suitcases to return to the United States, people came by to tell me good-bye. Ironically, Clarita, the diehard revolutionary, gave me three religious cards. She said,

> You said you did not have any room in your suitcase to take gifts back, so I thought long and hard. Here, these won't take up much space. They were my grandfather's. See, they still have the names in English: "Jesus," "Mary," and "Joseph." You don't have the revolution to live by in your country, but you need something to believe in.

Alma, Susana, and Adela asserted that if they had any say about my research, there was one image in particular they thought revealed the complexity of Cuban education, revolutionary values, and the intersection of my identity with Cuban culture. As I have shared everything else in my suitcase already, I will close with our favorite story.

I attended Pedagogia '99, an international education conference of several thousand participants held every other year in Cuba. Fidel, customarily, is the closing speaker, and I wanted to make sure to see him in person. This was an evening event far away from my home, so I opted to hitchhike one way, while it was still light outside, and, if necessary, I would take a taxi back.

A few cars passed me, and then a bulldozer stopped. I was confused because the driver's window was shut, and he was making a circling gesture with his hand. Finally I figured out that he wanted me to go to the other side. There was a long metal ladder leading to his open cab door, which contained a step to reach his seat. He pointed to the step next to his seat where I could sit. I climbed up, entered the dusty cab, and sat below him on the step. Because of the engine noise, we carried on our conversation practically yelling at each other. After telling me about his construction job in a new hotel zone, he asked me for my destination. Although I told him that letting me off near the Karl Marx Theater would be fine, in keeping with his generous manner he took me to its entrance. It was quite a scene. Security men were opening the doors of cars, taxis, and buses, but all eyes seemed to be on us as we rolled up in a bright yellow bulldozer and I climbed down in my skirt.

I had acquired a badge to attend the event, and the officials checked it, but they really did not seem to be able to make sense of a *yanqui* woman getting out of a bulldozer to hear Fidel at this special event. The irony lay in my wanting to hear Fidel speak on the future of education and value formation when my interaction with the laborer had already answered the question.

The laborer's thoughtfulness and unpretentiousness demonstrated the values of socialism that the inevitable economic change coming to Cuba will, I hope, never quell. He also represented Cuban education, prioritizing tourism over manual labor's original purpose of national agricultural and industrial development. Obviously, the most poignant data in my research came not from the anticipated formal interviews and events but rather from the unplanned, informal, daily interactions with people.

By this time I felt that I understood *lo espiritual y lo material* of revolutionary Cuba. Adela, Alma, Susana, Clarita, Bernardo, and Rosy, the participants in my interviews, MINED, and the laborer who gave me my first ride on a bulldozer to see Fidel were all pivotal in doing my research. They taught me how to live in Cuba and conduct my research in novel ways that seemed authentic, considering the identities and political obstacles involved. Inevitably, these methods, like all methods, are not without problematic concerns for researchers. Other researchers will time their jump rope and learn its ins and outs. Neither jumping rope nor packing my suitcases was easy for me. To protect my informants, I have packed and unpacked my suitcase with scrutiny. I close my emptied suitcase now and slide it under the bed. Anxiously, I await my next trip.

Surveys

My Cuban mentor encouraged me to create a survey on my own, which she would then check. My first drafts were found unacceptable, because my mentor felt I should specifically ask three simple questions (no fill-in-the-blanks or sentence completion format). In addition, I was told that if I asked more than three questions, the survey would be too time-consuming. In this appendix are my first drafts and then my final, accepted version.

In the first draft, "*encuesta de entrada*," my mentor did not like my question regarding organization affiliation. I explained that I wanted to see whether there was a link between family participation in organizations and revolutionary values. She found this idea to be ludicrous and asked me to cut that section. I also wanted to know the parents' employment. With the current economic situation I felt that employment might have something to do with the values lived and passed down to the children. Like the other sections of the survey, this one was struck down as well.

On the second draft, "*encuesta de salida*," with regard to questions five and six, which related to aspirations and students' advice to other students, I was told I had no business wanting to know what student aspirations were, for that information had nothing to do with revolutionary values. Question six I was told was "unimportant."

Encuesta de entrada (First draft—rejected by mentor)

Para los escolares de noveno grado de la Escuela Granma

Completa las frases y conteste las preguntas según te parezca adecuado. Gracias por tu participación.

número de grupo _____
sexo: H _____ V_____
fecha de nacimiento: _____

1. Para mí, ser pionero es
2. Cuando sea grande me gustaría ser

3. En el sistema de educación cubano existe la escuela al campo, ¿por qué?
4. ¿Cuál fue tu motivo para participar o no participar en la escuela al campo este año?
5. Relata tus experiencias de participar en trabajo socialmente útil.
6. Como persona, enuncia 3 cualidades de cómo quisieras ser.
7. Marca con una cruz las personas que viven contigo. En el caso de hermanos, tíos, primos, etc. especifique cuántos.

_____ madre _____ padre _____ abuelos _____ tíos

_____ hermanos mayores _____ hermanos menores _____ otros.

Explique el grado de parentesco. _____

8. Marca las organizaciones a qué pertenecen los miembros de la familia.

_____ UJC _____ FMC _____ CDR _____ CTC

_____ PCC ¿otra? _____

9. ¿Qué ocupación tienen las personas adultas que conviven contigo?

madre:

padre:

otros:

Encuesta de salida (First draft—rejected by mentor)

Para los escolares de noveno grado de la Escuela Granma

Completa las frases y conteste las preguntas según te parezca adecuado. Gracias por tu participación.
número de grupo _____

sexo: H _____ V _____
fecha de nacimiento: _____

1. Los tres mayores valores que aprendí participando en la escuela al campo este año fueron:
2. ¿Cuáles fueron los hechos que correspondieron a los valores que aprendiste?
3. ¿Qué sugieres para que la experiencia de la escuela al campo sea mejor?
4. ¿De qué manera es la escuela al campo socialmente útil?
5. Como el objetivo de la escuela al campo, en última instancia, no sólo es desarrollar labor agrícola, sino preparar a uno para la vida, ¿cuáles son tus mayores aspiraciones para la vida?
6. ¿Qué sugerencias darías a un pionero que va por primera vez a la escuela al campo para que tenga una buena experiencia?

Approved Survey

Cuestionario de preguntas (entrada)

PARA LOS ESCOLARES DE NOVENO
GRADO DE LA ESCUELA GRANMA

numero de grupo _____
sexo: H _____ V_____
fecha de nacimiento _____

1. ¿Qué significa para ti ser pionero?
2. ¿Qué importancia consideras que tiene el trabajo?
3. ¿Cuál fue el motivo para participar o no participar en la escuela al campo?
4. Enuncia 3 valores que quieres desarrollar en tu persona.

Cuestionario de preguntas para los padres de los
escolares de noveno grado de la Escuela Granma

Mi hijo/a es (sexo): H ____ V_____
y su fecha de nacimiento es _____

1. ¿Qué importancia Ud. concede a la participación de su hijo/a en la escuela al
   campo?
2. ¿Qué valores se ponen en manifesto en el Plan "la escuela al campo"?
3. Como madre/padre, ¿cuáles son los tres valores que mas contribuyen a formar
   en sus hijos?

Answers to Survey

Los resultados del cuestionario aplicado a los escolares de noveno grado de antes de su
étapa de la escuela al campo.

Pregunta No. 1

¿Qué significa para ti ser pionero?

1. H Para mí ser pionero significa ser parte del pueblo y conocer más sobre la
   patria.
2. V Para mi significa ser pionero un orgullo.
3. H Significa un privilegio que nos que demuestra nuestro país.
4. V "
5. V Para mi es un gran honor pues le estoy cumpliendo a mi patria estudiando y si
   algún día tiene más que cambiar nuestros lápices por fusiles ¡lo haremos!
6. H Para mí ser pionera significa mucho.
7. V Para mí ser pionero es como ser maestro.

8. H Para mí es muy importante ser pionero ya que eso es una tarea especial de todo niño.
9. H Para mí significa mucho ya que aprendo cada día más algo útil y válido.
10. V Significa para mí ser pionero algo muy grande porque estudiando ayuda a la revolución para revelar a los que se van.
11. V Significa ser parte de la Revolución.
12. V Significa todo pues ser pionero es el honor más grande que existe en el mundo.
13. V Significa mucho.
14. V Si significa algo muy grande para mi país y para mi comandante En jefe Fidel.
15. V Ser pionero para mí es como si tuviera una obligación familiar.
16. V Para mí significa ser pionero que hay que aprender porque después los conocimientos tienes que desarrollar y a mí no me gusta la escuela.
17. H Significa amar a la Patria y ser solidaria con mi país y me encanta la labor de ser Pionera.
18. V Lo significa todo para mí en la vida.
19. H Significa ser un buen estudiante.
20. H Significa algo muy importante y especial.
21. V Lo significa todo.
22. H Es ser ejemplo, es la palabra que nos coloca como símbolo de nuestra escuela, es cada día ser el mejor, continuar, realizar y desplegar los estudios a un triunfo. Es agurar conocimientos de todo tipo.
23. V Para mí significa ser pionero porque es un logro me he propuesto a medida de pasar los años como estudiar y siempre tomando de ejemplo a nuestro apostolo José Martí.
24. H Ser pionero para mí es ser un valor muy importante.
25. V Para mí significa ser pionero un orgullo y de tener tan buenos profesores.
26. H Para mí significa mucho pionero por que soy uno más de la patria como dijo José Martí.
27. V Para mí ser pionero significa ser buen estudiante hacer más tareas cumplir en todo.
28. H Para mí ser pionero lo es todo y significa mucho para mí.
29. H Ser pionero para mí es lo más importante en estos momentos ya que me siento bien serlo.
30. H Para mí ser pionero significa mucho, ya que por este medio aprendo bastante.
31. H Ser pionero para mí es dedicarme por entero al estudio y a la patria.
32. H Para mí ser pionero significa Cuba, trabajo, ayuda, estudio, solidaridad, porque ser pionero es un cargo que ayuda a los niños a relacionarse, a ser compañeros.

Pregunta No. 2

¿Qué importancia consideras que tiene el trabajo?

1. Lo considero importante para la vida cotidiana.
2. es que es muy importante para todo.
3. sin el trabajo no se puede desarrollar la economia en nuestro país.

4. "
5. nos forma y prepara para el futuro.
6. ya que forma al estudiante.
7. es muy bueno para aprender muchas cosas.
8. es una etapa para el ser humano muy importante
9. dependemos de nosotros mismos y de nuestros conocimientos.
10. cuando trabaje, sabré la importancia que tiene el trabajo.
11. para mí el trabajo es amor y ayuda a mi patria.
12. el trabajo tiene mucha importancia ya que el se sustentan las personas.
13. forma al estudiante.
14. significa algo muy grande para esta revolución y para nuestro comandante Fidel Castro.
15. por la asociación natural y por la Revolución.
16. no contestó.
17. sin él, nadie sería nada en la vida.
18. ayuda para la vida.
19. importante para el futuro.
20. forma al estudiante.
21. ayuda para la vida.
22. ayuda la economia del gobierno, el trabajo desprende raices necesarias para el desarrollo de un país, sin trabajo, ¿qué hubiera?
23. es factor fundamental que necesita la sociedad para su desarrollo.
24. tiene demasiado importancia y es muy útil.
25. sin el trabajo el hombre no es suficiente hombre para realizarse en la vida.
26. en él se ve muchas cosas de la vida.
27. significa una cosa útil para la vida porque todo ser humano tiene que trabajar para sobrevivir y mantener sus cosas.
28. por asi alcanzo a independencia económica y soy alguien en la vida.
29. por medio de él vivimos, sin él no creo que hubiéramos sobrevivido.
30. dependemos de nosotros mismos.
31. es la dedicación diaria con respeto a eso que a uno le gusta.
32. es una labor muy importante, con el trabajo nos desarrollamos, crecemos en la vida.

Pregunta No. 3

¿Cuál es tu motivo para participar o no participar en la escuela al campo?

1. voy porque me gusta el campo.
2. no voy porque tengo un tratamiento en el dentista y es muy complicado.
3. no voy porque estoy enfermo de hepatitis.
4. no voy porque no puedo coger sol en la cabeza.
5. no voy porque tengo una enfermedad en la rodilla y no me puedo agachar ni arodillar ni caminar por terrenos irregulares.
6. voy para contribuir con la escuela y con mis profesores.
7. voy porque a mí me gustan esas cosas.

8. no voy porque estoy enferma de la columna.
9. no voy por mi enfermedad.
10. voy porque me gusta ir a divertirme y trabajar en el campo.
11. voy para ayudar a mis maestros y amigos porque en la unidad está la fuerza.
12. los ganos de trabajan.
13. voy porque quiero tener una nueva experiencia.
14. voy porque quiero ayudar al pueblo de Cuba y al comandante.
15. no voy porque mi mamá va a ingresar y yo tengo que estar aquí para cualquier cosa.
16. no voy porque no hay dinero.
17. voy porque uno se divierte y se desarrolla.
18. no voy por problemas personales.
19. voy porque me gusta ir al campo.
20. no voy por problemas en los huesos.
21. voy porque es algo que me enseña que aprendes desde un principio para el futuro.
22. voy para enfrentarme ante cualquier cosa a la realidad y avivar mis voluntades y demostrar que soy más pionera y que puedo más que el miedo o el temor.
23. no voy porque tengo que operarme de la garganta.
24. voy porque es necesario ir.
25. no voy porque estoy enfermo de fiebre reumático y un sopro en el corazón.
26. voy porque me gusta.
27. voy porque es una cosa que te ponen en el expediente.
28. no voy porque estoy enfermo.
29. voy porque me gusta.
30. no voy porque mi mamá tiene un problema en los senos.
31. voy porque tengo interés por ayudar a la patria de tener más y más.
32. no voy porque soy asmático y alérgico. El polvo del campo me causa un gran daño.

Pregunta No. 4

Enuncia 3 valores que quieres desarrollar en tu persona.

1. inteligencia, amistad, honestidad
2. amistad, ser feliz, ser buena
3. honestidad, puntualidad, amistad
4. honestidad, valentia, solidaridad
5. pienso que ninguno, hasta ahora
6. amistad, solidaridad, honestidad
7. trabajador, decidido, amor
8. valentia, honestidad, sinceridad
9. amistad, amor, sencillez
10. trabajar, estudiar, crecer
11. amistad, compañerismo, independencia
12. solidaridad, valentia, responsabilidad
13. solidaridad, combatividad, honestidad
14. sinceridad, honestidad, valentia
15. amistad, intervivencia, honestidad

16. estudioso, inteligente, tener suerte en mi persona
17. honestidad, amistad, solidaridad
18. sinceridad, honestidad, humanitario
19. amistad, compañerismo, respetar a los demás
20. solidaridad, combatividad, humanitaria
21. sinceridad, honestidad, humanitaria
22. sinceridad, humanitaria, solidaridad
23. amistad, solidaridad, amor
24. amistad, cumplir con la escuela, mucho interés
25. ser más cariñoso, no decir más mentiras y no ser injusto
26. honestidad, sinceridad, amistad
27. ser una persona útil ayudarse uno mismo, honesto
28. honestidad, sencillez, camaradería
29. responsabilidad, sinceridad, amistad
30. amistad, amor, cariño
31. solidaridad, respeto, humanitaria
32. solidaridad, amistad, cortesia

Notes

Introduction

1. Ciudad Libertad is the real name of the educational compound. There are only two in Cuba: one in Havana and one in Santiago. Both of these compounds used to be military strongholds of Batista.

2. The study of anthropology was abolished at the time of the revolution and only in the past decade has emerged as a "working group" in Havana.

3. Several Cubans explained to me that the verb *inculcar* (to inculcate) is used to define the process and practice of teachers instilling or teaching revolutionary values, whereas *formar* (to form) is used to refer to the process in a more general or abstract way. Therefore, I have adopted the use of "inculcate" and "inculcation" instead of "form" or "formation" in keeping with this explanation, the prevalence of *inculcar* in educational documents, and its common use in conversations within and outside the classroom.

4. I have chosen not to translate *conciencia* throughout this book precisely because I do not find a single English translation that fully conveys the revolutionary commitment and call to action that this word implies in Cuba and other Latin American countries.

5. The U.S. dollar was penalized until 1993, when it became part of the Cuban economy. Beginning in 2003, the U.S. dollar is no longer used. Everything is measured against the euro.

Chapter 5

1. I found the ways in which education is conducted and interpreted to be varied and often conflicting among the Cuban populace.

2. See also Castro, "Estudio y trabajo," in *La educación en revolución* (Havana: Instituto Cubano del Libro, 1974), Chap. 7; M. Suz Pompa, M. Menéndez Blanco, and A. L. Bernal González, "La actitud comunista ante el trabajo," *Educación* 63 (October–December 1986): 110–116; Colaboradores, "Raíces históricas de la combinación del estudio con el trabajo," *Educación* 15, no. 56 (January–March 1985): 94–101; and

R. G. Paulston, "Changes in Cuban education," in *Educational innovations in Latin America*, ed. R. L. Cummings (Metuchen, N.J.: Scarecrow Press, 1973).

3. To protect the participants in this study, I have changed the names of neighborhoods, schools, children, teachers, and other adults. The only exceptions are Nancy, my mentor in Cuba, and Dr. Patiño, an official at the Ministry of Education, both of whom asked that I use their real names.

4. See also Chapter 7, on the schools to the countryside program.

5. No statistical information on race at the school or in the neighborhood was available at the time of this study. I did ask for this information at the school and municipality but was either put off or told that the information was not necessary for my study. I did not press the issue.

6. The exact citation is not given, to protect the anonymity of the informants.

7. The Pioneer organization is a mass organization for students ages 6–14. It is an integral part of the Cuban school system, organizing cultural and sports activities as well as reinforcing a cooperative, collective, ideological socialist teaching and learning atmosphere (see Chapter 6).

8. Santería is a noninstitutionalized religion in Cuba representing a synthesis of the Yoruba culture and Catholicism. Yemaya is the name of one of the primary saints, or Orishas.

9. Spiritualist leaders in Santería.

10. Spiritualist leader in Santería, a level above *santo*.

11. Hiring practices seemed to show a preference for lighter-skinned Cubans where tourism was involved.

12. I was not present for value-formation hour at Ciudad Libertad. Consequently, I have no information as to whether this discussion was as popular there.

13. By 1998, civic education had also been added to the seventh- and eighth-grade curriculum.

14. To promote European tourism, Cuba became in 2002 the first country outside of Europe to use the Euro. Currently, there are three currencies in circulation in Cuba: the convertible Cuban peso (CUC), the Cuban peso, and the Euro. Since the documentation made in this book predates 2002, references to currency do not include the Euro.

15. The family I lived with did not have or use Ivory soap.

16. Options for printing from a computer are scarcer than paper. Nancy found my handwritten work unacceptable, and it took many drafts before she approved my questionnaire.

17. With a self-owned or *cuenta propia* business, the owner is obligated to pay a flat tax to the state regardless of income. Thus, while this type of employment may give the individual some autonomy, it also places the individual in a high-risk situation while providing the state with a stable profit.

18. This Havana family told me that distribution was not always equal across the city, province, or the country. The state would often alternate the allotments to municipalities, trying to even out the supply. Often locations where the product was cultivated would have more access to it than areas where it was not, as in the case of coffee: those who lived in Havana received fewer rations of coffee than those who lived in the eastern part of the island, where it is principally grown.

19. In joint-venture businesses, where one might find more high-tech equipment, I saw screen savers with photographs of the main characters. The title song seemed to

be on the lips of every child; I even heard it in a school performance. Students in the school to the countryside program had found scripts of future episodes of the soap opera and read and talked about them all the time. A necklace that the grandmother wore in the soap opera became popular in Cuba. The necklace carried the depictions of *santos* from Santería.

20. Although the assault on the Moncada barracks took place in Santiago, on the other side of the island, I understood that this was a hideout used at some time before the assault—perhaps if there was a need to be in Havana.

Chapter 6

1. For further information on the Pioneer organization, see "The Pioneers," in MacDonald, *The making of a new people*, 176–181, and "The Young Pioneers," in Wald, *Children of Che*. As a word of caution, the structure and activities of the organization have changed quite a bit since the time of these publications. The structure has become more generalized (with fewer divisions), and some activities have been cut because of the economic crisis.

2. It oversees the Pioneers, grades one through nine; the Federation of Secondary Students, grades ten through twelve; and the Federation of University Students, college.

3. Prior to 1968, the Pioneers were an exclusive organization under the revolution. In addition, until 1977 the Pioneers included only students from first through sixth grades. In 1977 the Pioneer organization was extended to include students in seventh through ninth grades.

4. For more detail on the structure of the Pioneers, see *Compendio para el trabajo metodológico de la organización de Pioneros de José Martí* 1995.

5. At the end of ninth grade, students are selected for the Union of Young Communists (UJC). This is a highly selective process that may involve teachers or UJC representatives. If a student is not selected for the UJC, he or she may still be part of the mass organization for tenth through twelfth graders, the Federation of Students of Secondary School (FEEM). The socialization mechanisms of the Pioneers, starting as early as first grade, are in place to hone the values of vanguard students who will ultimately be members of the UJC (from age 15 to 25) and, later, members of the Communist Party of Cuba.

6. I have no idea what was done with respect to cleaning the bathrooms. The odor never dissipated.

7. La Flor is a fictitious name for the neighborhood where the school is located.

8. School is mandatory through ninth grade.

9. Ciudad Libertad is the real name of an educational compound containing several different showcase elementary and secondary schools in Havana.

10. In 1999 the Explorers program was extended to include tenth through twelfth graders.

11. See Medin 1990.

12. Probably because of the timing; I was granted permission for visits during my last week in Havana.

13. At this time, socialism is emphasized instead of communism.

14. When my informants knew I was sincerely interested, this type of interview

took the better part of the day. I felt as though they were revisiting a topic that had not been touched on in decades. It was as if they had mentally climbed the stairs to the attic and were looking for the dusty, cobweb-covered trunk from a time long ago. Once these memories and feelings were accessed, a new dimension of the person emerged. The process was emotionally complex for the interviewee, and for me.

15. Che's image was a popular commodity in the early 1970s, too. Alberta Korda had snapped the picture of Che in Havana early in the sixties. In 1967, just months before Che was sent to Bolivia, the Italian publisher Giangiacomo Feltrinelli asked Korda for a copy of his earlier photograph of Che that had appeared in the Cuban newspaper *Revolución*. Korda gave him two free copies as a gift. Shortly after Che was killed in Bolivia and rose to instant martyrdom, Feltrinelli capitalized on Che's death and had millions of posters of the Che photograph printed without Korda's permission. See *People Magazine*, October 25, 2000.

Chapter 7

1. See Laguna Vila et al. 1997.

2. This term was coined by Laurie Frederick as a play on the music label Trova, which developed into Nueva Trova and later Novísima Trova. See Frederik 2005.

3. I have been conducting research in Cuba since 1995. My experience in the EAC program took place in 1999, when I lived in Havana for eight months. "Granma," "La Flor," and the names of individuals used in this account are pseudonyms. At the time of this writing, the EAC program included only eighth and ninth graders.

4. This statement is based on my own observations and on conversations with teachers and administrators. When I asked for statistical data, those in charge denied having any. They also questioned the need for data in a study about values. As suspicion grew, I dropped the idea of pursuing these statistics.

5. Among those who practice Santería in Cuba, it is not uncommon to see soda cans used as a receptacle for flowers on a home altar dedicated to a saint. In addition, it is common practice to have flowers on the altar during a Catholic mass as an offering to evoke the spirits to call on one who has died.

6. A standard book of *matutinos* exists, with one for every day of the year.

7. A spiritual being or presence that is interpreted as one of the manifestations of God (Olofi) in the Santería religion.

8. Lizabet was one of the ninth-grade teachers who were asked to remain in the city with the students who could not undertake the field experience because of a family situation or health issues. She monitored another type of work in the city, working in the community garden for a half day, which was used as substitute work for those who did not attend the EAC.

Conclusion

1. Five Cubans infiltrated a right-wing anti-Castro group in Florida, were arrested, and were sent to prison.

2. The university degree program in social work ended in 1956 with the social tur-

moil related to events leading up to the Cuban Revolution. From 1959 on, the mass organizations became responsible for implementing social programs (De Urrutia Barroso n.d.).

3. R. Corral, cited in Strug 2006.

Appendix 1

1. Island Cubans still claim that Cuba is experiencing revolution. Foreigners have a tendency to label Cuba in ways that indicate that the revolution has died, using terms such as "post-revolutionary" and "post-socialist." I decided to follow the terminology of my informants and use "revolutionary Cuba," although considerable economic changes have affected what "revolutionary" looks like since 1989 and the fall of the Soviet bloc.

2. The phenomenon of forbidden research terrains is not new, as topics and locales can be politically sensitive for geographic, intellectual, or political reasons.

3. *Brigadistas* were teenage literacy workers.

4. Patria and Joanna requested that their real names be used; however, all other people's names used in my account are pseudonyms.

5. The "values crisis" in Cuba at the time was well publicized in the newspapers and other media. Several measures were being taken in the neighborhoods and schools to counter this crisis.

6. A term meaning a family-owned restaurant, borrowed from a popular Brazilian soap opera aired in Cuba at the beginning of the Special Period.

7. A fellow anthropologist told me she had tried for two years to gain access to the schools but was unsuccessful.

8. The Committee for the Defense of the Revolution, a neighborhood watch group made up of all the residents in the area.

9. *Santos* and *santeros* are spiritualist leaders in the noninstitutionalized Cuban religion of Santería. Santería involves a syncretization of the Yoruba and Catholic religions.

10. La Flor is a pseudonym for the neighborhood I resided in. However, Ciudad Libertad is the real name of the showcase school compound.

11. Toki is the Cuban equivalent of Kool-Aid, an inexpensive powdered drink mix.

12. The details of this event are still too politically sensitive for me to give a full account.

13. During the time I was in Cuba, I would conclude that very few Cubans had working ovens.

14. Photocopying facilities are hard to find and the process is very expensive— around fifty cents a copy.

15. The delivery is usually the baker's responsibility and is included in the U.S. $2.00 cost of the cake.

16. None of the tapes had any identifying marks on them regarding the informants, and we agreed on appropriate compensation.

Bibliography

Abascal López, J. 1980. Interview with José R. Fernández, Vice President of the Council of Ministers and Minister of Education. *Weekly Granma*, November 16, 2.

Ackerman, H. 1996. Mass migration, nonviolent social action, and the Cuban raft exodus, 1959-1994: An analysis of citizen motivation and internal politics. PhD diss., University of Miami.

Acosta, D. 1998a. Boarding-school system increasingly unpopular. InterPress Third World News Agency, November 4, 1-2.

————. 1998b. Retaining priority despite economic crisis. InterPress Third World News Agency, September 1, 1-2. END/IPS/tra-so/da/sm/98.

Addine Fernández, R. 1996. *Una alternativa en la formación de valores en la escuela media cubana*. Report. Havana: MINED.

Aguirre, B. E. 1984. The conventionalization of collective behavior in Cuba. *American Journal of Sociology* 90, no. 3:541-566.

Albert, M., and R. Hahnel. 1981. *Marxism and socialist theory*. Brooklyn, N.Y.: South End Press.

Anderson, B. 1991. *Imagined communities*. London: Verso.

Andrew, C., and Gordievsky, O. 1990. *KGB: The inside story*. New York: HarperCollins.

Apple, M. W. 1982. *Education and power*. Boston: Ark Paperbacks.

Araujo, M. F. 1976. The Cuban school in the countryside. *Prospects* 6, no. 1:127-131.

Arias Medina, M., and G. Ares Valdés. 1997. *Minas del Frió: Fragua de un nuevo maestro*. Havana: Editora Política.

Austin, J. L. 1971. Performative-constative. In *The philosophy of language*, ed. John R. Searle, 13-22. Oxford: Oxford University Press.

Azicri, M. 2000. *Cuba today and tomorrow: Reinventing socialism*. Gainsville: University Press of Florida.

————. 1988. *Cuba: Politics, economics and society*. New York: Continuum International Publishing.

Bakhtin, M. M. 1981. Discourse in the novel. In *The dialogic imagination: Four essays*, ed. Michael Holquist, trans. Caryl Emerson and Michael Holquist, 259-422. Austin: University of Texas Press.

Báez, L. 1994. Entrevista a Raúl Castro. *Granma*, September 17, 3-6.

Barkin, D. P., and N. R. Manitzas. 1973. *Cuba: The logic of the revolution.* Andover, Mass.: Warner Modular Publications.

Baudrillard, J. 1983. The precession of simulacra. Trans. Paul Foss and Paul Patton. *Art & Text* (Victoria, Australia) 11 (Spring): 3–47.

Báxter Pérez, E. 1999. La educación en valores, papel de la escuela. *Presentación en Pedagogía* 99.

———. 1990. Las orientaciones valorativas en los alumnos y maestros de la educación general. ICCP report. Havana: MINED.

Beatón, G. A., et al. 1992. *La atención a menores con trastornos de la conducta en Cuba.* Bogota: UNICEF.

Behar, R. 1996. *The vulnerable observer: Anthropology that breaks your heart.* Boston: Beacon Press.

———. 1993. *Translated woman: Crossing the border with Esperanza's story.* Boston: Beacon Press.

Bell, D. 1965. *The end of ideology.* New York: Free Press.

Bengelsdorf, C. 1994. *The problem of democracy in Cuba: Between vision and reality.* Oxford: Oxford University Press.

Benjamin, M. 1990. *No free lunch: Food and revolution in Cuba today.* Princeton, N.J.: Princeton University Press.

Bernardo, R. M. 1970. Moral stimulation as a nonmarket mode of labor allocation in Cuba. *Studies in Comparative International Development* 6, no. 6:119–134.

Betto, F. 1999. Para vivir en Cuba hay que saber amar. *Juventud Rebelde,* January 3, 5.

Bethell, L., ed. 1993. *Cuba: A short history.* Cambridge: Cambridge University Press.

Black, G. 1988. Cuba: The revolution toward victory always, but when? *The Nation,* October 24, 373–386.

Blum, D. 2001. Teaching about Cuba: The concientization of a US teacher-researcher. *International Journal of Qualitative Studies in Education* 14, no. 2:255–273.

Bohemia. 1995. A la raíz. January 6, B4–B7.

———. 1988. Heroísmo e inteligencia en Cuba. July 8, B22.

———. 1972. El primer acuerdo. April 7, 50.

———. 1962. March 30, 45.

Boletín FMC. 1982. A revolution within another revolution. Special issue, June, 21.

Bonfenbrenner, U. 1970. *Two worlds of childhood.* New York: Simon & Schuster.

Boorstein, E. 1968. *The economic transformation of Cuba.* New York: Modern Reader Paperbacks.

Booth, C. 1993. Here come the "yummies." *Time,* June 21. http://yachtingnet.com/time/magazine/article/0,9171,078733-1,00.html (accessed February 8, 2010).

Bourdieu, P., and J. C. Passeron. 1990. *Reproduction in education, society and culture,* trans. Richard Nice. London: Sage.

Bowles, S. 1971. Cuban education and the revolutionary ideology. *Harvard Educational Review* 41, no. 4:472–500.

Bowles, S., and H. Gintis. 1976. *Schooling in capitalist America.* London: Routledge and Kegan Paul.

Bunck, J. M. 1994. *Fidel Castro and the quest for a revolutionary culture in Cuba.* University Park: Pennsylvania State University Press.

Burchardt, H. 2002. Social dynamics in Cuba. *Latin American Perspectives* 29, no. 3:57–74.

Camnitzer, L. 1994. *New art of Cuba.* Austin: University of Texas Press.

Canfúx, J. 1981. A brief description of the "Battle for the Sixth Grade." J. A. Mateja, trans. *Journal of Reading.* December.

Carnoy, M. 1990. Educational reform and social transformation. In *Education and social transition in the Third World,* ed. M. Carnoy and J. Samoff. Princeton, N.J.: Princeton University Press.

———. 1989. Educational reform and social transformation in Cuba, 1959–1989. In *Education and social transition in the Third World,* ed. M. Carnoy and J. Samoff, 153–208. Princeton, N.J.: Princeton University Press.

Carnoy, M., and H. Levin. 1985. *Schooling and work in the democratic state.* Palo Alto, Calif.: Stanford University Press.

Carnoy, M., and J. Samoff, eds. 1990. *Education and social transition in the Third World.* Princeton, N.J.: Princeton University Press.

Carrobello, C. 1990. Job changes: Dissatisfaction discussed. *Bohemia,* September 13. FBIS-LAT-90-178, 4–6.

Castañeda, C. E. 1973. Study, work and military service in Cuba. In *Educational innovations in Latin America,* ed. R. L. Cummings, 145–149. Metuchen, N.J.: Scarecrow Press.

Castilla, B. 1971. Speech at the opening of the National Congress on Education and Culture. *Granma Weekly Review,* May 9, 4–5.

Castro, F. 1992. Castro addresses teachers' conference 30 May. FBIS-LAT-92109, June 5, 6–18.

———. 1991. Castro speaks at opening. FBIS-LAT-91-199-S, October 15, 3–26.

———. 1989. Ni una sola piedra de las trincheras de la moral y del honor de Cuba puede quedar sin reparar. *Granma,* July 3, 1.

———. 1987. *Granma,* November 15, 1987, 1.

———. 1986. Main report to the Third Congress of the Cuban Communist Party. *Granma Weekly Review,* February 16, 5.

———. 1985. Playboy interview: Fidel Castro. *Playboy* 32, August, 183.

———. 1980. Informe central al segundo congreso [del Partido Comunista de Cuba]. *Bohemia,* December, 59.

———. 1978. Speech delivered on 4 September 1978 for opening of the 1978–1979 school year. *Weekly Granma,* September 17, 2–4.

———. 1974. *La educación en revolución.* Havana: Instituto Cubano del Libro.

———. 1972a. La historia me absolverá. In *La revolución cubana: 1959–1962,* 31–32. Mexico City: Editorial ERA.

———. 1972b. Report on the Cuban economy. In *Cuba in revolution,* ed. R. Bonachea and N. Valdés. Garden City, N.Y.: Doubleday Anchor Books.

———. 1972c. Speech at the 2nd Congress of the Young Communist League, April 5. Castro Speech Data Base, Latin American Network Information Center, University of Texas. http://infor-smtp.lanic.utexas.edu/project/castro/db/1972/19720405.html (accessed January 3, 2010).

———. 1972d. Speech at the final session of the 2nd Congress of the Young Communist League, April 16, 2–4.

———. 1971a. La escuela en el campo. *Educación* 1, April–June, 13.

———. 1971b. Speech on the Tenth Anniversary of the Creation of the Ministry of Interior. *Granma Weekly Review,* June 13, 4–6.

————. 1969. Edita "El militante," 4.

————. 1968. *Granma Weekly Review*, December 15, 2.

————. 1967. March 13 anniversary speech. Castro Speech Data Base, Latin American Network Information Center, University of Texas. http://info-smtp.lanic .utexas.edu/project/castro/db/1967/19670314.html (accessed January 15).

————. 1966a. *Granma Weekly Review*, June 19, 1966.

————. 1966b. Speech at the closing of the National Meeting of School Monitors, in Chaplin Theater. September 17.

————. 1962. Radio interview, Moscow Domestic Service, January 29.

————. 1961a. Speech to intellectuals on June 30, 1961. In *Palabras a los intelectuales* (Words to intellectuals), pamphlet. Havana: National Cultural Council.

————. 1961b. Universidad popular sexto ciclo. *Educación y revolución*, 231–319. Havana: Publicación de la Universidad Popular.

Castro, R. 1973. Important battles are being waged in the field of production. *Granma Weekly Review*, August 12, 7–8.

CETSS (Comité Estatal de Trabajo y Seguridad Social). 1981. *Censo de población, viviendas y electoral, 1953*. Havana: CETSS.

Charcon Arteaga, N. 1998. *La formación de valores morales: Propuesta metodológica y experiencias aplicadas*. ICCP report. Havana: MINED.

Comisión Nacional Cubana de la UNESCO. 1962. *Cuba y la conferencia de educación y desarrollo económico y social*. Havana: Editorial Nacional de Cuba.

Compendio para el trabajo metodológico de la organización de Pioneros de José Martí. 1995. Guantánamo, Cuba: Presidencia Provincial.

Conde, Y. M. 1999. *Operation Pedro Pan: The untold exodus of 14,048 Cuban children*. New York: Routledge.

Consejo de Ministros. 1971. Ley No. 1231. *Gaceta Oficial*, March 26, 1–4.

Córdova, E. 1992. *El mundo del trabajo en Cuba socialista*. Caracas: Fondo Latinoamericano de Ediciones Sociales.

Csikszentmihalyi, M. 1990. *Flow*. New York: Harper Perennial.

CubaInfo. 1994. Education minister announces greater link between college and ideology. No. 6 (September), 10.

de Certeau, M. 1984. *The practice of everyday life*. Berkeley and Los Angeles: University of California Press.

de la Torre, C. 1995. "¿Cómo somos los cubanos?" *Revista Cubana de Psicología* 12, no. 3:209–234.

de Urrutia Barroso, L. n.d. El trabajo social en Cuba: Desarrollo de una profesión. In *Selección de lecturas sobre sociología y trabajo social: Curso de formación de trabajadores sociales*. Havana: University of Havana.

Declaración del Primer Congreso Nacional de Educación y Cultura. 1971.

Díaz-Briquets, S. 1993. Collision course: Labor force and educational trends in Cuba. In *Cuban Studies*, vol. 23, ed. J. Pérez-López. Pittsburgh: University of Pittsburgh Press.

Dolgoff, S. 1996. *The Cuban revolution: A critical perspective*. Minneapolis: Black Rose Books.

Domínguez, J. 1993. Cuba since 1959. In *Cuba: A short history*, ed. L. Bethell, 95–148. London: Cambridge University Press.

———. 1989. *To make a world safe for revolution: Cuba's foreign policy*. Cambridge: Harvard University Press.

———. 1978. *Cuba: Order and revolution*. Boston: Belknap Press.

Domínguez, M. I., M. E. Ferrer, and M. V. Valdés. July 1990. Las generaciones en la sociedad cubana actual (cuarta parte): Características generacionales de los estudiantes y los desvinculados del estudio y el trabajo. Havana: Departamento de Sociología, Centro de Estudios Psicológicas y Sociológicas/Academia de Ciencia de Cuba.

dos Santos López, J. 1997. *Hasta el último grano: Primer gran desafío productivo de los estudiantes cubanos*. Havana: Editorial Pueblo y Educación.

Dubois, J. 1959. *Fidel Castro: Rebel-liberator or dictator?* Indianapolis: Bobbs-Merrill.

DuBois, W. E. B. 1990. *The souls of black folk*. New York: Vintage.

Duranti, A. 1993. Intentions, self, and responsibility: An essay in Samoan ethnopragmatics. In *Responsibility and evidence in oral discourse*, ed. Jane Hill and Judith Irvine, 24–37. Cambridge: Cambridge University Press.

Eckstein, S. 1994. *Back from the future: Cuba under Castro*. Princeton, N.J.: Princeton University Press.

Economic Intelligence Unit (EIU). 2000. *Country profile 2000: Cuba*. Kent, U.K.: Redhouse Press.

Edelman, M. 1985. *The symbolic uses of politics*. Chicago: University of Illinois Press.

———. 1971. *Politics as symbolic action: Mass arousal and quiescence*. Chicago: Markham.

Educación. 1990. Diálectica de la educación cívica. Colectivo de autores del Dpto. de Marxismo-Leninismo del IPE Nacional. January–March, 100–103.

———. 1989. Carta del Ministro. 19 (October–December), 20–24.

———. 1987. Sobre los maestros primarios y el Servicio Militar Activo. October–December, 67.

Educación contemporánea: Revista internacional de países socialistas. 1976. Havana: Ministry of Education.

Eisenstadt, S. N., ed. 1968. *Max Weber: On charisma and institution building*. Chicago: University of Chicago Press.

Elizalde, R. M. 1996. Prostitution in Cuba: The truth about women in Cuba called *jineteras*. *Granma International*, September 4, 8–9.

El Militante Comunista. 1987. La calidad de la educación: Tema de análisis permanente. September, 16–25.

El País. 1987. May 1, 7.

Epstein, E. H. 1987. The peril of paternalism: The imposition of education on Cuba by the United States. *American Journal of Education* 96, no. 1:1–23.

Erikson, E. H. 1968. *Youth: Identity and crisis*. New York: Norton.

Errante, A. 2000. But sometimes you're not part of the story: Oral histories and ways of remembering and telling. *Education Researcher*, March, 16–27.

Fagen, R. R. 1969. *The transformation of political culture in Cuba*. Palo Alto, Calif.: Stanford University Press.

Federación de Mujeres Cubanas. 1990. *Proyecto de informe*. Havana: Author, 7–8.

Fernández, D. J. 2000. *Cuba and the politics of passion*. Austin: University of Texas Press.

Fernández, G. A. 1982. The freedom flotilla: A legitimacy crisis of Cuban socialism? *Journal of Interamerican Studies and World Affairs* 24, no. 2:196.

Fernández, J. R. 1981. Informe a la asamblea nacional. *Ciencias Pedagógicas* 3 (June–December): 3–25.

Fernández, N. 1996. Race, romance, and revolution: The cultural politics of interracial encounters in Cuba. PhD diss., University of California, Berkeley.

Fernández Perera, R., R. Ferrer Pérez, T. Aguilar Abreu, J. Canfúx Gutiérrez, L. Rabre Alvarez. 1985. *La batalla por el sexto grado.* Havana: Editorial Pueblo y Educación.

Ferrer, C. 1987. El movimiento pioneril. In *Apuntes para la historia del movimiento juvenil comunista y pioneril cubano,* ed. L. Vizcaíno, Z. Gómez, A. Pérez, and C. Ferrer. Havana: Editora Política.

Figueroa, M. 1975. Improvement of the Educational System: On a thesis of the First Congress of the Party. *Granma Weekly Review,* June 29, 2.

Figueroa, M., A. Prieto, and R. Gutiérrez. 1974. *The basic secondary school in the country: An educational innovation in Cuba.* Paris: UNESCO Press.

Fitzgerald, F. 1989. The reform of the Cuban economy, 1976–86: Organization, incentives, and patterns of behaviour. *Journal of Latin American Studies* 21, no. 2:283–310.

Foreign Broadcast Information Service (FBIS). 1992a. Majority of students to enter polytechnics. FBIS-LAT-92-073. April 15, 7.

———. 1992b. Civil defense tunnels. FBIS-LAT-92-066. April 6, 3–4.

———. 1991a. Need for university students questioned. FBIS-LAT-91-129. July 5, 6–8.

———. 1991b. Official discusses private enterprise restrictions. Notimex News Service (April 8, 1991). FBIS-LAT-91-076-A. April 19, 2.

Frank, R. 1988. A theory of moral sentiments. In *Beyond self-interest,* ed. J. S. Mansbridge. Chicago: University of Chicago Press.

Franqui, C. 1989. *Vida, aventuras y desastres de un hombre llamado Castro,* 1st ed. Barcelona: Planeta.

Frederik, L. A. 2005. Cuba's national characters: Setting the stage for the Hombre Novísimo. *Journal of Latin American Anthropology* 10, no. 2:401–436.

Freire, P. 1970. *Pedagogy of the oppressed.* New York: Continuum Books.

French, H. 1990. Cuba flirts with capitalism to stave off collapse. *New York Times,* December 5, 18.

Friedman, J. 1992. The past in the future: History and the politics of identity. *American Anthropologist* 94:837–859.

Fuller, L. 1992. *Work and democracy in socialist Cuba.* Philadelphia: Temple University Press.

———. 1988. Fieldwork in forbidden terrain: The U.S. state and the case of Cuba. *American Sociologist* 19, no. 2:99–120.

Gal, S., and G. Klingman. 2000. *The politics of gender after socialism.* Princeton, N.J.: Princeton University Press.

García Galló, G. J. 1973. Educating the "New Man" in Cuba. Radio Free Europe, research report, February 9.

———. 1967. La escuela en el campo. *Educación en Cuba,* January–February, 1.

Geertz, C. 2000. *Available light: Anthropological reflections on philosophical topics.* Princeton, N.J.: Princeton University Press.

———. 1983. *Local knowledge: Further essays in interpretive anthropology.* New York: Basic Books.

————. 1964. Ideology as a cultural system. In *Ideology and discontent,* ed. D. E. Apter. New York: Free Press.

Gillette, A. 1972. *Cuba's educational revolution.* Fabian Research Series no. 302. London: Fabian Society.

Giroux, H. 1981. *Ideology, culture, and the process of schooling.* Philadelphia, Pa.: Temple University Press.

Goffman, E. 1959. *The presentation of self in everyday life.* New York: Anchor Books.

González, E. 1974. *Cuba under Castro: The limits of charisma.* Boston: Houghton Mifflin.

Goodenough, W. H. 1963. *Cooperation and change: An anthropological approach to community development.* New York: Russell Sage Foundation.

Granma. 2002. Fidel presides over graduation ceremony for first group of junior high school teachers. July 16.

————. 1989. Recibe el Papa con satisfacción invitación para visitar a Cuba. May 29, 6.

————. 1987a. Clausuro Fidel: El V Congreso de la UJC. April 6, 2.

————. 1987b. La política de cuadros: Una tarea priorizada después del tercer congreso del partido. March 17, 3.

————. 1982. Al colero lo mordió el cocodrilo. March 26, 3.

————. 1981. Ser maestro significa ante todo serlo en todos los órdenes de la vida. July 8, 1.

————. 1973. Aprueba el consejo de ministros las leyes de organización del sistema judicial y de procedimiento penal y otros textos legales. May 25, 1.

————. 1970a. Los trabajadores opinan sobre: Austentismo y ausentistas, ley contra la vagancia, y un pasado de explotación que ya no volverá nunca más. September 22, 2.

————. 1970b. Inician maestros en todo el país periodo intensivo de estudios. July 1, 3.

————. 1969. Edita "El militante comunista" la monografía: La productividad del trabajo y factores de su aumento. March 3.

————. 1968a. Hacia la primera región comunista de Cuba: Panorama de la educación en la isla de muchos hombres. August 14, 5.

————. 1968b. Construirán en la calle 100 la "Ciudad Cordón," que contará con doscientos cincuenta viviendas. August 14, 3.

————. 1966. September 27, 2.

Granma Weekly Review. 1986. A consciousness, a communist spirit, a revolutionary will and vocation were, are and will always be a thousand times more powerful than money. December 14, 9.

————. 1972. Final declaration of the 2nd Congress of the Young Communist League. April 23, 7–8.

Grogg, P. 2008. CUBA: Shoring up the educational system. http://ipsnews.net/news .asp?idnews=43734 (accessed February 18, 2009).

Guerrero Borrego, N. 1999. Males por exceso de amor. *Juventud Rebelde,* April 24, 2.

Guerrero, N., and E. Socarrás. 1979. La construcción de la base económica del socialismo: Nueva Moncada para la juventud. *Investigación e Información Juvenil* 10:54–65.

Guevara, E. 1979. *¿Qué debe ser un joven comunista?* Managua: Secretaria Nacional de Propaganda y Educación Pública, F.S.L.N.

————. 1968. *Episodes of the revolutionary war.* New York: International Publishers.

————. 1965. El socialismo y el hombre en Cuba. *Semanario Marcha* (Montevideo, Uruguay).

————. 1964. *Obra revolucionaria,* vol. 10, 14. Mexico City: ERA.

————. 1962. *What should a young communist be?* (brochure to FSLN). Havana: Imprenta Nacional de Cuba.

Guillén, N. 1972. *Obra poética 1958–1972.* Havana: UNEAC.

————. 1964. *Tengo.* Havana: Instituto Cubano del Libro.

Habel, J. 1991. *Cuba: The revolution in peril.* London: Verso.

————. 1989. *The revolution in peril.* London: Verso.

Hall, B. 1975. Moral incentives and socialist development: The case of Cuba. *Journal of Sociology* 11, 47–52.

Hammersley, M., and P. Atkinson. 1995. *Ethnography: Principles in practice,* 2nd ed. New York: Routledge.

Haraszti, M. 1988. *The velvet prison: Artists under state socialism.* London: I. B. Taurus.

Haraway, D. 1988. Situated knowledges: The science question in feminism and the privilege of partial perspective. *Feminist Studies* 14, no. 3:575–599.

Hart, A. 1962. Comisión Nacional Cubana de la UNESCO. *Cuba y la Conferencia de la Educación.* March.

Hildago, A. 1984. Cuba, the Marxist state and the new class. Photocopy.

Hoffer, E. 1951. *The true believer: Thoughts on the nature of mass movements.* New York: Harper & Row.

Huberman, L., and P. M. Sweezy. 1969. *Socialism in Cuba.* New York: Modern Reader Paperbacks.

International Bank for Reconstruction and Development, Economic and Technical Mission to Cuba. 1952. *Report on Cuba.* Baltimore, Md.: International Bank.

Jatar-Haussmann, A. 1999. *The Cuban way: Capitalism, communism and confrontation.* Sterling, Va.: Kumarian Press.

Jennings, M. K., and R. G. Neimi. 1974. *The political character of adolescence: The influence of family and schools.* Princeton, N.J.: Princeton University Press.

Jimenez, G. 1991. Podemos desarrollarnos sin obreros? *Granma,* May 31, 3.

Johnson, P. 1993. The nuanced lives of the intelligentsia. In *Conflict and change in Cuba,* ed. A. Baloyra and J. A. Morris, 137–163. Albuquerque: University of New Mexico Press.

Jolly, R. 1964. The educational aims and programs of revolutionary government. In *Cuba: The economic and social revolution,* ed. D. Seers, 175–189. Chapel Hill: University of North Carolina Press.

JUCEPLAN. 1968. *Compendio estadístico de Cuba, 1968.* Havana: Ministerio de Educación.

Kahl, J. A. 1969. The moral economy. In *Cuban communism,* ed. I. L. Horowitz. New Brunswick, N.J.: Transaction Books.

Karol, K. S. 1970. *Guerrillas in power: The course of the Cuban revolution.* London: Jonathan Cape Publishers.

Kaufman, G. 1974. The meaning of shame: Toward a self-affirming identity. *Journal of Counseling Psychology* 21:568–574.

Kirk, J. 1989. *Between God and the party: Religion and politics in revolutionary Cuba.* Tampa: University of South Florida Press.

Kondo, D. K. 1990. *Crafting selves: Power, gender, and discourses of identity in a Japanese workplace.* Chicago: University of Chicago Press.

Kozol, J. 1991. *Savage inequalities: Children in America's schools.* New York: Harper Perennial.

―――. 1978. *Children of the revolution: A Yankee teacher in the Cuban schools.* New York: Delacorte Press.

La Belle, T. J., and C. R. Ward. 1990. Education reform when nations undergo radical political and social transformation. *Comparative Education* 26, no. 1:95–106.

Laguna Vila, D., M. L. Martínez Sierra, H. A. Mesa Hernández, E. Herrera Orúa, and J. Rodríguez Ben. 1997. *Educación Cívica: 9 grado.* Havana: Editorial Pueblo y Educación.

Lamore, J. 1970. *Cuba.* Paris: Presses Universitaires de France.

Lataste, A. 1968. *Cuba: ¿Hacia una nueva economía política del socialismo?* Santiago de Chile: Editorial Universitaria.

Latin American Weekly Report. 1980. April 18, 1. http://www.latinnews.com/lwr%5F/LWR_2315.asp.

Latin American Regional Reports (Caribbean). 1980. January 18, 5.

Llanusa, J. 1969. Creando una nueva conciencia. *Bohemia,* January 24, 60 ff.

―――. 1967. Hacer hombres como el Che. *Revolución y cultura,* November 30, 18–20.

Leiner, M. 1994. *Sexual politics in Cuba: Machismo, homosexuality, and AIDS.* Boulder, Colo.: Westview Press.

―――. 1987. The 1961 national Cuban literacy campaign. In *National literacy campaigns: Historical and comparative perspectives,* ed. R. F. Arnove and H. J. Graff. New York: Plenum Press.

―――. 1985. Cuba's schools: 25 years later. 1959–1984. In *Cuba: Twenty-five years of revolution,* ed. S. Halebsky and J. M. Kirk. New York: Praeger.

―――. 1975. Schools to the countryside. In *Education for rural development: Case studies for rural development,* ed. M. Ahmed and P. H. Coombs. New York: Praeger.

―――. 1970. Cuba's schools: Ten years later. *Saturday Review,* October 17, 69.

Lewis, O., R. Lewis, and S. Rigdon. 1977. *Four men.* Urbana: University of Illinois Press.

Llerena, M. 1966. Mario Llerena memoirs. Hoover Institution Archives, Stanford, Calif.

Lorenzetto, A., and K. Neys. 1965. *Methods and means utilized in Cuba to eliminate illiteracy.* UNESCO report. Havana: Editora Pedagógica.

Loewen, J. W. 2007. *Lies my teacher told me: Everything that your American history book got wrong.* New York: Simon & Schuster.

Lutjens, S. 1996. *The state, bureaucracy, and the Cuban schools: Power and participation.* Boulder, Colo.: Westview Press.

MacDonald, T. 1985. *Making a new people.* Vancouver, B.C.: New Star Books.

Mahmood, S. 2001. Feminist theory, embodiment, and the docile agent: Some reflections on the Egyptian Islamic revival. *Cultural Anthropology* 16, no. 2:202–236.

Malloy, J. M. 1971. Generation of political support and allocation of costs. In *Revolutionary change in Cuba,* ed. C. Mesa-Lago. Pittsburgh: University of Pittsburgh Press.

Márquez, R. 1972. Foreword. In *Cuba's educational revolution,* ed. A. Gillette. Fabian Research Series no. 302. London: Fabian Society.

Martí Pérez, J. 1976. *Escritos sobre educación.* Havana: Editora Ciencias Sociales.

———. 1975. *Obras completas,* vol. 8. Havana: Editora Ciencias Sociales.

Martín, J. L. 1999. Investigación social en Cuba. *Temas* 16–17:143–153.

———. 1991. Youth and the Cuban revolution: Notes on the road traversed and its perspectives. Trans. A. Yañez. *Latin American Perspectives* 69, no. 2 (Spring): 95–100.

Martuza, V. 1981. A conversation with Abel Prieto. *Journal of Reading,* December, 261–270.

Maurer, R. 1975. Work: Cuba. In *International documentation,* ed. W. L. Kaiser, 22–26.

Mayor, J., Z. Regalado, and L. Rodríguez. 1999. Pioneros con experiencia. *Juventud Rebelde,* April 11, 2.

Mayor Lorán, J. 2009. Maestros, con todo el amor de la palabra. *Granma,* 5, July 13.

———. 2007. En Cuba cada estudiante cuenta. *Granma,* 6, December 27.

Mbembe, A. 2001. *On the postcolony.* Berkeley and Los Angeles: University of California Press.

McPherson Sayu, M. 1994. El círculo de interés, una vía para la formación de una cultura turística en los escolares del consejo popular de plaza vieja. Unpublished manuscript.

McManus, J. 2000. *Cuba's island of dreams: Voices from the Isle of Pines and Youth.* Gainesville: University of Florida Press.

Medin, T. 1990. *Cuba: The shaping of revolutionary consciousness.* Boulder, Colo.: Lynne Rienner Publishers.

Menéndez Quintero, M. 1994. Hay que buscar estrellas. *Juventud Rebelde* 9, February 1.

Mesa-Lago, C. 1978. *Cuba in the 1970s: Pragmatism and institutionalization.* Albuquerque: University of New Mexico Press.

———. 1971. Economic policies and growth. In *Revolutionary change in Cuba,* ed. C. Mesa-Lago, 277–338. Pittsburgh, Pa.: University of Pittsburgh Press.

Ministerio de Educación (MINED). 1997. *Métodos de investigación pedagógica.* Havana: Editorial Pueblo y Educación.

———. 1992. *Programa educación cívica: Noveno grado.* Havana: Editorial Pueblo y Educación.

———. 1989. Análisis del cumplimiento de las medidas derivadas del XII Seminario Nacional y otros aspectos del trabajo educacional. In *Seminario Nacional a Dirigentes, Metodólogos e Inspectores de las Direcciones Provinciales y Municipales de Educación y de los Institutos Superiores Pedagógicos (documentos normativos y metodológicos).* Havana.

———. 1977. *Report of the Republic of Cuba to the Twenty-sixth International Conference on Public Education.* Havana: Empresa Impresoras Gráficas.

———. 1968. *Report to the Thirty-first International Conference on Public Instruction Convened by the OIE and UNESCO.* Havana: Ministerio de Educación.

Miranda, J. 1984. La transformación radical del sistema educacional de educación. *Educación* 53 (April–June): 76–83.

Mohanty, C. T. 2003. *Feminism without borders: Decolonizing theory, practicing solidarity.* Durham, N.C.: Duke University Press.

Moreno, J. 1971. From traditional to modern values. In *Revolutionary change in Cuba,* ed. C. Mesa-Lago, 471–497. Pittsburgh: University of Pittsburgh Press.

Moses, C. 2000. *Real life in Castro's Cuba*. Wilmington, N.C.: Scholarly Resources.

Mtonga, H. L. 1993. Comparing the role of education in serving socioeconomic and political development in Tanzania and Cuba. *Journal of Black Studies* 23, no. 3 (March): 382–402.

Musgrove, F. 1964. *Youth and the social order*. London: Routledge and Kegan Paul.

New York Times. 1989. April 2, A1.

Oppenheimer, A. 1992. *Castro's final hour: The secret story behind the coming downfall of communist Cuba*. New York: Simon & Schuster.

Orientaciones "Fuerza de acción pioneril." 1998. (Document of the Pioneer Organization). Havana.

Padula, A. 1993. Cuban socialism: Thirty years of controversy. In *Conflict and change in Cuba*, ed. E. A. Baloyra and J. A. Morris, 15–37. Albuquerque: University of New Mexico Press.

Paulston, R. G. 1971. Education. In *Revolutionary change in Cuba*, ed. C. Mesa-Lago. Pittsburgh: University of Pittsburgh Press.

Perera, A. 1999. Profesores de historia recibirán curso intensivo. *Juventud Rebelde*, May 5, 2.

Perera, A., and I. Rosquete. 1999. Conducta responsable. *Juventud Rebelde*, April 17, 3.

Pérez, A. 1987. La unión de jóvenes comunistas. In *Apuntes para la historia del movimiento juvenil comunista y pioneril cubano*, ed. L. Vizcaíno, Z. Gómez, A. Pérez, and C. Ferrer. Havana: Editora Política.

Pérez, L. 1977. The demographic dimensions of the educational problem in socialist Cuba. *Estudios Cubanos* 7, no. 1:33–58.

Pérez-López, J. 1995. *Cuba's second economy: From behind the scenes to center stage*. New Brunswick, N.J.: Transaction Publishers.

Pérez-Stable, M. 1993. *The Cuban Revolution: Origins, course, and legacy*. North Carolina: Oxford University Press.

Pogolotti, G. 1977. Para una cultura revolucionaria: Nuevos y viejos valores. *Casa de las Americas* 18, no. 104:108–113.

———. 1967. La revolución universitaria cubana. *Latinoamerica: Anuario de Estudios Latinoamericanos* (Mexico) 13:17.

Portelli, A. 1981. "The time of my life": Functions of time in oral history. *International Journal of Oral History* 2, no. 3:162–180.

Portuondo, J. A. 1980. La revolución universitaria cubana. *Latinoamerica: Anuario de Estudios Latinoamericanos* 13, 17.

Prensa Latina. 2004. Number of social workers grows in Cuba. December 24. http://www.A49-4FBF-BOCI-AA5EBEA03249}&LanguagesEN (accessed January 15, 2010).

Price, R. F. 1977. *Marx and education in Russia and China*. Totowa, N.J.: Rowman and Littlefield.

Provenzo, E., Jr., and C. García. 1983. Exiled teachers and the Cuban Revolution. *Cuban Studies/Estudios Cubanos* 13, no. 1 (Winter): 1–13.

Radio Havana Cuba. 2000. Future Cuban teachers receive official banner. November 27. http://www.mailarchive.com/kominform@lists.eunet.fi/msg04640.html (accessed January 15, 2010).

Read, G. H. 1970. The Cuban revolutionary offensive in education. *Comparative Education Review* 14, no. 2:131–143.

Regalado, Z., and I. Rosquete. 1999. Eternas interrogantes. *Juventud Rebelde*, February 28, 3.

Resolución Ministerial No. 462/64. 1964. Havana: Ministerio de Educación.

Retzinger, M. S. 1991. *Violent emotions: Shame and rage in marital quarrels.* Newbury Park, Calif.: Sage.

Richmond, M. 1990. Revolution, reform and constant improvement: 30 years of educational change in Cuba. *Compare* 20, no. 2:101–114.

Rock Around the Blockade Newsletter. 2003. The battle of ideas and improving socialism. May–June. http://www.rat.org/uk/vc/vc_27_battle.htm (accessed January 15, 2010).

Rodríguez, A. M. 1995. Te invito a hablar de. . . . *El Habanero*, December 29, 3.

Rodríguez, C. R. 1980. An interview with Carlos Rafael Rodríguez, December 1980. In *Building Socialism in Cuba: Fidel Castro speeches, vol. 2, 1960–1982,* ed. Michael Taber, 316–321. College Park, Ga.: Pathfinder Press.

Roig Izaguirre, J. S. 1987. Las escuelas de oficios: Objetivos y perspectivas. *Educación*, October–December, 58–61.

Romero Fernández, E. 1994. Los valores morales en el proyecto revolucionario cubano: Reflexiones a partir del derrumbe del socialismo real. *Islas* 108:149–155.

Rosaldo, M. Z. 1984. Toward an anthropology of self and feeling. In *Culture theory: Essays on mind, self, and emotion,* ed. R. A. Shweder and R. A. LeVine, 137–157. Ithaca, N.Y.: Cornell University Press.

Rose-Ackerman, S. 1997. The political economy of corruption. In *Corruption and the global economy,* ed. K. A. Elliott, 31–60. Washington, D.C.: Institute for International Economics.

Rosendahl, M. 1997. *Inside the revolution: Everyday life in socialist Cuba.* Ithaca, N.Y.: Cornell University Press.

Rubio, V. 1999. La escuela debe fomentar una conducta más responsable. *Granma*, April 17, 2–3.

Salva, J. S. 1977. ¿Pioneros en la secundaria? *Bohemia*, 38, September 23, 30–32.

Silverman, B. 1971. *Man and socialism in Cuba.* New York, Athenaeum.

Soto, L. 1967. Lo importante es que desarrollemos nuestro camino. *Cuba Socialista* 7, no. 65 (January): 37–61.

———. 1965. Las escuelas de instrucción revolucionaria en el ciclo político-técnico. *Cuba Socialista* 5, no. 41 (January): 67–82.

———. 1963. Dos años de instrucción revolucionaria. *Cuba Socialista* 4, no. 18 (February): 30–44.

"Special Period" affects agricultural work. 1991. September 13. FBIS-LAT-91-178.

Spradley, J., and D. W. McCurdy. 1972. *The cultural experience: Ethnography in complex society.* Chicago: Science Research Associates.

Strug, D. 2006. Community-oriented social work in Cuba: Government response to emerging social problems. *Social Work Education* 25, no. 7:749–762.

Suarez, A. 1971. Leadership, ideology and political party. In *Revolutionary change in Cuba,* ed. C. Mesa-Lago. Pittsburgh: University of Pittsburgh Press.

Suchlicki, J. 1997. *From Columbus to Castro and beyond,* 4th ed. Washington, D.C.: Potomac Books.

Teski, M. C., and J. J. Climo, eds. 1995. *The labyrinth of memory: Ethnographic journeys.* Westport, Conn.: Bergin and Garvey.

Theroux, P. (1989). *The Old Patagonian Express: By Train through the Americas.* New York: Houghton Mifflin Harcourt.

Thomas, H. S., G. A. Fauriol, and J. C. Weiss. 1984. *The Cuban Revolution, 25 years later.* Boulder, Colo.: Westview Press.

Trabajadores. February 5, 1985. Havana.

Trento, A. 2000. *Castro and Cuba: From the revolution to the present.* New York: Interlink Books.

Tucker, R., ed. 1972. *The Marx-Engels reader.* New York: Norton.

Turner, L. 1987. Cinco preguntas acerca del Perfeccionamiento Continuo del Sisteman Nacional de Educación. *Educación,* 66, 3–14.

Turner, V. 1992. *Blazing the trail: Way marks in the exploration of symbols.* Tucson: University of Arizona Press.

———. 1982. *From ritual to theater: The human seriousness of play.* New York: Performance Art Journal Publications.

———. 1974. *Dramas, fields and metaphors: Symbolic action in human society.* Ithaca, N.Y.: Cornell University press.

Turquino. 1959. *Informaciones diversas (La Marcha del País).* November.

Tzulc, T. 1986. *Fidel: A critical portrait.* New York: Avon Books.

UNESCO. 2008. Institute for Statistics, Data Centre. January. http://stats.uis.unesco.org/unesco/ReportFolders/Report olders.aspx (accessed January 2, 2009).

———. 1962. Proyecto principal de educación. *Boletín Trimestral* 14 (April–June): 146.

Universidad Popular. 1961. *Educación y Revolución,* ser. 6, 271. Havana: Imprenta Nacional de Cuba.

Uriarte, M. 2008. Social impact of economic matters. In *A contemporary Cuban reader: Reinventing the revolution,* ed. P. Brenner, M. Jiménez, J. M. Kirk, and W. M. LeoGrande, 285–391. Lanham, Md.: Rowman and Littlefield.

U.S. Department of Health, Education and Welfare. 1976. *The educational system of Cuba.* HEW Publication no. 75-193. Washington, D.C.: U.S. Government Printing Office.

Valdés, N. P. 2001. Fidel Castro, charisma and *santería:* Max Weber revisited. In *Caribbean charisma: Reflections on leadership, legitimacy and populist politics,* ed. A. Allahar. Kingston, Jamaica: Ian Randle Publishers.

———. 1992. Cuban political culture: Between betrayal and death. In *Cuba in transition: Crisis and transformation,* ed. S. Halebsky and J. M. Kirk. Boulder, Colo.: Westview Press.

———. 1988. The changing face of Cuba's Communist Party. In *The Cuba reader: The making of a revolutionary society,* ed. Phillip Brenner et al., 172–175. New York: Grove Press.

———. 1972. Radical transformation of Cuban education. In *Cuba in revolution,* ed. N. P. Valdés and R. E. Vonachea, 422–455. New York: Anchor.

———. 1971. *The Cuban Revolution: A research study guide (1959–1969).* Albuquerque, N.M.: University of New Mexico Press.

Valencia, M. 1997. Young people: Interrupted dreams. *Granma International,* January 29, 8–9.

Verde Olivo. 1976. January 11, 44.

———. 1972. April 9, 19.

————. 1961. June 14, 7.

Volkan, V. D. 1988. *The need to have enemies and allies: From clinical practice to international relationship.* New York: James Aronson.

Wald, K. 1978. *Children of Che: Childcare and education in Cuba.* Palo Alto, Calif.: Ramparts Press.

Wallace, A. F. 1966. Revitalization movements. *American Anthropologist* 59:64–265.

————. 1961. *Culture and personality.* New York: Random House.

Weber, M. 1978. *Economy and society.* Berkeley and Los Angeles: University of California Press.

————. 1947. The nature of charismatic authority and its reorganization. In *On charisma and institution building,* ed. S. N. Eisenstadt, 48–65. Chicago: University of Chicago Press.

Willis, P. 1993. Symbolic creativity. In *Studying culture: An introductory reader,* ed. A. Gray and J. McGuigan, 209–216. London: Edward Arnolds.

Wirtz, K. 2004. *Santería* in Cuban national consciousness: A religious case of the *doble moral. Journal of Latin American Anthropology* 9, no. 2:409–438.

Wooden, W. W. 2004. Youth culture in the post-Soviet Cuba: The vanguards, pessimists, and antirevolutionaries. htp://216.239.41.104/search?q5cache:79BfozT-Ig0J.www.blockcuba.com/youth.htm+in+the+postsoviet+cuba&hl5en (accessed January 15, 2010).

World Bank. 1998. *World development indicators.* New York: World Bank.

Young, A. 1984. *Gays under the revolution.* San Francisco: Grey Fox Press.

Yurchak, A. 2005. *Everything was forever, until it was no more: The last Soviet generation.* Princeton, N.J.: Princeton University Press.

Zimbalist, A. 1989. Incentives and planning in Cuba. *Latin American Research Review* 24, no. 1:65–93.

Index